BRITISH SOCIALISM

DOCUMENTS IN POLITICAL IDEAS

General editor: *Bernard Crick*

BRITISH SOCIALISM

Socialist thought from the 1880s to 1960s

Anthony Wright

LONGMAN
London and New York

LONGMAN GROUP LIMITED
Longman House, Burnt Mill, Harlow
Essex CM20 2JE, England
Associated companies throughout the world

*Published in the United States of America
by Longman Inc., New York*

First published 1983

BRITISH LIBRARY CATALOGUING IN PUBLICATION DATA

Wright, Anthony
  British socialism. – (Documents in political ideas)
  1. Socialism in Great Britain – History
  I. Title   II. Series
  335'.00941   HX243

  ISBN 0-582-29561-0

LIBRARY OF CONGRESS CATALOGING IN PUBLICATION DATA

Main entry under title:

British socialism.

  (Documents in political ideas)
  1. Socialism – Great Britain – History.
I. Wright, Anthony, 1948–   II. Series.
HX243.B67 1983   335'.00941   82-17295
ISBN 0-582-29561-0

Set in 10/11 pt Linotron 202 Plantin
Printed in Hong Kong
by Hing Yip Printing Co.

CONTENTS

EDITOR'S PREFACE

Students of political ideas will be familiar with the debate among their teachers about texts and contexts, whether the study of political ideas primarily concerns the meaning of a text or an understanding of the main ideas of an epoch. Both should be done but not confused; and texts need setting in their context. But it is easier for the student to find and to read the texts of political philosophers than to be able to lay his hands upon the range of materials that would catch the flavour of the thinking of an age or a movement, both about what should be done and about how best to use common concepts that create different perceptions of political problems and activity.

So this series aims to present carefully chosen anthologies of the political ideas of thinkers, publicists, statesmen, actors in political events, extracts from State papers and common literature of the time, in order to supplement and complement, not to replace, study of the texts of political philosophers. They should be equally useful to students of politics and of history.

Each volume will have an authoritative and original introductory essay by the editor of the volume. Occasionally instead of an era, movement or problem, an individual writer will figure, writers of a kind who are difficult to understand (like Edmund Burke) simply by the reading of any single text.

B. R. C.

AUTHOR'S PREFACE

This book contains a selection from the vast literature produced by British socialists over the last century. Its aim is to give a sense of what 'British socialism' has come to mean at the level of ideas and theory. It is not, therefore, about policy debates or political organisations. Although its emphasis is predominantly upon what it regards as mainstream British socialism (and so does not deal with some socialist traditions that have had a presence in Britain), the harsh disciplines of selection and compression have meant that many subsidiary figures have not found a place here. This is regrettable, but I hope that enough remains to fulfil the purpose of the book.

An important feature of this anthology is that the extracts from key texts are of substantial length. They are designed to be long enough to allow their authors to present an argument with sufficient coherence and example. In addition to these substantial extracts, shorter items are also included to fill out the historical picture or to illustrate other tendencies. At present there is no source book on British socialism of this kind, and it is hoped that it will fill an important gap – especially at a time when there is so much discussion about the nature of British socialism. It remains, of course, only an introduction to a political tradition and not a substitute for independent exploration. If this is a standard warning from all compilers of anthologies, it is because they are most aware of what they have done and they want to share the responsibility.

I am very grateful to Bernard Crick for asking me to undertake this work and for encouraging me along the way; to my wife, Moira, for taking on an unfair share of the domestic routine while it was being completed; and to Audrey Elliott, who typed the whole text with her usual cheerful efficiency and never complained once. Finally, I dedicate this book to my two small sons, Benjamin

Tomos and Timothy Rhys, so that when they can read what it contains they may at least understand their father a bit better.

Anthony Wright

ACKNOWLEDGEMENTS

We are grateful to the following for permission to reproduce copyright material:

George Allen & Unwin Ltd for extracts from *Democracy in Crisis* by H. J. Laski and *Equality* by R. H. Tawney; Bell & Hyman Ltd for an extract from *Self-Government in Industry* by G. D. H. Cole; Jonathan Cape Ltd and the Estate of C. A. R. Crosland for extracts from *The Future of Socialism* by C. A. R. Crosland; the author and Chatto & Windus Ltd for extracts from *The Long Revolution* by Raymond Williams; Faber & Faber Ltd for an extract from *The Socialist Case* by Douglas Jay; Fabian Society for extracts from *Programme for Victory*, 1941 by G. D. H. Cole, *The Irresponsible Society*, 1960 by Richard Titmuss and *The Sickness of an Acquisitive Society* by R. H. Tawney; Victor Gollancz Ltd and Mrs Elizabeth Al Qadhi for extracts from *Contemporary Capitalism* by John Strachey; Independent Labour Publications, I. L. P. (formerly Independent Labour Party) for an extract from *Socialism and Society*, 6th edition 1908 by J. R. Macdonald; The London School of Economics and Political Science for extracts from *Socialism in England*, 1890 by Sidney Webb and *A Constitution for the Socialist Commonwealth of Great Britain* by Sidney & Beatrice Webb.

INTRODUCTION

Ideas are consequences, but also havé consequences. They are
shaped by experience, but also shape experience. This is just a way
of saying that political ideas are important and deserve to be taken
seriously, and this includes those ideas (of the kind represented
here) that are associated with particular political traditions and experiences. Political ideas of this kind provide a bridge between past
and future, and between pure reflection and unreflective action.
However, they may of course perform other functions too. They
may, for example, serve as obfuscating ideology, or attain the status
of myth. They also have their characteristic limitations, preferring
to address themselves to the historically specific rather than the philo-
sophically universal and often being less concerned with theoretical precision than with political relevance. It is also useful to remember that the dominant ideas of a political movement or tradition may find their source in the movement's inarticulate major
premises (or 'ethos'[1]*) as well as in its more formal doctrines.

With these preliminaries in mind, it is possible to turn to the
political tradition that is represented in this anthology. To write of
'British socialism' (thus acknowledging its status as a distinctive
tradition) is to refer both to a political movement and a body of
ideas. The concern here, rather unfashionably, is with the latter
more than the former. Herbert Morrison's immortal formulation
that 'socialism is what Labour Governments do' was designed to
close down any distinction of this kind in favour of a necessary fusion. A recent literature has been organised around a new formulation and a necessary fission: socialism is what Labour Governments

* References to material in this anthology are given in the text inside [square]
brackets, indicating the number of the document in this book in which the extract
occurs. Other references are given in the normal way, and are listed at the end of
this introduction.

fail to do.[2] Yet this represents its own form of closure, in this case a closure of any serious exploration of the theoretical tradition of British socialism. Certainly there has been a remarkable paucity of historical and critical studies in this area, while a striking feature of much of the contemporary argument within the Labour Party is its divorce from any real encounter with its own intellectual tradition. Yet it is still possible that it is Tawney rather than Trotsky who has more to contribute to these arguments.

The centenary of modern British socialism, the passage from the 'socialist revival' of the 1880s to the ideological controversies of the 1980s, invites retrospection and reassessment. What are the distinctive characteristics of the tradition represented here? What has 'British socialism' come to denote in the wider universe of political ideas? There are a number of more or less familiar answers to questions of this kind. Perhaps the most familiar concerns the reputed moralism of British socialism, its preference f presenting the socialist argument in 'the language of moral revolt' (Thompson, [4.8]) rather than in the categories of economic analysis or of historical determination. This does not mean that British socialism 'owes more to Methodism than to Marx' (as that misleading adage would have it), but it does mean that it has consistently insisted that the world of political economy should be regarded as an arena of moral choice. The 'ethical socialism' associated with Keir Hardie and the Independent Labour Party (ILP) gave early popular expression to this approach, although its influence was still more pervasive. Perhaps its most eloquent and compelling statement is to be found in the work of R. H. Tawney. Tawney always insisted that social institutions had to be subjected to the test of moral purpose; and this sort of 'Tawneyism' shaped and expressed the thinking of a whole generation of British socialists.

The centrality of moralism carried with it a cluster of associated characteristics and consequences. Socialism was envisaged not as an era of abstract economic justice but of a remoralised social order in which a new moral life could be practised. Significantly, this emphasis was also shared by such creative British Marxists as William Morris and Belfort Bax, and expressed in their concern with the development of a 'socialistic ethics' [1.6]. The language of fellowship and fraternity within British socialism was employed both to express this general conception and to prefigure the new society. The Continental 'comrade' became the British 'brother'. Not merely was a socialism of fellowship often out of sympathy with the politics of class warfare, but an ethical socialism tended to make its appeal to the moral conscience of all individuals and not merely to the self-interest of a particular class, even if in practice one class was likely to be more responsive to the socialist call. This mode of thought testifies of course to the failure of Marxism to establish a central presence within British socialism during its formative period, a failure that is properly regarded as a British idiosyncrasy in the context of the development of European socialism as a whole.

This British idiosyncrasy has been reflected in other familiar characteristics of the tradition. It has been, overwhelmingly, a reformist tradition, expressed in its commitment to a parliamentary Labourism. The State was not to be smashed from without but captured from within, and parliamentary elections on the basis of universal suffrage and democratic procedures were regarded as the key terrain of socialist struggle. Aneurin Bevan recorded how, as a young Marxist auto-didact, 'quite early in my studies it seemed to me that classic Marxism consistently understated the role of a political democracy with a fully developed franchise'.[3] The ascendancy of this view meant that British socialism escaped the pitched battles between revisionism and orthodoxy that marked the growing pains of Continental social democracy. It also meant that, once established, the Labour Party won the allegiance of almost all the figures represented here, despite the tensions inherent in their attachment. This dominance of the British Left by the Labour Party, and in particular the acceptance of this dominance by such key intellectuals as Cole, Laski and Tawney, has been significant in defining the context in which theoretical inquiry has taken place and, perhaps, in closing off alternative theoretical explorations.

Yet a tradition takes its shape from the materials that are at hand (and, of course, from the use that is made of these materials). Thus, modern British socialism drew upon the materials that were available in British society of the late nineteenth century. Its moralism, for example, drew heavily upon its inheritance of a Ruskinian tradition of ethical protest and aesthetic criticism, as well as responding to the religious crisis of the period which was providing an increasing audience for a secular message in a religious idiom. Bernard Shaw described the contemporary appeal of a socialism of this kind: 'The working-man who has been detached from the Established Church or the sects by the Secularist propaganda, and who, as an avowed Agnostic or Atheist, strenuously denies or contemptuously ridicules the current beliefs in heavens and devils and bibles, will, with the greatest relief and avidity, go back to his old habits of thought and imagination when they reappear in this secular form. The Christian who finds the supernatural aspect of his faith slipping away from him recaptures it in what seems to him a perfectly natural aspect as Christian Socialism.'[4]

A fashionable social Darwinism provided materials for biological, organic and collectivist modes of thought, while positivism exercised a diffuse influence.[5] An older radical democratic tradition also made itself available (old Chartist symbols were raised at a miners' rally attended by Keir Hardie in 1880[6]), as did an earlier Owenism. Then there was the pervasive influence of English liberalism, and of its advanced radical varieties such as that of Henry George. Eric Hobsbawm has written of 'the broad and generic sense in which virtually all Englishmen of the left were at least the illegitimate offspring of the radical–liberal tradition'.[7] Finally, there was the fact that an accommodative ideology of 'labourism' was already securely established in the consciousness of the British working class by the time of the socialist revival of the 1880s, so that 'when socialist ideas and a socialist movement returned to Britain in the last twenty years of the century, the most serious obstacle to the acceptance of a position of intellectual and political independence was the strength and tenacity of this labourist tradition.'[8] Even a brief inventory of this kind cautions against any surprise that British socialism should have expressed itself in a distinctive idiom rather than simply borrowing from socialist materials that were already available, in different form, elsewhere.

It is certainly the case that British socialists have generally wanted to recognise, even assert, the distinctiveness of their own national tradition. This is as true for William Morris as for the Fabians, for the Guild Socialists as for George Orwell. The latter described a British socialist future that would 'not be doctrinaire, nor even logical', abolishing the House of Lords but probably preserving the monarchy [3.7]. In the hands of a Ramsay MacDonald the domestic credentials of British socialism, its separateness from a 'foreign' Marxism or syndicalism, could be invoked as a propaganda weapon both in internal socialist arguments and in the presentation of socialism to a wider public. Nor is it without significance that the pioneer of British Marxism, H. M. Hyndman, first tried to fuse a Marxist with a national tradition and finished up by abandoning the former because of the pull of the latter. Tawney expressed a general view when he insisted, against the background of the ideological controversies of the 1930s, that British socialism had necessarily to 'wear a local garb'.[9] In more recent times there have been those who have wanted to disrobe British socialism of its shoddy local garb and replace it with purer material of foreign importation. This was evidently necessary because of its contamination by a diseased history and culture that had produced the ascendancy of a sterile bourgeois empiricism.[10] However, there remained those who were unconvinced by both the analysis and the prescription when set against 'the peculiarities of the English'.[11] The lack of theoretical sweep and philosophical grandeur within British socialism has been apparent enough of course, and in some respects has undoubtedly had disabling effects. In general, though, British socialists (at least until recently) have felt little inclination to be apologetic on this account. As Keir Hardie wrote to Engels: 'We are a solid people, very practical and not given to chasing bubbles.'[12]

So far this characterisation of British socialism has been in general terms and, if left there, would be seriously misleading. Indeed, it may be suggested that part of the neglect and misreading of British socialism derives from the easy attribution to it of such familiar labels as reformism, moralism, labourism, empiricism and collectivism. The point is not that such labels are inaccurate but that they are inadequate. They do scant justice to the actual historical contours of the tradition and reduce a diverse tradition to a unitary one. Perhaps most serious of all, this has the effect of silencing arguments and blocking off alternative traditions and, in doing so, making them less available to us today. A relevant example here is the historical treatment of William Morris whose political legacy, ignored or dismissed by the wider society, was generally compressed either into an 'orthodox' Marxism or an 'ethical' anti-Marxism; until Edward Thompson presented Morris in terms of a critically important fusion of traditions ('a transformed romantic', 'a communist utopian'[13]) that enabled him to escape from the historical closet and become an active presence within British socialism and within the wider socialist tradition. The argument here is that this sort of open and critical approach should be brought to bear on the actual historical experience of British socialism itself.

If this approach is adopted, the distinctiveness of British socialism will remain, but it will be less easy to regard it simply as a unitary tradition. Instead, areas of significant argument will emerge and subsidiary (sometimes conflicting) traditions will surface. Just as socialism in general may be regarded as having presented itself in a number of different forms and tendencies,[14] so too with British socialism. Thus, even if it has often expressed itself in the language of moralism (capitalism is immoral), it has also expressed the socialist argument in other terms too: for example, in the language of rationalism (capitalism is inefficient) and of historical determinism (capitalism is doomed), or as a fulfilment and extension of other traditions, notably the democratic and the liberal. Not only has the socialist argument taken different forms at different periods, but different forms in the same period and this frequently, because of the eclectic character of British socialism, from the same pen. An extensive and varied typology could be constructed of the modes in which the socialist argument has been articulated in Britain.

It is possible to offer further examples of the benefits that accrue from a more open (and historical) approach to British socialism. For example, the 'absence' of Marxism within British socialism has to take account of its very real presence at crucial periods (the 1880s, 1930s), the nature and impact of this presence, and the general treatment of Marxism by British socialists. Similarly, any account of the parliamentary reformism of British socialism would be inadequate if it failed to take account of the serious engagement with the dilemmas of a reformist strategy on the part of some British socialists (as in the early 1930s, in the wake of the demise of the Labour Government) and their discussion of the conditions in which a radical gradualism might succeed. So too with the collectivism of British socialism, expressed in the familiar Fabian inheritance of bureaucratic centralism. So familiar is this account that it overlooks the fact that even Fabian collectivism (like much early British socialism) was predominantly localist and multiform rather than centralist and uniform in orientation. In 1890 that arch-Fabian, Sidney Webb, was to be found trying to disabuse people of the 'misapprehension' that socialism implied 'a rigidly centralised national administration of all the details of life', whereas socialists had 'as yet contributed nothing to the difficult problem of political science as to the proper line of division between the functions of the central government and those of the local authorities'.[15] What the familiar account of British collectivism also misses is the existence of an important tradition of socialist pluralism and participatory democracy (associated especially with G. D. H. Cole and the Guild Socialists)[16] within British socialism. These examples could be extended and multiplied: the point is simply that it is necessary to come to terms with an actual tradition and not merely with one of its familiar caricatures.

The material collected here, though necessarily small in size and selective in scope, provides an introduction to some of these matters. It covers the period from the 1880s, which is the period during which socialism in Britain has had a continuous existence. Its focus is what it takes to be the mainstream and distinctive tradition of British socialism, therefore does not deal with those other traditions (such as syndicalism and communism) that have their own derivation and continuity. The material has been ordered chronologically and grouped into a number of broad periods. The chronological presentation is intended to give a sense of a tradition in development and debate in its actual historical context, and this would be difficult with a more abstracted thematic treatment. The periodisation is not intended to indicate rigid lines of historical or theoretical demarcation, merely to suggest some staging-posts at which it seems appropriate to pause for reflection on the journey so far. Some preliminary and necessarily brief observations on the route to be followed are offered here.

The starting-point is the decade of the 1880s, which marked the revival of socialist ideas and popular agitation after the long interlude of mid-Victorian quiescence. There was little expectation at the beginning of the decade that such a revival was imminent. Then Marx was still railing at the suffocating grip of 'Brit. Philistinism' and Engels was writing from London to disabuse those who might be 'deluded into thinking there is a real proletarian movement going on here'.[17] However, by the end of the decade the 'collection of oddities' (as the early pioneers were once described to Morris) had become an incipient mass movement and Engels could now announce to the world that the English proletariat had finally awakened from 'its long winter sleep'.[18] Not only were the Social Democratic Federation (SDF), Socialist League and Fabian Society already in existence, but the 'new unionism' was spreading the movement throughout the country and preparing the way for a genuine workers' party, in the shape of the Independent Labour Party that was founded in the mid-1890s and which, at the turn of the century, combined with the trade unions to form the Labour Party. However, the concern here is less with the organisational history of Labour and socialist politics in this formative period, which is richly documented elsewhere,[19] than with the character of socialist thought at the time.

The material anthologised here opens appropriately with H. M. Hyndman, a reminder that Marxism established its presence in Britain at the very beginning of the socialist revival but also raising questions about why that presence did not prove more secure and influential thereafter. Hyndman has had a bad press, getting off to a poor start by earning the wrath of Marx and Engels (the latter describing him as 'an arch-conservative and an extremely chauvinistic but not stupid careerist'), and his domineering manner has generally been linked to those characteristics of the SDF (for example, its sectarianism, and neglect of the trade unions) that have been held responsible for the failure of the SDF to become a mass Marxist party on the model of European social democracy.[20] Yet individual Marxists (as Hobsbawm and Cole pointed out[21]) could have assumed leadership roles in the working-class politics of the 1890s if possessed of a better political sense, for the movement was still sufficiently open for that to happen, and Hyndman had done more than anyone else to make Marxism (or at least 'Anglo-Marxism' as it has been called) available to British socialists at a crucial period. As the extract included here shows, his *Historical basis of socialism in England* was intended as a 'really scientific' [1.1] presentation of the socialist argument, wholly different from an earlier utopianism, and its account of historical development and of the theory of surplus value made it a respected source of information and argument even among those British socialists who preferred to state their socialism in a different idiom. Yet Hyndman's schematic account also reflected a narrowed Marxism and one which had undergone no creative adaptation to British conditions. It sat uneasily alongside his political strategy, which was a 'curious blend of political opportunism and theoretical dogmatism'.[22] Indeed, at times it seemed that Marxism was invoked to press home a message about the irresistible march of history that was designed to frighten the English governing class into abdication as an alternative to inevitable 'national decrepitude and decay' [1.1] accompanied by bloody class warfare. Not for nothing did Hyndman warn that the centenary of 1789 was fast approaching.

It was William Morris who offered a more creative fusion of Marxism with a domestic tradition. Unversed in the intricacies of Marxist economics and philosophy although mastering what he could (and assisted in this by his regular 'Baxination', as he called it, at the hands of his friend and Socialist League comrade, the philosopher Belfort Bax), Morris nevertheless effected a remarkable marriage between Ruskin and Marx, romanticism and rationalism, moralism and materialism, and utopianism and scientific socialism. This was a heady mixture that exercised a wide influence upon British socialists, coupled with a deep personal respect for Morris himself, even though his political strategy of socialist purity and the 'making of socialists' left him organisationally isolated. No mere utopian, Morris found in Marxism a secure theoretical and historical anchorage and sought to make this anchorage accessible to others, as in his translation of the theory of surplus value into 'this elementary piece of honesty' [1.2]. Yet no confined Marxist either, Morris drew upon other traditions in his indictment of the 'civilisation' of industrial capitalism (with its leisure class, machine tyranny, destruction of nature and general vulgarity) and was most distinctive of all in his 'constructive' anticipations of the Society of the Future, with its equality of condition and democratic fellowship. If these were the 'spaces' which Marxism had failed to occupy (as Edward Thompson suggests), then Morris's exploration of them provided his central contribution to British socialism and the one which was most readily absorbed by that tradition.

By contrast, the claim of Fabianism (that most distinctive school of British socialism) was not merely to occupy any spare theoretical ground left vacant by Marxism but to replace Marxism as the theoretical framework of British socialists. Thus the official historian of the Fabian Society records its first historic achievement as having been to 'break the spell of Marxism in England'.[23] In fact, there was scarcely a spell of this kind to break, although Fabians like Webb and Shaw nevertheless set about the task with vigour. Thus a Marxist economics of surplus value was judged to be much inferior as a tool of economic analysis than a revised Fabian theory of rent, and a Marxist revolutionary politics much inferior to a Fabian tactic of permeation of existing institutions supported by a social scientific presentation of the case for reform. Yet Fabianism resembled Marxism in its claim to be scientific rather than utopian, and its claim to have uncovered the motor of historical development. It should not be forgotten that the 'inevitability of gradualness' was about inevitability as much as gradualness, as is clear in Sidney Webb's description of the relentless march towards collectivism as 'the inevitable outcome of Democracy and the Industrial Revolution' [1.3], and buttressed by the anti-individualist view of organic evolution and social organisation that derived from the influence of social Darwinism and Comtean positivism. The Fabians are usually regarded simply as the bureaucratic technicians of reform within British socialism, the rational apostles of a planned social and economic order. Yet this makes Fabianism too monolithic, and neglects the extent to which it derived its collectivism from its own search for a new moral consensus for society. Thus Sidney Webb could regard collectivism as 'the positive stage of Comtism' and his socialism was really a 'primarily moral'[24] doctrine rooted in a conception of the growth of social feelings and the construction of a new moral world of social solidarity and interdependence.

According to Shaw, the Fabians alone were exempt from the 'illusions' [1.7] that characterised the other varieties of socialist thought at the time, whether Marxist or utopian. It was not necessary to admire the 'sordid, slow, reluctant, cowardly path to justice'[25] of Fabian reformism, only to recognise its inevitability as an extension of the present. Fabian proposals would succeed where others would fail because they 'have on them that stamp of the vestry which is so congenial to the British mind. None of them compel the use of the words Socialism or Revolution; at no point do they involve guillotining, declaring the Rights of Man, swearing on the altar of the country, or anything else that is supposed to be essentially un-English'.[26] Shaw's anticipation of the central role for a Fabian practical reformism in the evolution of British politics proved substantially correct, and in the 1890s it made itself available to the new Independent Labour Party despite its own earlier disbelief in the need for a separate workers' party. Yet, as has been seen, there were other socialist traditions available to the ILP and it drew freely upon these too. Its own brand of plain moralism indicated that during the early 1890s socialism had 'found a British idiom',[27] and this 'ethical socialism' soon established itself as the characteristic note of British socialism. It enabled British socialism to extend its political reach, but at the cost of weakening its intellectual grasp. Yet ethical socialism was not an exclusive doctrine, and the propaganda of the ILP, as with Blatchford's *Merrie England* [1.5], reflected an eclecticism that testified to the continued openness of British socialism in this period.

It was an openness that revealed certain characteristics and left many questions unanswered. There was little enthusiasm for a centralised State (not even among the Fabian collectivists) and Morris and Bax envisaged a system of federated communes. There was a widespread desire to roll back factory industrialism and urbanism, a desire that has been regarded as one expression of a more general anti-industrial culture in Britain.[28] Many of those who looked forward to a socialist future did so by reaching back for inspiration and example to a lost past. Existing inequalities were frequently linked to a moral corrosion, reflected in a leisure class and 'the canker of effete gentility' (Carpenter, [1.4]), with socialism presented in terms of a remoralised social order. But these preoccupations, which were expressed in the powerful visions of Morris or Blatchford, had increasingly to live alongside the programmatic and strategic needs of the developing world of labour politics. If socialism as class power was rejected, how was socialism as moral growth to be achieved? How did the qualitative transformation implied by ethical socialism relate to the needs of a concrete political programme? What was to be the character of a socialist reformism and who was to define it? How did the Society of the Future relate to the politics of the present?

If questions of this kind had been raised by the 1890s, they became more acute early in the new century as British socialism began its 'journey from fantasy to politics',[29] with the consolidation of a distinctive Labour politics in the form of a marriage between trade union interest and socialist purpose. The socialist wing of this new coalition, as the bearer of mainstream British socialism, had increasingly to confront the implications of its commitment to a practical reformism and to a comprehensive social transformation. In fact, rather than endeavouring to establish a serious link in action and theory in this matter it seemed too often to operate in separate realms. The Fabians were on hand to supply the programmatic needs of reform (secure in their knowledge that such instalments of reform would achieve their painless consummation in collectivism), while the ethical socialists of the ILP continued to preach their gospel of moral fundamentalism. The two traditions stood sharply contrasted in the almost simultaneous presentation in the first decade of this century of the socialist future in terms of a scientific rationalism, 'a general plan of social life' from the Fabian convert H. G. Wells [2.5], and in terms of a moral transformation that would 'make the material environment correspond to the ethical spirit' from the ILP leader Keir Hardie [2.4]. Yet what these two different visions shared was a utopianism that built no real bridge between present and future. Thus Wells had to invent his Samurai élite, while Hardie dismissed any attempt to 'dogmatise about the form which the Socialist State shall take' and assured his readers that the establishment of full communism would prove 'a comparatively easy task as the natural successor to State Socialism' [2.4]. In much ILP literature 'socialism' stood as a distant beacon, unsullied and untroubled by the practical concerns of the present, with the gulf that this opened up being filled with rhetorical gush.[30]

The grand master of rhetorical gush was J. R. MacDonald, and he deployed this talent to the full at this time in defining the developing shape and identity of 'British socialism', both for the socialist movement itself and for a wider audience. This was an important role, at a crucial period. MacDonald's eclecticism drew freely upon available traditions in his construction of an accommodative ideal, welding an organic evolutionism with a rationalist appreciation of its collectivist implications and a conception of moral citizenship. What this meant was that 'Socialism marks the growth of Society, not the uprising of a class'; and its watchword was 'not class consciousness but community consciousness' [2.1]. If socialism was about 'organic wholeness' and the moral growth of a whole society, it could not also be about social divisions and class struggles: and so MacDonald's eclecticism had to stop short at socialist traditions of this kind. It was necessary instead to refute the claims of Marxism (and later of syndicalism) and to distance and distinguish British socialism from them, and this was a role that MacDonald made his own. Yet this involved a contraction of the theoretical perspectives available to British socialism compared to an earlier period, in the pursuit of a moderate respectability consistent with a participant in British parliamentary politics.[31] This pursuit was successful, but its theoretical foundations provided a shaky basis for a concrete political strategy (as MacDonald himself was to find out).

Despite such attempts to set the mould of British socialism in the first two decades of this century, it remained a period of considerable theoretical diversity and argument. Indeed, the second decade of the century and early part of the third has good claim to be regarded as the most theoretically vibrant period of twentieth-century British socialism, certainly more so than the superficially more adventurous 1930s. Despite MacDonald's essays in theoretical contraction and the consolidation of a parliamentary Labourism rooted in Fabian collectivism, it was still possible to feel that British socialism was a tradition in the making and that there was room for argument about its goals and strategy. An important argument of this kind was mounted by the Guild Socialists, who drew upon an increasing antipathy to the State (reflected variously in pluralism and syndicalism) to construct a comprehensive theoretical challenge to Fabian collectivism in the form of a strategy of industrial action directed towards the establishment of a decentralised system of democratic 'guilds' throughout industry and the wider society. According to G. D. H. Cole, the leading theorist of Guild Socialism, the Fabian State would simply be 'the Earthly Paradise of bureaucracy' [2.2] whereas Guild Socialism (claiming to draw upon the inheritance of William Morris) would offer real freedom and self-government to the worker, because it was rooted in a creative synthesis of syndicalism and collectivism, producer and consumer, industry and politics. Guild Socialism had not felt it necessary to draw upon Marxism in making its challenge to Fabianism, for what it offered was not an ideology of class power but a 'constructive ideal' [2.2] of self-government. The commitment to the workers' education movement on the part of Cole and Tawney may be seen as an expression of their belief in the need for workers to acquire the cultural tools to frame an ideal of this kind and the confidence to pursue it.

Both Tawney and Laski emerged as significant figures within British socialism during this period of theoretical vitality. Moreover, they both identified themselves to some extent with Guild Socialism, although from different perspectives. Laski was a leading academic critic of theories of State sovereignty and an advocate of a philosophical pluralism, and this gave him some (though not uncritical) sympathy with Guild Socialism. However, by the early 1920s he had moved into a Fabian orbit and undertaken at least a partial rehabilitation of the State as 'a public service corporation' [2.7]. From the perspective of an economic historian and Christian moralist, Tawney approached matters rather differently. He echoed the Guild Socialist view that poverty was merely a symptom and lack of freedom the disease, and that producers had particular rights in relation to their functions. However, his central concern was with the proposition that 'social institutions are the visible expression of the scale of moral values which rules the minds of individuals, and it is impossible to alter institutions without altering that moral valuation' [2.3]. An 'acquisitive' society had to be replaced by a 'functional' one, and for Tawney this change in the dominant moral principle of society was more important than (and even made redundant) much Guild Socialist system building. The goal was a new moral unity, not an elaborate division of powers. However, unlike many 'ethical' socialists Tawney's moralism had a hard cutting edge. It did make connections between moral valuation and social institutions, with direct consequences for political practice.[32]

It seemed that the theoretical departures of this period might produce some lasting effects on the developing shape of British socialism. For example, the Webbs were obliged to take up the challenge to Fabian collectivism that came from the Guild Socialists, and although they spoke disparagingly of these 'impatient democrats' and claimed that the problem of democratic authority would increasingly be resolved by the operation of 'the searchlight of published knowledge' [2.6], they nevertheless sought a *modus vivendi* with the Guild Socialists. Sidney Webb conceded that socialists had 'contributed so far very little to the theory or practice of Democracy'.[33] The young Clement Attlee declared that Guild Socialism had taught the lesson that 'no form of society will be satisfactory that leaves the worker a wage-slave',[34] and Labour's 1918 statement of its socialist basis reflected the contemporary climate in its coupling of public ownership with democratic control. The Guild movement also indicated the continuing openness of British socialism, for its composition stretched from neo-anarchists to proto-Communists and from Christian socialists to radical individualists. Yet the environment in which this was possible was soon to change under the impact of external events, so that by 1920 a new model Labourism confronted an official Communism. This historic rupture had important theoretical consequences, for it meant the loss of an earlier plurality and of an arena in which an independent Left might operate. One important effect of this bifurcation was the 'self-conscious isolation of Marxism from the national mainstream',[35] but it also involved a more general closure against diverse theoretical traditions. Socialism became Labour Socialism and Marxism became official Communism, and the loss of theoretical vitality within British socialism in the 1920s paralleled the development of these increasingly monolithic political blocs.

The inter-war years have been described as the 'socialist generation'[36] in British Labour politics. This may seem a curious description for a period in which the Left, both domestically and internationally, suffered such serious defeats and was generally on the defensive. It was a period of economic slump, of the failure of the General Strike, of the political catastrophe of 1931, of the rise of fascism. The workers' control movement was halted, and the State again embraced as a practical instrument of social improvement and economic amelioration. Thus Beatrice Webb could welcome the defeat of the General Strike as marking 'the death gasp of that pernicious doctrine of "workers' control"',[37] and the Labour politician Herbert Morrison could smuggle in the model of the independent public corporation as the bureaucratic form of nationalisation. Yet the period was also a socialist generation, in the sense that the Labour Party's formal adoption of a socialist constitution in 1918 ushered in an era of Labour Socialism, a doctrine which combined a strategy of parliamentary reformism with a commitment to a new social order. However, it also raised questions about the nature of this combination, and in a context in which socialist argument was now necessarily tied to considerations of organisational loyalty. Much socialist thought of the period turned on these matters.

It was possible to overcome difficulties of this kind by adopting the traditional practice of keeping current politics and doctrinal goals in different compartments, and this too was a feature of the 'socialist generation' in Labour politics. However, although this practice might escape serious consequences in the early days of ILP propaganda, it proved disabling (as with MacDonald) as a guide to action on the assumption of office. A tradition which simply attributed contemporary ills, notably unemployment, to capitalism and shrugged off all responsibility for them in the contemplation of a future socialism in which they (necessarily) would not exist was unlikely to be well equipped for the sort of practical policy-making which a reformist strategy implied. And so it proved with the Labour Government of 1929 – 31, especially in the key area of anti-depression economics, and actually impeded the adoption of a radical programme.[38] However, this testifies less to the essential perils of an ideological socialism than to the failure to relate it to a concrete strategy of reform and transition, resulting in a relapse into the arms of orthodoxy (and the bearers of that orthodoxy) and an inability to explore available alternatives.[39]

The trauma of 1931 severely dented the confident assumptions of Labour Socialism and, coupled with the further traumas presented by the 1930s, produced a flurry of theoretical alarums and excursions. Everyone claimed to be busily learning the 'lessons'[40] of 1931 and new groups were formed on the Left (notably the Socialist League) to press these lessons home, with the rump of the ILP disaffiliating from Labour in the name of an independent Marxism (which meant that it took its international viewpoint during the 1930s almost straight from Trotsky).[41] The central lesson concerned the viability of the strategy of parliamentary reformism and it was argued (for example, by Cole, Laski and Cripps) that a future socialist administration would need to implement a rapid programme of socialisation, that new constitutional powers would be needed to accomplish this, and that there should be a preparedness to meet the unconstitutional opposition that this might provoke. All this produced a magnificent storm about a socialist threat to parliamentary democracy.[42] Yet an important argument of substance underpinned this cluster of proposals. It was claimed that hitherto socialist reformism had been rooted in a concessions policy, a belief that an expansive capitalism would go on yielding its concessions to socialism. Yet what this overlooked was, firstly, that capitalism was no longer expanding but in crisis and, secondly, that it was anyway unrealistic to expect capitalism to go on functioning normally in the face of serious socialist incursions that weakened its operating principles. It was claimed that a serious socialist reformism had to learn these lessons, abandon the philosophy of concessions, and think through the economic and political implications of the enterprise it was engaged upon. A failure to do this would simply mean a repeat of the MacDonaldism that had produced the capitulation of 1929–31. The most articulate exponent of this position was probably G. D. H. Cole, but it was widely shared and is reflected in Laski's remark that 'the whole philosophy of concession has been seriously called into question' [3.2].

Yet Laski also reflected the wider argument within which the question of reformism was increasingly set as the decade of the 1930s progressed. Issues of strategy were fused with a more comprehensive assault on the theoretical structure of Labour Socialism, turning on such matters as the nature of the State, political method and the analysis of capitalist economic crisis. Thus although Laski vacillated between capitalism's failure 'to win assent to its hypotheses' and its deteriorating economic performance as the cause of its impending downfall, he argued that 'for the masses . . . it is not attacked because it is regarded as inherently wrong . . . it is attacked because it is unsuccessful' [3.2]. The economic failure of capitalism prevented it from meeting the expectations generated by political democracy and this guaranteed crisis and challenge. Laski's passing note that 'large-scale economic recovery might permit the resumption of the policy of concessions' [3.2] was intended to illustrate just how unlikely was any permanent rescue for capitalist democracy. Whereas much earlier socialist thought in Britain had been predominantly ethical, in the 1930s it became heavily economic. The economic crisis of capitalism shaped the character of socialist argument in general, whether that crisis was believed to be final and fatal (as with Laski or Strachey) or amenable to an economics of recovery (as with the neo-Keynesianism of G. D. H. Cole). For example, the chaos of capitalism, reflected in its inability to prevent slumps and unemployment, was contrasted with the rationality of socialist economic planning. The tradition of socialism as rationalism was drawn upon to promote 'planning' as a cornerstone of socialist argument in the 1930s, sustained in part by the Soviet example. As the title of an influential book by Barbara Wootton put it, the issue was *Plan or no plan.*[43]

The widespread belief in capitalist collapse had a profound influence on socialist thinking, especially when linked to developing political events throughout Europe. Many of the theoretical supports of a parliamentary gradualism seemed to have been kicked away by these economic and political developments, and this produced a renewal of interest in Marxism among many British socialists (just as it also produced a renewed interest in, and attachment to, the Soviet Union[44]). Thus G. D. H. Cole could write in 1933 that: 'to look around on the world of today with seeing eyes is to be a Marxist, for Marxism alone explains what is going on'.[45] Only Marxism seemed sufficiently comprehensive to encompass and explain the seeming disintegration of an entire civilisation and to offer the promise of a successful reconstruction. This sense of a civilisation in crisis and decay was undoubtedly decisive in John Strachey's embrace of Marxism and his proclamation of 'the end of British socialism',[46] but it was reflected also in Laski's liberal despair that was converted into a Marxisant proclivity for global and schematic propositions about the course of contemporary history (contrary to his earlier dismissal of Marx,[47] and often with scant regard for actual events and tendencies). Thus Strachey emphasised the need for acceptance of 'the fact of finality' [3.4] in relation to modern European civilisation, and Laski argued that there was 'no prospect of final adjustment' within existing society because it lacked 'that area of common agreement about fundamentals which makes possible the unity needful for peace' [3.2]. It is difficult to feel that approaches of this kind, generally rooted in a schematic Marxism (or 'Marxism plus habeas-corpus' as Laski's position was once described[48]), were adequate guides to analysis or action in the 1930s. They fostered a neglect of the recuperative powers of capitalism and an exaggeration of socialist possibilities, as well as a dismissal of reformist social democracy (at one period in the language of 'social fascism') and an uncritical identification with the Soviet Union. Most serious of all, a facile economic determinism issued in a grim misreading of fascism as (necessarily) the death agony of capitalism (or 'nothing but monopoly-capitalism imposing its will on those masses whom it has deliberately transformed into its slaves' as Laski described it[49]) and a consequent failure to explore the real implications for socialist theory and practice of this new, twentieth-century type of political formation.

Despite the mythology of the Red Decade, it was not neo-Marxism but a New Fabian neo-Keynesianism that proved a more durable product of the 1930s. A group of younger socialist economists (like Jay, Durbin and Gaitskell), as well as the older G. D. H. Cole, denied that the collapse of capitalism was inevitable and drew upon a Keynesian economics of recovery to argue that the case for socialism had therefore to be stated in other terms. Thus Douglas Jay argued for an egalitarian definition of socialism as 'the abolition of private unearned or inherited incomes rather than of the private ownership of the means of production' and pointed out that John Strachey's conception of socialism in terms of planning and social-ised production was 'perfectly compatible with all the most unbridled abuses of private capitalism' [3.5]. Strachey himself later identified the work of Jay and Keynes as important in his reconciliation with reformism, because of their demonstration that economic recovery was possible and collapse avoidable.[50]

It was not merely in economic thinking that the decade of the 1930s left its mark on socialist thought in Britain, with important consequences for policy and outlook. An economic reformism was paralleled by a political commitment to a 'democratic socialism' as a distinctive tradition. This commitment was felt to be necessary as a response to the varieties of unfreedom and undemocratic practice that had revealed themselves in the 1930s, some of them wearing socialist labels. As Orwell observed, recent experience had shown that centralised ownership could just mean 'a self-elected political party, and oligarchy and privilege can return, based on power rather than on money' [3.7], and therefore a new definition of socialism was required. Evan Durbin argued that 'to betray democracy is to betray socialism' [3.6] and presented the essential task as the delineation of a socialist programme in terms of the democratic method. At this same time G. D. H. Cole (a socialist who *had* understood the nature of fascism) sought to reconstruct Fabianism by assembling the credentials of a 'liberal socialism', combining central planning with democratic control and liberal freedoms, and regarded the possibility of such an enterprise as 'the great question that confronts us in building our Socialist civilisation for tomorrow' [3.3]. It is clear then that, despite the allurements of other theoretical traditions, the real impact of the 1930s on British socialism was in terms of a clarifying redefinition of its own tradition. Characteristically, R. H. Tawney had felt no distracting allurements in the 1930s, knowing that socialism was about the morally desirable and not the historically or economically necessary. At the beginning of the decade he had prefaced his eloquent exposition of the democratic socialist case for equality by reminding his readers that the only test of new forms of social organisation was whether they were 'more favourable than the old to a spirit of humanity and freedom in social relations' [3.1]. Armed with this test, Tawney was unlikely to find much to attract him in a decade in which (as he later remarked) 'invitations to hunt tigers were issued by sportsmen with whom a brave man might well hesitate to shoot rabbits'.[51]

The post-war Labour Government, with its programme of limited nationalisation and welfare provision, was the culmination of 'the road to 1945' and of the 'socialist generation'.[52] Its very achievements emptied the cupboard of practical reformism (even before the end of the Government's lifetime) and raised the question of what socialism now meant, both theoretically and programmatically. Moreover, this was a question that had to be answered in conditions of renewed capitalist prosperity and political quiescence, and against the background of the political and economic experience of the 1930s. It demanded an analysis of the developing nature of post-war society, and of the relationship between these developments and traditional socialist objectives. There were both collective (*New Fabian essays, Conviction, Twentieth century socialism, Out of apathy*) and individual efforts (Crosland, Strachey) addressed to this problem in the immediate post-war decades, with a widespread belief in the need for some kind of 'revision' in the socialist position to take account of a changing environment. Even a stout defender of a traditional collectivism like Aneurin Bevan thought that society was now 'between two worlds' and that the necessary primacy of public property would need to incorporate the fact 'that a mixed economy is what most people of the West would prefer' [4.5].

Just as much socialist writing in the 1930s was economic in orientation, in the 1950s and 1960s it became markedly sociological. The key arenas were now those of class, power and culture. The need for this shift of emphasis was expressed most forcefully in C. A. R. Crosland's declaration that 'today traditional capitalism has been reformed and modified almost out of existence, and it is with a quite different form of society that socialists must now concern themselves' [4.1]. In other words, the economic problem was effectively solved and socialists should therefore divert their attention to an original ethical concern with the achievement of social equality. It is easy enough with hindsight to mock Crosland's economic optimism, but it did nevertheless represent a damaging assumption as far as his general position was concerned (as did his acceptance of the benign and domesticated nature of contemporary capitalism). It is interesting to reflect that Raymond Williams (not an economist, unlike Crosland) was better able to notice the 'ominous signs' that meant that 'the ordinary optimism about Britain's economic future can be reasonably seen as simple complacency' [4.3].

Introduction

It was possible to argue for a switch of emphasis within socialist thought without also maintaining that capitalism had effectively disappeared or that economic analysis no longer mattered. John Strachey achieved a comprehension in his account of contemporary capitalism (as befitted a former Marxist) that distinguished it from much other writing of this period, and in which he argued that capitalism had undergone a 'mutation' towards a more concentrated and centralised system ('last stage capitalism') that ran contrary to the democratic trend towards the diffusion of power. In Strachey's view, 'such contradictory trends can hardly co-exist indefinitely' and it was now the essential task to establish democratic political power over the new concentrations of private economic power, 'for political power and economic power are, in the last resort, merely aspects of one indivisible whole, namely power itself' [4.2]. There was a wider concern with questions of power at this time, if at a somewhat less comprehensive theoretical level. Experience of the 1930s contributed to this, as did contemporary concern about the 'managerial society'. Thus Crossman announced that 'the planned economy and the centralisation of power are no longer socialist objectives' and that 'the main task of socialism today is to prevent the concentration of power in the hands of *either* industrial management *or* the state bureaucracy' [4.4]. Richard Titmuss identified the new 'massive concentrations of interlocking economic, managerial and self-regarding professional power' [4.7] as the contemporary accelerators of inequality and argued that the pursuit of social equality (even in Croslandite terms) depended upon bringing this 'growth of irresponsible power' under new forms of social control.

As a contributor to *Conviction*, the philosopher and novelist Iris Murdoch argued that the Welfare State should be regarded as marking 'the successful end of the first road along which the Socialist movement in this country elected to travel' and that it was 'time now to go back and explore the other road, to go back to the point of divergence' [4.6] (although another contributor to the same volume showed how far from completion was even the first road[53]). This meant the restatement of socialism in terms of an 'autonomous moral conception', and Murdoch argued for a return to the concerns of the Guild Socialists. That veteran Guild Socialist, G. D. H. Cole, had also returned forcefully to these earlier concerns as his contribution to the theoretical deadlock of the 1950s, and at the very end of his life was to be found addressing himself to the question 'Socialism: centralist or libertarian?' 'To my mind', he wrote, 'there have always been two fundamental cleavages in Socialist thought – the cleavage between revolutionaries and reformists, and the cleavage between centralisers and federalists'. He argued that the first cleavage had received most attention traditionally, at the expense of the second.[54]

Cole also provided a bridge from an older socialist tradition to the 'New Left' of the late 1950s and early 1960s. The New Left were originally Marxist intellectuals who broke from the Communist Party in 1956 over Hungary and devoted themselves to restoring Marxist theory after its Stalinist accretions; at first keeping their distance from the 'bourgeois' Labour Party but were influential in the student movements of the 1960s, many of whose members a decade later entered the Labour Party. A revaluation of William Morris and of Guild Socialism formed part of the reworking of cultural history that (linked to contemporary cultural analysis) seemed an essential political project for the New Left. In his foreword to the New Left volume *Out of apathy*, Norman Birnbaum announced that: 'We have enlarged the usual scope of political discussion to consider (with Richard Hoggart and Raymond Williams) the possibility of a common culture in industrial Britain . . . The problem of the quality of daily life in industrial society ought to be at the centre of socialist thought and not, where it is usually found, at its periphery'.[55] It was necessary to find neglected traditions and sources of renewal for the task of challenging the suffocating culture of a commercial and bureaucratic society. Inchoate and emotional as it often was, New Left writing did represent an attempt to break the moral and intellectual deadlock of social democracy in the face of consumer capitalism. This meant talking about values, class and power, and reopening such closed issues as workers' control and industrial democracy (about which Crosland contentedly noted that 'today one scarcely hears a whisper of these matters at Labour Party or Trade Union conferences'[56]). An important influence on the New Left was Raymond Williams, whose powerful cultural analysis of the 'contradictions' within existing society pointed the way towards new meanings, values and institutions aimed at the creation of a genuine community and away from a current deadlock in which, in trying to think about social change, 'we seem reduced to a choice between speculator and bureaucrat' [4.3]. One important way in which the area of choice could be expanded was that 'the pressure now, in a wide area of our social life, should be towards a participatory democracy, in which the ways and means of involving people much more closely in the process of self-government can be learned and extended' [4.3]. Such was the climate of the times that

Labour's return to power in 1964, after a long winter in the wilderness, could be regarded by socialists as at least an opening towards the kind of project that Williams had described.[57] The closure of this opening, sealed off by a Wilsonian ideology of 'modernisation' (an echo of an earlier MacDonaldite rhetoric of unitary progress), was to be the signal for a new era of socialist theorising. But now a main object of such theory was social democracy itself.

Thus it is not just the fear of a loss of historical perspective that explains why the material collected here does not extend beyond the early 1960s. The point is not that there has been no socialist theorising since then, but that it has been theoretical activity of a different kind. The material anthologised here is recognisably a common tradition, in the way that much subsequent socialist literature is not. However, it is not yet possible to say whether this represents an interlude in the British socialist tradition or a permanent rupture and fragmentation. It has its source in the conjuncture of a post-1956 unattached Marxism with a post-1964 demoralised Labour Socialism. As one product of that conjuncture put it, 'a definition has failed, and we are looking for new definitions and directions'.[58] In fact, two definitions were judged to have failed, both official Communism and official Labourism, and this created a space in which new theoretical and organisational excursions could be embarked upon.

The character of Labour's tenure of office in the 1960s and 1970s is of inescapable importance here, just as the experience of 1929–31 was decisive in shaping socialist thought during the decade that followed. The deification of 'pragmatism' and the denigration of theory *of any kind* had crippling consequences both for Labour's performance and for the theoretical credentials of a whole political tradition. It was not that Labour was 'revisionist' in these years, but that there was not even a coherent egalitarian revisionism of the kind espoused by Crosland or Gaitskell. The discovery that inequality had actually increased during a period of Labour rule provided damning testimony to this.[59] The dismal experience of these years presented a stark contrast (and challenge) to the sweeping and optimistic rationality of 1950s social democratic revisionism, but this challenge was not seriously taken up in the resulting theoretical vacuum. Crosland restated his belief in the essential correctness of the revisionist reformulation of socialist ends, but confessed to an excessive optimism in his earlier work about the means to their achievement and concluded that 'a move to the Left is needed'[60] if further progress was to be made. Less robust social democrats (like Roy Jenkins) simply suggested the need for more 'idealism' in tackling particular social problems.[61] From the Left it was argued that the revisionist thesis had exaggerated the power of the State in relation to contemporary capitalism and that the development of increasingly concentrated economic power required new forms of socialist control and planning. It was claimed that the traditional distinction between 'macro' and 'micro' economic levels was no longer adequate because of the power now wielded by a small number of giant multinational firms over national economies, and that this new 'meso-economic'[62] sector provided the grounds for new forms of State intervention.

What was lacking in all of this was any attempt at a comprehensive restatement of the socialist position in terms of the tradition represented in this anthology. Instead there was fragmentation, and attempts to move 'beyond the fragments' were cast in a different idiom. The period had provided an object lesson in the degenerative potential of social democracy, and much theoretical activity was devoted to an exposition of social democracy's role in a developing British corporatism[63] and the need for different theoretical perspectives than those that had sustained British socialism in the past.[64] It was a case of Tawney out, Gramsci in (the work of the early century Italian communist Gramsci, with its focus on 'cultural hegemony' and the role of the intellectuals, was embraced enthusiastically at this time by those intellectuals in search of a new political strategy). The 'revival of Marxism' in this period coincided with an institutional expansion of social science and this had important consequences for the tradition represented here. Perhaps most important of all, a distinctive British socialism (identified wrongly but understandably with the recent performance of social democratic politicians) was set aside in favour of a denationalised social science of Marxist provenance. Moreover, a public, persuasive literature of socialism (as was the material collected here) was increasingly displaced by a private literature in a private language (of 'problematics', 'hegemonic perspectives', etc.) circulating among the academies and the sects. In a nice parody of the thing described, one observer saw the problem as that of 'a routineised and compulsive internalisation of sectarian dialogue'.[65]

The effect of all this was to make it difficult to define the theoretical shape of British socialism at the centenary of its modern revival. The social democratic offensive of the 1950s had issued in the bankruptcy of ideas of the 1970s. The basis of a traditional ethical socialism had been eroded, displaced by the harsher disciplines of an abstracted social science. Neither the Fabian head nor the ILP heart of British socialism seemed in healthy condition. The denuded theoretical cupboard of Labour politics was increasingly restocked with an uneasy mixture of sub-Marxism and radical populism, and some of this restocking was eagerly undertaken by envoys from previously hostile traditions who sometimes contributed an intolerant disregard for political and procedural values (a disregard often proclaimed as 'democracy' or, in its own unlovely idiom, as 'democratisation'). The politics of Mr Benn represented a renaissance of socialist enthusiasm (at least in some quarters), but scarcely a creative extension of British socialist ideas. His radical populism, announced as 'home-grown British',[66] had a motley and precarious theoretical base (claiming a direct passage from the Bible to 'the moving words of Clause IV' and embracing every popular movement, notably Chartism, on the way) that seemed to draw only tenuously upon a specifically socialist tradition. Moreover, his style of saintly didacticism did not convey the impression of a mind seriously grappling with a difficult argument, and this left key issues (such as the link between central planning and local self-management) massively unresolved and prevented him building upon an earlier Guild Socialist tradition with which, curiously, he failed to establish a vitalising connection. Likewise, his insistent distinction between 'social democracy' and 'democratic socialism' was not accompanied by any serious attempt to explore the theoretical pedigrees of these traditions in order to establish what distinction (if any) there actually was, apart from the fact that one sounded rather more muscular than the other. Nor was this project undertaken by the social democrats themselves,[67] despite the fact that the centenary of modern British socialism was also the occasion for a schism within its broad church. Some social democrats became Social Democrats (a nice touch of centennial irony, since the term 'social democracy' had once been historical shorthand for organised Marxism, hence its adoption by Hyndman's Social Democratic Federation in the 1880s) and they sought to appropriate at least part of the British socialist tradition for their cause.[68] However, the problem of capitalism now seemed to be replaced by the 'crisis of industrialism'[69] in their hands, and the goal of a self-managing society reduced to assorted calls for more 'participation' and 'decentralisation'. The socialist content of this new Social Democracy seems insecure, and likely to be further eroded by the corrosive influence of electoral pressures and its Liberal alliance.

However, the continued disintegration of the Labour Party might create enough political and theoretical space for the new movement.

Thus a century after the socialist revival of the 1880s the 'radiant ambiguities of the word socialism' (Tawney's phrase) seemed more radiant than ever. However, some of these ambiguities and their possible consequences had been apparent to the most prescient of the socialist pioneers. William Morris, with an eye on the Fabians, had warned of the dangers of a 'sham, utilitarian socialism' resulting from a social reformism and wondered pessimistically 'whether the Society of Inequality might not accept the quasi-socialist machinery . . . and work it for the purpose of upholding that society in a somewhat shorn condition, maybe, but a safe one . . . The workers better treated, better organised, helping to govern themselves, but with no more pretence to equality with the rich, nor any more hope for it than they have now'.[70] A similar anticipation was voiced by Bernard Shaw, although he cheerfully accepted the achievement of such a 'somewhat shorn condition' as the inevitable culmination of the socialist project, for 'it will have so completely relieved the pressure to which it owes its force that it will recede before the next great movement in social development' [1.7]. Both Morris and Shaw could have found support for their anticipations in the situation a century later, as their descendants endeavoured to reformulate the socialist argument in the difficult light of an intervening, twentieth-century experience.

One recent book asked simply *What went wrong?*[71] with the socialist dream. Much had gone right of course, in terms of such things as greater economic security and a diminution of social inequality. Thus Attlee could remind Laski, in a celebrated exchange of letters in 1944, of 'the extent to which what we cried in the wilderness five and thirty years ago has now become part of the assumptions of the ordinary man and woman. The acceptance of these assumptions has its effect both in legislation and administration, but its gradualness tends to hide our appreciation of the facts.'[72] Yet Britain of the 1980s was clearly not the 'socialist commonwealth' envisaged by the socialist pioneers of the 1880s (and even some of the real gains seemed again to be threatened). Perhaps the very notion of a 'socialist commonwealth' was simply one of the socialist 'illusions' described by Shaw, except that the Fabian project had come to seem scarcely less illusory. An optimistic historical rationality, whether Marxist or Fabian, seemed to have had its (nineteenth-century) day, unable to withstand the weight of twentieth-century experience. A casualty of this was the idea of planning, once central to the socialist alternative to capitalism but now unable to carry its former conviction (a disability shared by experts in general and by social scientists in particular). Nor could the State be so easily embraced as the benign agency of planning and general social improvement, when it was felt (at best) to have inaugurated a system of bureaucratic welfare collectivism and (at worst) to have been the instrument of totalitarian tyranny. If the nineteenth century had demonstrated the evils of capitalism, the twentieth century had warned of the problems and perversions of socialism. Considerations of this kind are reflected in some contemporary socialist thinking, for example in the renewed interest (among socialists of otherwise different persuasions) in questions of scale and participation and the search for non-bureaucratic forms of socialism both in relation to industry and the wider society.[73] However, it cannot yet be claimed that this task has been pursued with sufficient rigour or system, and the impression is created of a cluster of ideas in search of a theory. What is so far lacking, it might perhaps be suggested, is a convincing theory of community socialism, of an 'enabling' State which combines sufficient central control to secure a socialist framework of social policy and economic activity with an active sponsorship of varieties of local and functional initiative to secure a participatory diversity of organisational forms in relation to industry and public services.

This points towards a post-Fabian socialism, and in a context in which international and technological developments have intensified the economic problems confronting British socialists. However, far from being obsolete or irrelevant in this situation much of the British socialist tradition represented in this anthology addresses itself to concerns that seem decidedly contemporary. If it is a tradition 'dosed with eclecticism' (as E. P. Thompson has described it[74]), this has allowed it to draw upon a large reservoir of sources and to speak in a local idiom. Even the absence of a Marxist orthodoxy may be seen as having an expansive effect on socialist ideas, in so far as it prevented political thinking being inhibited by the test of political and doctrinal correctness. Whatever its other defects, Fabian tolerance has had a civilising effect on the conduct of political argument and contributed to the diversity of socialist opinion. In a century in which political methods have shown themselves to be inextricably connected to political products this is a not inconsiderable asset. Even a British (Fabian) empiricism may be seen as a useful antidote to some contemporary meta-theory and at least a reminder that socialism has to keep an eye on the real world. Also in this heretical vein, there is the standing reminder from George Orwell that socialist writing need not be incompatible with clear prose, and that we should be on our guard when it seems to be.

Many of the substantive concerns of British socialism over the last century seem also to have a new, contemporary relevance. The search for a social basis for 'community' and for the practice of 'fellowship' has been at the centre of much socialist thought in Britain, and it is central to modern preoccupations too. The vision (from William Morris) of an active community of free and equal individuals remains a stubborn challenge both to the passive, vicarious and unequal society of commercial capitalism and to many contemporary varieties of socialism. The early British socialist concerns with the nature of work, machinery and the environment once again seem entirely contemporary, as does the concern with self-government and decentralisation. There are materials (from Cole and the Guild Socialists) for a socialist tradition that is decentralist and participatory. There is the lesson (powerfully taught by Tawney) that socialist means should never be confused with socialist ends; that even equality, let alone nationalisation, found its real justification in so far as it contributed to the socialist goal of a common life ('fellowship') and that the connecting thread between means and ends had always to be kept in view. Orwell taught the terrible lesson that Tawney already knew, that inequality was also about power and that the socialist project could be disfigured and debased by its abuse of State power in the technical conditions of the twentieth century. Perhaps most distinctive and important of all, the British socialist tradition was 'unashamedly ethical',[75] even when it was other things too. Its message was that socialism was about values, and that to be a socialist was to make a moral choice and not merely to assert an economic interest or to recognise a historical necessity.

At times this sort of moralism could be divorced from any serious analysis of capitalism, or even serve as a substitute for such analysis and for effective political action. Sometimes this was a generous (if disabling) error, at other times it allowed politicians to practise a moral rhetoric of obfuscation. Yet it is simply not true that British socialism has always failed to make the necessary linkages, for at its best it has combined ethical valuation with analytical power in a combination that has provided the materials for a serious socialist politics. This political practice would be reformist, but a reformism that was coherent and purposive (which is surely the essential point in this matter). The reality has been, of course, that so much socialist reformism has been incoherent and purposeless, and this has cast a contemporary shadow of neglect over British socialism as a body of ideas. Yet such neglect would be a considerable loss in the present reformulation of the socialist project, at a time when the loosening of some of the traditional theoretical and organisational rigidities within British and international socialism is creating an opening towards new ideas and the retrieval of submerged traditions. Whether British socialism can find in this situation a source of renewal cannot be foreseen, but it can at least take heart from William Morris's description of 'how men fight and lose the battle, and the thing they fought for comes about in spite of their defeat, and when it comes, it turns out not to be what they meant and other men have to fight for what they meant, under another name'.

NOTES

1. See H. M. Drucker, *Doctrine and ethos in the Labour Party*, Allen and Unwin: London, 1979.
2. Some examples are R. Miliband, *Parliamentary socialism* (2nd edn), Merlin Press: London, 1973; D. Coates, *The Labour Party and the struggle for socialism*. CUP: Cambridge, 1975; and D. Howell, *British social democracy*, Croom Helm: London, 1976.
3. Aneurin Bevan, *In place of fear*, Quartet: London, 1978, p. 39.
4. Bernard Shaw, 'The illusions of socialism' in E. Carpenter (ed.), *Forecasts of the coming century*, The Labour Press: Manchester, 1897, p. 157.
5. On the positivist influence, see Royden Harrison, *Before the socialists*, Routledge: London, 1965.
6. F. Reid, *Keir Hardie*, Croom Helm: London, 1978, p. 51.
7. E. J. Hobsbawm, *Labouring men*, Weidenfeld and Nicolson: London, 1964, p. 253.
8. John Saville, 'The ideology of labourism' in R. Benewick, R. N. Berki and B. Parekh (eds), *Knowledge and belief in politics*, Allen and Unwin: London, 1973, pp. 214–15.
9. R. H. Tawney, *Equality* (4th edn), Allen and Unwin: London, 1964, p. 200.
10. See especially the articles by Perry Anderson ('Origins of the present crisis') and Tom Nairn ('The nature of the Labour Party') which first appeared in *New Left Review* in 1964 and then in P. Anderson and R. Blackburn (eds), *Towards socialism*, Fontana: London 1965.

11. E. P. Thompson, 'The peculiarities of the English' in R. Miliband and J. Saville (eds), *The socialist register*, Merlin Press: London, 1965. This essay also appears in E. P. Thompson, *The poverty of theory*, Merlin Press: London, 1978.

12. Hardie to Engels 21 May 1889; quoted in K. O. Morgan, *Keir Hardie*, Weidenfeld and Nicolson: London, 1975, p. 40.

13. E. P. Thompson, *William Morris: romantic to revolutionary*, Merlin Press: London, 1977, p. 792. The rival accounts of Morris are represented by J. Bruce Glasier, *William Morris and the early days of the socialist movement*, Longman: London, 1921, and R. Page Arnot, *William Morris: a vindication*, Lawrence and Wishart: London, 1934.

14. For a useful description of the 'tendencies' within socialism, see R. N. Berki, *Socialism*, Dent: London, 1975.

15. S. Webb, *Socialism in England*, Swan Sonnenschein: London, 1890, p. 109.

16. See A. W. Wright, *G. D. H. Cole and socialist democracy*, Clarendon Press: Oxford, 1979.

17. Marx to Sorge, 15 Dec. 1881; Engels to Bebel, 30 Aug. 1883; in Marx and Engels, *Selected correspondence*, Lawrence and Wishart: London, 1936.

18. F. Engels, 'The fourth of May in London' (1890) cited in ibid., p. 469.

19. The best account remains H. Pelling, *The origins of the Labour Party 1880–1900* (2nd edn), Clarendon Press: Oxford, 1965.

20. See for example H. Collins, 'The Marxism of the Social Democratic Federation' in A. Briggs and J. Saville (eds), *Essays in labour history 1886–1923*, Macmillan: London, 1971. On Hyndman the standard history (though not strong on his thought) is C. Tsuzuki, *H. M. Hyndman and British socialism*, Clarendon Press: Oxford, 1961.

21. E. J. Hobsbawm, 'Hyndman and the SDF' in Hobsbawm, op. cit., p. 237; G. D. H. Cole, *A history of socialist thought, Vol. 2. Marxism and anarchism 1850–1890*, Macmillan: London, 1954, p. 409.

22. S. Pierson, *Marxism and the origins of British socialism*, Cornell: Ithaca and London, 1973, p. 67.

23. E. R. Pease, *The history of the Fabian Society*, Fabian Society and Allen and Unwin: London, 1916, p. 236. Pease's claim is contested by A. M. McBriar, *Fabian socialism and English politics 1884–1918*, CUP: Cambridge 1962, pp. 347–8 and E. J. Hobsbawm, 'The Fabians reconsidered' in Hobsbawm, op. cit., pp. 250–71.

24. W. Wolfe, *From radicalism to socialism: men and ideas in the formation of Fabian socialist doctrines 1881–1889*, Yale: New Haven and London, 1975, p. 280 and *passim*.

25. Bernard Shaw, 'The transition to social democracy' in *Fabian Essays* (6th edn), Allen and Unwin: London, 1962, p. 235.

26. ibid, p. 235.

27. Pierson, op. cit., p. 140.

28. On this see M. J. Wiener, *English culture and the decline of the industrial spirit 1850–1980*, CUP: Cambridge, 1981.

29. This is the theme of S. Pierson, *British socialists: the journey from fantasy to politics*, Harvard: Cambridge, Mass. and London, 1979.

30. See the introduction by Robert Dowse to his edition of James Keir Hardie, *From serfdom to socialism*, Harvester: Brighton, 1974.

31. On MacDonald's thought, see R. Barker, 'Socialism and progressivism in the political thought of Ramsay MacDonald' in A. J. A. Morris (ed.), *Edwardian radicalism 1900–1914*, Routledge: London, 1974; R. Barker, 'Political myth: Ramsay MacDonald and the Labour Party', *History*, Vol. 61, Feb. 1976; and Bernard Barker's introduction to his edition of *Ramsay MacDonald's political writings*, Allen Lane: London, 1972.

32. See Ross Terrill, *R. H. Tawney and his times: socialism as fellowship*, Andre Deutsch: London, 1973.

33. S. Webb, 'A stratified democracy', *New Commonwealth*, Supplement, 28 Nov. 1919, p. 2.

34. C. R. Attlee, 'Guild v. municipal socialism', *Socialist Review*, May 1923. Attlee also said of Cole that 'he has caused me, like many others, to revise my previous views as to the future industrial structure of society' (*idem*).

35. S. Macintyre, *A proletarian science: Marxism in Britain 1917–1933*, CUP: Cambridge, 1980, p. 234.

36. Most notably by S. Beer, *Modern British politics*, Faber: London, 1965.

37. B. Webb, *Diaries 1924–1932*, M. I. Cole (ed.), Longman: London, 1956, pp. 92–3 (entry for 4 May, 1926).

38. See R. Skidelsky, *Politicians and the slump*, Macmillan: London, 1967.

39. There were (contrary to Skidelsky) available socialist alternatives on offer, from J. A. Hobson's ILP grouping and from G. D. H. Cole. So the socialist 'failure' can be seen rather differently: see R. H. Tawney, 'The choice before the Labour

Party', *Political Quarterly*, **3**, July–Sept. 1932, and Royden Harrison 'Labour government: then and now', *Political Quarterly*, **41** Jan.–Mar. 1970.

40. See R. Eatwell and A. W. Wright, 'Labour and the lessons of 1931', *History*, **63**, Feb. 1978, 38–53.

41. On the politics of this period see B. Pimlott, *Labour and the Left in the 1930s*, CUP: Cambridge, 1977.

42. See for example R. Bassett, *The essentials of parliamentary democracy*, Macmillan: London, 1935; and A. H. Hanson, 'The Labour Party and House of Commons reform' in his *Planning and the politicians*, Routledge: London, 1969.

43. For a discussion of planning ideas within the Labour Party at this time, see A. Oldfield, 'The Labour Party and planning–1934, or 1918?', *Society for the Study of Labour History Bulletin* **25**, autumn 1972.

44. See D. Caute, *The fellow-travellers*, Weidenfeld and Nicolson: London, 1973; and B. Jones, *The Russia complex: the British Labour Party and the Soviet Union*, Manchester University Press: Manchester, 1978.

45. In a contribution to a symposium on Marx in *Plebs*, Mar. 1933. However, this has to be read alongside Cole's particular version of Marxism, as set out at this time in his *What Marx really meant*, Gollancz: London, 1934.

46. This phrase is used as a chapter heading in Strachey's *What are we to do?*, Gollancz: London, 1938.

47. See Laski's essay on *Karl Marx*, Fabian Society and Allen and Unwin: London, 1922; and his Home University Library study of *Communism*, Williams and Norgate: London, 1927.

48. By Felix Frankfurter, cited in M. Peretz, 'Laski Redivivus', *Journal of Contemporary History*, **1**, No. 2, 1966. On Laski's political thought, see H. A. Deane, *The political ideas of Harold J. Laski*, Columbia University Press: New York, 1955, and B. Zylstra, *From pluralism to collectivism: the development of Harold Laski's political thought*, Van Gorcum: Netherlands, 1968. There is still no study of Laski as a British socialist, rather than as an academic political theorist.

49. In his Foreword to R. A. Brady, *The spirit and structure of German fascism*, Gollancz: London, 1937.

50. See his remarks in his contribution on 'Tasks and achievements of British Labour', in R. H. S. Crossman (ed.), *New Fabian essays*, Turnstile Press: London, 1952. Here he cites Keynes and Jay as important influences on his revised position, which he dates from 'about 1938'.

51. R. H. Tawney, *Equality* (4th edn), Allen and Unwin: London, 1964, p. 198.

52. See Beer, op. cit. and P. Addison, *The road to 1945*, Cape: London, 1975.

53. See the pioneering essay by Brian Abel-Smith, 'Whose Welfare State?', *Conviction*, N. Mackenzie (ed.), MacGibbon and Kee: London, 1958.

54. G. D. H. Cole, 'Socialism: centralist or libertarian?' 1959; an article written to introduce an Italian collection of his work.

55. E. P. Thompson (ed.), *Out of apathy*, Stevens: London, 1960, pp. x–xi. This meant a revaluation of such earlier figures as the Guild Socialists, whose emphasis remained 'creative and indispensable' (Raymond Williams, *Culture and society 1780–1950*, Penguin: Harmondsworth, 1961, p. 191).

56. C. A. R. Crosland, *The Conservative enemy*, Cape: London, 1962, p. 217.

57. How widely this view was shared (and later abandoned) can be seen in the distance between the first (1961) and second (1973) editions of R. Miliband's *Parliamentary socialism*. A new post-script in the second edition distanced itself from the perspective of the earlier edition, in which 'the concluding section of the book left open the possibility that the Labour Party might yet become an adequate agency for that radical transformation of British society to which it had for so long been formally committed' (2nd edn, Merlin: London, 1973, p. 350). Similarly, even a New Left Reviewer like Tom Nairn had written of Labour's arrival in power in 1964 that 'socialists everywhere should see its advent with a certain hope, a certain critical confidence, and not merely as the futile repetition of an old illusion' ('The nature of the Labour Party' in *Towards Socialism*, Fontana: London, 1965, p. 217).

58. R. Williams (ed.), *May Day manifesto 1968* Penguin: Harmondsworth, 1968, p. 14.

59. See P. Townsend and N. Bosanquet (eds), *Labour and inequality*, Fabian Society: London, 1972.

60. Anthony Crosland, *Socialism now*, Cape: London, 1974, p. 44.

61. Roy Jenkins, *What matters now*, Fontana: London, 1972.

62. The term was coined in the central work of this new revisionism, S. Holland, *The socialist challenge*, Quartet: London, 1975.

63. See for example, L. Panitch, *Social democracy and industrial militancy*, CUP: Cambridge, 1976; and the historical analysis of 'corporate bias' in K. Middlemas, *Politics in industrial society*, Andre Deutsch: London, 1979.

64. Thus Miliband declared that: 'A serious revolutionary party, in the circumstances of advanced capitalism, has to be the kind of 'hegemonic' party of which Gramsci spoke ...' R. Miliband, *The state in capitalist society*, Weidenfeld and Nicolson: London, 1969, p. 274.

65. Bernard Crick, 'Some socialist books', *Political Quarterly*, **48**, Jan.–Mar. 1977, p. 92.

66. Tony Benn, *Arguments for socialism*, Penguin: Harmondsworth, 1980, p. 146. See also his *Arguments for democracy*, Cape: London, 1981.

67. But see John Mackintosh, 'Socialism or social democracy?', *Political Quarterly*, **43**, Oct.–Dec. 1972, and 'Has social democracy failed in Britain?', *Political Quarterly*, **49**, July–Sept. 1978.

68. Thus Shirley Williams sought to appropriate Tawney in her *Politics is for people*, Penguin: Harmondsworth, 1981; and David Owen laid claim to Cole and the Guild Socialists in his *Face the future*, OUP: Oxford, 1981.

69. Williams, op. cit., p. 16.

70. William Morris, 'Communism', a lecture delivered in 1893 and published as a Fabian Tract in 1903, and in his *Collected Works*, Vol. 23, pp. 264–76.

71. J. Seabrook, *What went wrong?*, Gollancz: London, 1978.

72. Attlee to Laski, 1 May, 1944; quoted in K. Martin, *Harold Laski*, Gollancz: London, 1953, p. 152.

73. This contemporary trend is evident in such different works as those by Benn, op. cit.; E. Luard, *Socialism without the state*, Macmillan: London, 1979; G. Radice, *Community socialism*, Fabian Tract 464, Fabian Society: London, 1979; F. Cripps *et al.*, *Manifesto: a radical strategy for Britain's future*, Pan: London, 1981; and the books by Shirley Williams and David Owen quoted in note 68 above.

74. E. P. Thompson, 'An open letter to Leszek Kolakowski', in R. Miliband and J. Saville (eds), *Socialist register*, Merlin: London, 1978.

75. R. H. Tawney, 'British socialism today' (June 1952) in *The radical tradition*, R. Hinden (ed.), Penguin: Harmondsworth, 1966, p. 176.

Part one
1880–1900

I.I H. M. HYNDMAN: BRITISH MARXISM

H. M. Hyndman was the key figure in the introduction of Marxist ideas into Britain during the socialist revival of the 1880s. Founder and leader of the Social Democratic Federation, the first socialist organisation of this period, Hyndman had drawn upon Marx, though without attribution, in his early book *England for all* (1881) and this had earned the wrath of Marx and contributed to the lasting antagonism of Engels and the Marx family circle. The book from which the following extracts are taken, *The historical basis of socialism in England* (1883), may be regarded as the first significant native Marxist text. In introducing it, its author carefully acknowledged his 'indebtedness to the famous German historical school of political economy headed by Karl Marx'.

. . . I have briefly passed through the economical and social transition from the England of the feudal times, when men were for the most part in command of their means of production which they handled for the purpose of obtaining articles of immediate use, only the superfluity being brought forward for exchange, they themselves also being bound to one another to their feudal superiors and to the Church by personal and not by mere pecuniary relations – from this period, which in the main represented rude wealth and prosperity for the people, the development of a race of landless families has been traced contemporaneously with a growth of large landowners, considerable farmers and capitalists, and an artisan and agricultural-labourer class, but few of whom could become masters of a business, or who could hope to obtain, either as owner or tenant, any large extent of land. During the whole of this 250 or 300 years, the condition of the mass of the people had been becoming more and more dependent upon the good pleasure of the classes above them. Exchange, which in the earlier period had been a secondary consideration for production, now gradually became the paramount object; the means of production also, as well as the control of individual exchange, instead of being very widely distributed, had become concentrated to a large extent in the hands of a class . . .

And now what is the basis and what the measure of the exchange-value of the commodities produced in our modern society? What is the meaning of the utility which they must possess ere such exchange can be carried on? It is on the correct answer to these two questions that an understanding of our complicated society depends, as well as a reasoning appreciation of the history of the great industrial revolution which dates from the end of the eighteenth century . . .

The capitalist, whether farmer or manufacturer, buys his labour as cheap as he can, and applies it to the land which he holds or rents, or to the raw material which he has purchased, so that he may produce food or commodities for exchange at a profit. When also the capitalist buys the labour-force it is the owner of the labour who sells on credit. The labourer works, with few exceptions, for a day, week, fortnight, month, before he receives his wages. He advances his labour as embodied in the commodity or part of the commodity to the capitalist: the capitalist advances nothing to him. This gives the employer every advantage. If he fails the labourers suffer: they are not paid under our law, for the labour has been sold beforehand, and duly delivered by the expenditure of force from the labourer's body. And this consumption of force of labour produces not only commodities but surplus value – an additional value which belongs to the capitalist besides. Everything else which is needed for the purposes of production – raw material, machinery, &c. – have been bought by the capitalist at their actual market value and paid for at their actual market price. It is from labour only, the labour-force of human beings compelled to compete against one another for a bare subsistence wage, that the actual employer derives his surplus value, and the merchant, &c., his profit. Out of this, his last purchase, bought on credit, the capitalist makes his capital breed. This labour-force, bought of its owner in the open market and then embodied in the commodity – this it is which gives the capitalist the additional value he hungers for . . .

In practice, of course, the labourer only gets back a small fraction of the value he produces in the shape of the money-wages he receives. For the working man who has sold his labour works under the control of the capitalist to whom his labour now belongs for an agreed period, and whose object it is that he should work hard and continuously. The reason why it seems that the capitalist does pay the labourer is because he possesses the means of production to start with, and the product in which the worker's force of labour is embodied is the property of the capitalist at the end. Wages, therefore, are paid by the capitalist in the same way as he would pay the hire of a horse or a mule. Then the employer applies this human merchandise which he has thus bought 'on the cheap' to his raw materials and machinery. The result is a social value; and not only such value, but a surplus value for the capitalist himself, derived from this purchased labour . . .

This exposition gives in brief Karl Marx's famous theory of surplus value, which, though stated by more than one English writer before him, and put forward in a philosophical form by Rodbertus was first elaborated and proved as the basis of our modern system of profit-making by Marx himself. It is clear that it quite changes the view of the distribution of wealth which finds favour with ordinary economists even now. We have seen that inventions and progress in various directions are not due to any particular class, that the organisation of labour is not the result of the skill of individuals, but is the outcome of the growth of society; yet one class is called upon to do all the labour, whilst others live enfranchised from all manual and even, in many cases, useful mental work . . .

Let it never be forgotten that the means of production, the constant capital, exist in the hands of a class only in order that with each ounce of work that is employed a proportional amount of unpaid labour may be embodied in surplus value for the benefit of the easy classes. It is the business of the capitalist to get out of his capital the largest possible amount of extra labour . . .

This is the system which gained complete predominance in English production at the end of the eighteenth century. Capital represents, therefore, an epoch in social production, and expresses a whole system of definite social relations. It does not exert its full power until the instruments of production are concentrated in the hands of one class, who then necessarily can obtain possession of all future improvements; whilst the members of another class, deprived of the means of production, either as individuals or as parts of the community, are obliged to sell their force of labour in the market in order to gain, on the average, but a bare subsistence, and render more and more surplus value – rent, profit, interest – to those who buy their labour and live upon it. Never at any previous period has capital in this form obtained complete control of any human society; yet what is really in the present shape only two hundred years old is frequently spoken of as eternal; and the competitive ideas which are the necessary growth of the society in which we live, just as the ideas of personal superiority and ecclesiastical hierarchy were the ideas of the middle ages, are applied to all the centuries, and treated as if they must necessarily be permanent.

Unfortunately the full explanation of surplus value, the exposition of how it is that, under the guise of freedom, the workers hand over the bulk of the value they produce to other classes for nothing was not fully given until within the last twenty or five-and twenty-years. Even now the overwhelming majority of employers and employed are either ignorant of the truth or cannot understand it. Had mankind seen two or three hundred years ago, or even a hundred years ago, that the growth of capital, the increased socialisation of labour, and the extension of exchange at the command of the individual, could not but mean the slavery of the producing class, some remedy might have been provided to control the development for the common good. But in a class struggle it is not reason but force that wins the day. From the date of about a hundred years ago force, economical, social, and political, became more and more at the disposal of capitalists either in one way or another. Their power extended over the whole field with a rapidity quite unexampled in the records of any other age or country; and before any steps were taken to regulate the process in the interests of the nation at large, the class struggle which hitherto has been the necessary companion or fore-runner of all progress had begun. The endeavours of the middle class to obtain control of the political, as they practically had of the economical, and in the strict sense social sphere of action, were accompanied by hopeless efforts to keep back their extending power from below. A fight between the proletariat and the middle class has kept pace step by step with the more manifest antagonism between the capitalist or mercantile class and the landowner . . .

Even while we are discussing the conditions around us, the historical movement, which, if neglected, renders all political economy utterly worthless, is pressing steadily onwards. The utopian socialists and reorganisers of society passed over the details of growth almost as lightly as the bourgeois economists. 'The eagle eye of the idealist' saw the imperfections of the society of his own day, and could suggest a better form for the future, but the development proceeding from the past and going on relentlessly through the present into the future, was too often hidden from even his gaze. The really scientific process takes account of the past and of the present, knowing right well that in this way alone is it possible to forecast, in any sound sense, the economy of the future. Those who desire to trace the origin and the effect of the machine industry must first grasp that antagonism of classes which has led irresistibly to our existing anarchy. Alike in agriculture and in manufacture, the constant improvements of machinery, the incalculable revolutions which may be wrought by new discoveries and inventions, render absolute plans or forecasts impossible. But this we can discern, that by great corporations, made up of many shareholders, who employ salaried officials to organise production or distribution; by the growing disposition of the State, even in its present bourgeois form, to take control of various departments also with a hierarchy of salaried officials, the old individualism, pure and simple, is being broken down, and collective in some degree substituted for individual effort. The revolt of the organised method of production, where each worker is more and more dependent on his fellow, against the anarchical system of exchange, where each is against all, becomes more pronounced with every successive crisis. The middle-class is incapable of handling its own social system, and the proletariat must at last come by its own. From the worse side of our existing civilisation a new and better form must be evolved, if any beneficial change takes place...

Of the organisation of the Trade Unions or their principal objects there is no need to speak at length... They constitute, in fact, an aristocracy of labour who, in view of the bitter struggle now drawing nearer and nearer, cannot be said to be other than a hindrance to that complete organisation of the proletariat which alone can obtain for the workers their proper control over their own labour... Being also fundamentally unsectarian and unpolitical, they prevent any organised attempt being made by the workers as a class to form a definite party of their own, apart from existing factions, with a view to dominate the social conditions – a victory which, of course, can only be peaceably gained by resolute political action.

Trade unions, however, whether in town or country, must lead to wider and more powerful combinations of the working classes if they are to raise the proletariat of Great Britain from their present degraded state. Those very jealousies between trades or portions of trades, as well as between the Unionist officials themselves, throw back the movement, whilst the mere existence of an aristocracy of labour tends to disguise the economical pressure under which all suffer. Trade unions have done good work in the past; so far as they defend their own people from oppression and maintain a higher standard of life they are doing good work today; but by holding aloof from the political struggle, and by refusing to strive for the control of the machinery of production in concert with their fellows they keep back the advance of their own class as a class and prepare even for their own members a sad future in view of the constant changes which are going on in every branch of human industry . . .

But the waste of Trades Union funds on strikes or petty benefits to the individuals who compose them is still more deplorable. Enormous sums have been spent or lost, directly, or indirectly, in consequence of strikes which, if applied by the Unionists to an active propaganda against the existing system, whereby a class is permitted to crush them under the pretence of scientific economy, would long since have produced a serious effect. Even the return of working-class members to Parliament, as in Germany, with a definite mandate from their fellows to uphold the claims of those who produce all wealth and live in comparative misery, would have gained the Unionists far more than they have secured by mere strikes. Twenty working-class members even in our present ill-chosen middle-class House with a thorough determination to force the economical and social oppression of their fellows upon the attention of the remaining 638 pensioners upon labour around them would soon, if thoroughly supported out of doors, change the whole course of legislation. And to bring this about would be a slight strain upon the workers compared with what unsuccessful strikes have often cost them. It is in this direction, at any rate, that we must look for any complete reform. The producing classes themselves must work out their own enfranchisement from the tyranny they suffer from. Our present suffrage, though still far from what it ought to be, gives far greater power to the workers than they have ever used to force forward their own claims . . .

Now I beg any man, no matter to what class he belongs, to look rapidly again over the official facts and figures . . . and then ask himself whether as an Englishman he can wish to perpetuate a system which results in such misery and degradation for the workers? Some there are who will not be convinced by official reports, or who believe perhaps that these things are in the nature of the case.

Examine them yourselves. Take a very simple test. Rise early in any great industrial city and watch the working men and women going to their work between five and six o'clock in the morning; note their appearance, their height, their weight, their general bearing; wait four or five hours, you can go to bed again and have breakfast, and then go out and consider the middle and upper middle class as they come into their various businesses. The contrast is but too sad and too conclusive . . .

So long as the people thought that all this misery was inevitable, so long might they possibly bow down in silence and quiet. Now that they learn each day how they suffer and are oppressed in order that others may wax fat on the fruits of their labour, is it probable that they will eternally submit? When revolution is prepared in the womb of society, he is a fool indeed who thinks he can prevent it from manifesting itself in open and declared shape. That very decay of Parliamentarism and so-called representative government which is now apparent to all helps on and is in itself indicative of the coming change. Politics, it cannot be too often repeated, are but the outcome and manifestation of the form of production and the class antagonism below. No doubt the form of government reacts in part upon the production, as religious ideas in time react in the same way. But the conflict between the socialised system of production and the individualist system of exchange has in England reached a most critical point. Though the workers of all nations must of necessity combine in order to bring about a new and better system, England is the country where the economical evolution has reached its highest development, and where the reconstruction must consequently begin.

It is a noble rivalry in which all nations may fitly take a part. The day when an abstract theorist will be a practical statesman may never come; the day when the practical statesman can dispense with being a well-grounded theorist is gone by already. Nowhere is this more true than in our own country. For to sum up our present position –

First. In no civilised country in the world is there such a monopoly of land as in Great Britain.

Second. In no country are capital, machinery, credit, and the means of production generally so concentrated in the hands of a class.

Third. In no country is there such a complete social separation between classes.

Fourth. In no country is the contrast between the excessive wealth and luxury of the few and the grinding and degrading poverty of the many so striking.

Fifth. In no country is the machinery of government so entirely in the hands of the non-producing classes, or are the people so cajoled out of voting power and due representation.

Sixth. In no country are the people so dependent for their necessary food on sources of supply thousands of miles away.

Seventh. In no country is it so difficult for a man to rise out of the wage-earning class.

Eighth. In no country is justice so dear or its administration so completely in the hands of the non-producing classes who make the laws.

Here then, are a series of indisputable facts, to which may be added the truth that the revolutionary character of our present system of production already noted is becoming more marked each day. Electricity threatens to subvert entirely the whole of our processes in every department of industry; education, imperfect as it is, teaches our workers to appreciate their surroundings, and circumstances force them to combine. No change can be for the worse in their condition. Let, then, all classes take account of the inevitable antagonism, and endeavour to help those who produce the wealth of the country to enter upon their inheritance without bloodshed, to the glory of England and to the benefit of all. Those who urge that class ought not be set against class, belong themselves to that very class which is producing and intensifying the antagonism they hypocritically deplore. Let the capitalists and their hangers-on, the landowners, strive with the workers for a peaceable change, and England may set an example of peaceful reconstruction to the world. But at present there is very little sign of any such wise and farsighted action on the part of the classes in possession; history teaches us that only resolute combination on the part of the oppressed classes has ever gained them anything. It is sad that the men in possession should be thus blind to their own best interests, and refuse to recognise facts in the society around them which point steadily in one direction. But with the misery due to the existing system, it is impossible to hold any terms. That has reached a point where national decrepitude and decay must inevitably follow, unless wholesale changes are immediately brought about. These changes are being steadily prepared all the while by the very oppression and misery themselves, as well as by the new forces placed at the disposal of humanity. It is to the control of these forces by the whole community that we must look for improvement in the near future . . .

In considering the future in any branch of human knowledge, it is absolutely necessary to base all attempts at prognostication upon the most careful records of past events. This is true of every field of inquiry, and specially true, though not always so clearly admitted, in regard to the most complicated field of all, that of human society. The study of social and economical problems is now seen to be as hopeless when divorced from sound historical methods as anatomy or surgery which took no account of lower forms of life on the work of previous generations. Not many centuries have elapsed since any man who said he could predict the return of a comet or calculate the recurrence of an eclipse would have been set down as a magician or a maniac. The elaborate diagnosis which will today enable a first-rate pathologist to state precisely the course of physical, and through physical of mental disease in a manner surprising even to the educated, is due to as carefully recorded observations as those which have guided the astronomer to his irrefragable conclusion. Rigid accuracy, so far as possible, in the tabulation of facts, guided all the while by scientific imagination, has taken the place of the slip-shod guess-work of old time led astray by theological crazes. The same with the study of the movements and relations of mankind in civilised society today. Just in so far as we can trace the evolution through the long ages of social development, precisely to that extent may we fairly hope to forecast correctly the next stages of our growth . . .

Such is the scientific and abstract record of the past and analysis of the future. The idea of the appropriation of the land and the other means of production by the State has long had a hazy existence in the minds of men who wished well to their kind. The utopian Socialist bears the same relation to the Socialist of science as the able alchemist or astrologer bears to the chemist or the astronomer of the nineteenth century. There is no possibility of bringing about the great change until men's minds are prepared for it, and the evolution has reached the necessary point. Then utopia ends and actual practice begins . . .

The ideals of Plato, More, Bellers, Rousseau, Saint Simon, Fourier, even Owen, are replaced in fact by the scientific ideals, so to say, of the student of modern social conditions, who sees in the future near or far human society with its production, its education, its life, its entire existence, organised not to the advantage of any classes however well-born or however dexterous in accumulation, but for the benefit, the well-being, and the true happiness of all. In England the early commencement of this great class struggle is assured . . .

This process we see going on under our eyes, and the only question is whether we wish to hasten or to slacken an advance inevitable in either case. The succession of world-wide crises, of which we have now had six in this century, the last having been almost a permanent crisis since 1878, prove conclusively that apart from any mere currency questions or local difficulties the workers are subject to periods of fearful privation, owing to the manner in which production at large is carried on and international exchange is conducted. No mere half measures, no ingenious sophistries evolved out of fortnightly settlements, three months' bills and bankers' balances, will suffice to deal with the anarchy due to a radically injurious system. We in England must face this question at once. The increasing dependence upon foreign sources of food supply, the growth of foreign competition in open markets, the fearful condition of the fringe of labour, force us to national and international socialism as the only way of escape from an insupportable situation at home for the mass of the people.

That the land, and with the land, mines, rivers, &c., will come under the control of the people we have already seen, nor is it reasonable to suppose that any compensation will be given to the landholders, the fund-holders, or the railway or water shareholders, when it has been determined to assume administration of all for the public benefit. To compromise in order to avoid bloodshed, may be a course that would recommend itself to the workers; but this would be a mere transfer of holdings for a time. In the end the entire power and means of production will belong to the State or its delegates, who will then be like the State itself, simply one great body of equal men organised to act in concert, with leaders chosen by themselves. It is for this purpose and not from any theoretical political grievance, that the proletariat or wage-earners must necessarily take hold of the governing power, through the medium of universal suffrage, putting an end for ever to hereditary authority and class distinctions. Centralisation and decentralisation would thus have free play in the politics of the whole community, as collective action in production would leave the freest play to individual faculty in every direction, save the accumulation of wealth at the expense of the labour of others . . .

Monopoly by a class of land, of machinery, of capital, of credit, dominates the globe. But if the power of capitalism is thus worldwide, so also is the power of Socialism, which is slowly but surely organising for its overthrow. Throughout the civilised world the workers are learning slowly that they at least have no interests at variance. The commercial wars which are waged in Asia, in South Africa, in Cochin China, in Egypt, do not profit them; the returns they bring to the capitalist class do but strengthen the domestic tyranny. In every country new associations of workers and thinkers are being formed today, and old associations are gaining strength, which have for their sole object to bring mankind together on the safe ground of a common interest. That there are different schools, some of which desire at once to resort to that destruction which modern explosives so readily lend themselves to, is undoubted. But the desire for common social organised action grows with working-class education, just as mere individual anarchism has its foundation in middle-class ideas and middle-class ignorance. It is true that the great International organisation of 1864 fell to pieces after the Paris Commune, but the basis of international agreement remains, and common action is being everywhere prepared for which cannot but have stupendous results. We are approaching the end of the century; 1889 is the centenary of the great French Revolution. The ideas of the enfranchisement of mankind from capitalist domination are everywhere abroad among the working men. In these days, when communication is so rapid and news spreads so fast, simultaneous action has a cumulative effect, economical, social and political. It is childish to overlook class antagonism as the great factor in all human progress throughout history from the break-up of village communities to our own time. Rather is it wise to reflect that the present capitalism, with its attendant mercenary militarism and dominant officialism, bears with it the certainty of early destruction; rather is it well to make ready, soberly and scientifically, for the Socialist organisation of production, exchange, and international relations which – however threatening the aspect of affairs at this moment – must inevitably take its place as the future of our race. It is in no spirit of narrow patriotism or petty jealousy of other peoples that I long to see my own country cut out the canker that gnaws away her prosperity, and stand forth before the world as the leader in a reorganisation which will mean enlightenment and happiness for the entire human race.

I.2 WILLIAM MORRIS: UTOPIAN COMMUNISM

William Morris, artist, writer and craftsman, is widely regarded as the greatest and most original of the early British socialist thinkers of the modern period. He joined Hyndman's Social Democratic Federation and embraced Marxism, but a split within the SDF caused him to leave and to establish the Socialist League, for which he worked tirelessly throughout the mid and late 1880s until it in turn was torn apart by disputes between anarchists and parliamentarists. However, Morris continued to preach his socialist gospel of utopian communism until his death in 1896. His best-known socialist writing is the utopian romance *News from nowhere* (1890), but his many socialist lectures are the most characteristic expression of his ideas. The lecture printed in full here, 'The society of the future', was first delivered in 1887 and is a good summary of his mature socialist position.

In making our claims for the changes in Society which we believe would set labour free and thus bring about a new Society, we Socialists are satisfied with demanding what we think necessary for that Society to form itself, which we are sure it is getting ready to do; this we think better than putting forward elaborate utopian schemes for the future. We assert that monopoly must come to an end, and that those who can use the means of the production of wealth should have all opportunity of doing so, without being forced to surrender a great part of the wealth which they have created to an irresponsible owner of the necessaries to production; and we have faith in the regenerative qualities of this elementary piece of honesty, and believe that the world thus set free will enter on a new cycle of progress. We are prepared to face whatever drawbacks may accompany this new development with equanimity, being convinced that it will at any rate be a great gain to have got rid of a system which has at last become nearly all drawbacks. The extinction of the disabilities of an effete system of production will not, we are convinced, destroy the gains which the world has already won, but will, on the contrary, make those gains available to the whole population instead of confining their enjoyment to a few. In short, considering the present condition of the world, we have come to the conclusion that the function of the reformers now alive is not so much prophecy as action. It is our business to use the means ready to our hands to remedy the immediate evils which oppress us; to the coming generations we must leave the task of safeguarding and of using the freedom which our efforts shall have won them.

Nevertheless, we do partly know the direction which the development of the world will take in the immediate future; the evolution of past history teaches us that. We know that the world cannot go back on its footsteps, and that men will develop swiftly both bodily and mentally in the new Society; we know that men in general will feel the obligations of Society much more than the latter generations have done, that the necessity for co-operation in production and life in general will be more consciously felt than it has been; that the comparative ease of life which the freeing of labour will bring about will give all men more leisure and time for thought; that crime will be rarer because there will not be the same temptation to it; that increased ease of life and education combined will tend to free us from disease of body and mind. In short, that the world cannot take a step forward in justice, honesty and kindliness, without a corresponding gain in all the material conditions of life.

And besides what we know, a knowledge without which we should not take the trouble to agitate for a change in the basis of Society, we cannot help guessing at a great deal which we cannot know; and again, this guessing, these hopes, or if you will, these dreams for the future, make many a man a Socialist whom sober reason deduced from science and political economy and the selection of the fittest would not move at all. They put a man in a fit frame of mind to study the reasons for his hope; give him courage to wade through studies, which, as the Arab king said of arithmetic, would otherwise be too dull for the mind of man to think of.

There are, in fact, two groups of mind with whom Social Revolutionists like other people have to deal, the analytical and the constructive. Belonging to the latter group myself, I am fully conscious of the dangers which we incur, and still more perhaps of the pleasures which we lose, and am, I hope, duly grateful to the more analytical minds for their setting of us straight when our yearning for action leads us astray, and I am also, I confess, somewhat envious of the beatitude of their dreamy contemplation of the perfection of some favourite theory; a happiness which we who use our eyes more than our reasoning powers for noting what is going on in the world, seldom or never enjoy.

However, as they would and do call our instinctive vision dreaming, and as they almost always, at least in their own estimation, have the better of us in argument when we meet in friendly battle, I must be careful what I say of them, and so will for the present at least only deal with the visionaries or *practical people*. And one thing I must confess from the beginning, which is that the visions of us visionary or practical people differ largely from each other, and that we are not much interested in each others' visions; whereas the theories of the analysts differ little from each other, and they are hugely interested in each others' theories – in the way that a butcher is interested in an ox – to wit, for cutting up.

So I will not attempt to compare my visions with those of other Socialists, but will simply talk to you of some of my own, and let you make the comparison yourselves, those of you who are visionaries, or let you unassisted by me criticise them, those of you who are analytically given. In short, I am going to give you a chapter of confessions. I want to tell you what it is I desire of the Society of the Future, just as if I were going to be reborn into it; I daresay that you will find some of my visions strange enough.

One reason which will make some of you think them strange is a sad and shameful one. I have always belonged to the well-to-do classes, and was born into luxury, so that necessarily I ask much more of the future than many of you do; and the first of all my visions, and that which colours all my others, is of a day when that misunderstanding will no longer be possible; when the words poor and rich, though they will still be found in our dictionaries, will have lost their old meaning; which will have to be explained with care by great men of the analytical kind, spending much time and many words over the job, and not succeeding in the end in making people do more than pretend to understand them.

Well now, to begin with, I am bound to suppose that the realization of Socialism will tend to make men happy. What is it then makes people happy? Free and full life and the consciousness of life. Or, if you will, the pleasurable exercise of our energies, and the enjoyment of the rest which that exercise or expenditure of energy makes necessary to us. I think that is happiness for all, and covers all difference of capacity and temperament from the most energetic to the laziest.

Now, whatever interferes with that freedom and fulness of life, under whatever specious guise it may come, is an evil; is something to be got rid of as speedily as possible. It ought not to be endured by reasonable men, who naturally wish to be happy.

Here you see is an admission on my part which I suspect indicates the unscientific mind. It proposes the exercise of free will on the part of men, which the latest scientists deny the possibility of, I believe; but don't be afraid, I am not going into argument on the matter of free will and predestination; I am only going to assert that if individual men are the creatures of their surrounding conditions, as indeed I think they are, it must be the business of man as a social animal, or of Society, if you will, to make the surroundings which make the individual man what he is. Man must and does create the conditions under which he lives; let him be conscious of that and create them wisely.

47

Has he done so hitherto? He has tried to do so, I think, but with only moderate success, at any rate at times. However, the results of that moderate success he is proud of, and he calls it *civilization*. Now, there has been amongst people of different minds abundant discussion as to whether civilization is a good thing or an evil. Our friend Bax in his very able article on the subject, did, I think, really put the matter on its true footing when he pointed out that as a step to something better, civilization was a good, but as an achievement it was an evil. In that sense I declare myself an enemy of civilization; nay since this is to be a chapter of confessions, I must tell you that my *special* leading motive as a socialist is hatred of civilization; my ideal of the new Society would not be satisfied unless that Society destroyed civilization.

For if happiness be the pleasurable exercise of our energies and the enjoyment of necessary rest, it seems to me that civilization, looked at from the static point of view, as Bax phrases it, tends to deny us both these good things, and thereby tends to reduce man to a machine without a will; to deprive him gradually of all the functions of an animal and the pleasure of fulfilling them, except the most elementary ones. The scientific ideal of the future of man would appear to be an intellectual paunch, nourished by circumstances over which he has no control, and without the faculty of communicating the results of his intelligence to his brother-paunches.

Therefore my ideal of the Society of the future is first of all the freedom and cultivation of the individual will, which civilization ignores, or even denies the existence of; the shaking off the slavish dependence, not on other men, but on artificial systems made to save men manly trouble and responsibility: and in order that this will may be vigorous in us, I demand a free and unfettered animal life for man first of all: I demand the utter extinction of all asceticism. If we feel the least degradation in being amorous, or merry, or hungry, or sleepy, we are so far bad animals, and therefore miserable men. And you know civilization *does* bid us to be ashamed of all these moods and deeds, and as far as she can, begs us to conceal them, and where possible to get other people to do them for us. In fact, it seems to me that civilization may almost be defined as a system arranged for ensuring the vicarious exercise of human energies for a minority of privileged persons.

Well, but this demand for the extinction of asceticism bears with it another demand: for the extinction of luxury. Does that seem a paradox to you? It ought not to do so. What brings about luxury but a sickly discontent with the simple joys of the lovely earth? What is it but a warping of the natural beauty of things into a perverse ugliness to satisfy the jaded appetite of a man who is ceasing to be man – a man who will not work, and cannot rest? Shall I tell you what luxury has done for you in modern Europe? It has covered the merry green fields with the hovels of slaves, and blighted the flowers and trees with poisonous gases, and turned the rivers into sewers; till over many parts of Britain the common people have forgotten what a field or a flower is like, and their idea of beauty is a gas-poisoned gin-palace or a tawdry theatre. And civilization thinks that is all right, and it doesn't heed it; and the rich man practically thinks, 'Tis all right, the common people are used to it now, and so long as they can fill their bellies with the husks that the swine do eat, it is enough. And all for what? To have fine pictures painted, beautiful buildings built, good poems written? O no: those are the deeds of the ages before luxury, before civilization. Luxury rather builds clubs in Pall Mall, and upholsters them as though for delicate invalid ladies, for the behoof of big whiskered men, that they may lounge there amidst such preposterous effeminacy that the very plushed-breeched flunkies that wait upon the loungers are better men than they are. I needn't go further than that: a grand club is the very representative of luxury.

Well, you see I dwell upon that matter of luxury, which is really the sworn foe of pleasure, because I don't want workmen even temporarily to look upon a swell club as a desirable thing. I know how difficult it is for them to look from out of their poverty and squalor to a life of real and manly pleasure; but I ask them to think that the good life of the future will be as little like the life of the present rich as may be: that life of the rich is only the wrong side of their own misery; and surely since it is the cause of the misery, there can be nothing enviable or desirable in it. When our opponents say, as they sometimes do, How should we be able to procure the luxuries of life in a Socialist society? answer boldly, We could not do so, and we don't care, for we don't want them and won't have them; and indeed, I feel sure that we cannot if we are all free men together. Free men, I am sure, must lead simple lives and have simple pleasures: and if we shudder away from that necessity now, it is because we are not free men, and have in consequence wrapped up our lives in such a complexity of dependence that we have grown feeble and helpless. But again, what is simplicity? Do you think by chance that I mean a row of yellow-brick, blue-slated houses, or a phalangstere like an improved Peabody lodging-house; and the dinner-bell ringing one into a row of white basins of broth with a piece of bread cut nice and square by each, with boiler-made tea and ill-boiled rice-pudding to follow? No; that's the philanthropist's ideal, not mine; and here I only note it to repudiate it, and to say, Vicarious life once more, and therefore no pleasure. No, I say; find out what you yourselves find pleasant, and do it. You won't be alone in your desires; you will get plenty to help you in carrying them out, and you will develop social life in developing your own special tendencies.

So, then, my ideal is first unconstrained life, and next simple and natural life. First you must be free; and next you must learn to take pleasure in all the details of life: which, indeed, will be necessary for you, because, since others will be free, you will have to do your own work. That is in direct opposition to civilization, which says, Avoid trouble, which you can only do by making other people live your life for you. I say, Socialists ought to say, Take trouble, and turn your trouble into pleasure: that I shall always hold is the key to a happy life.

Now let us try to use that key to unlock a few of the closed doors of the future: and you must remember, of course, in speaking of the Society of the future, I am taking the indulgence of passing over the transitional period – whatever that may be – that will divide the present from the ideal; which, after all, we must all of us more or less form in our minds when we have once fixed our belief in the regeneration of the world. And first as to the form of the position of people in the new Society – their political position, so to say. Political society as we know it will have come to an end: the relations between man and man will no longer be that of status or of property. It will no longer be the hierarchical position, the office of the man, that will be considered, as in the Middle Ages, nor his property as now, but his person. Contract enforced by the State will have vanished into the same limbo as the holiness of the nobility of blood. So we shall at one stroke get rid of all that side of artificiality which bids us sacrifice each our own life to the supposed necessity of an institution which is to take care of the troubles of people which may never happen: every case of clashing rights and desires will be dealt with on its own merits – that is, really, and not legally. Private property of course will not exist as a right: there will be such an abundance of all ordinary necessaries that between private persons there will be no obvious and immediate exchange necessary; though no one will want to meddle with matters that have as it were grown to such and such an individual – which have become part of his habits, so to say.

Now, as to occupations, we shall clearly not be able to have the same division of labour in them as now; vicarious servanting, sewer-emptying, butchering, letter-carrying, boot-blacking, hairdressing, and the rest of it, will have come to an end: we shall either make all these occupations agreeable to ourselves in some mood or to some minds, who will take to them voluntarily, or we shall have to let them lapse altogether. A great many fidgety occupations will come to an end: we shan't put a pattern on a cloth or a twiddle on a jug-handle to sell it, but to make it prettier and to amuse ourselves and others. Whatever rough or inferior wares we make, will be made rough and inferior to perform certain functions of use, and not to sell: as there will be no slaves, there will be no use for wares which none but slaves would need. Machinery will probably to a great extent have served its purpose in allowing the workers to shake off privilege, and will I believe be much curtailed. Possibly the few more important machines will be very much improved, and the host of unimportant ones fall into disuse; and as to many or most of them, people will be able to use them or not as they feel inclined – as, e.g., if we want to go a journey we shall not be compelled to go by railway as we are now, in the interests of property, but may indulge our personal inclinations and travel in a tilted waggon or on the hindquarters of a donkey.

Again, the aggregation of the population having served *its* purpose of giving people opportunities of inter-communication and of making the workers feel their solidarity, will also come to an end; and the huge manufacturing districts will be broken up, and nature heal the horrible scars that man's heedless greed and stupid terror have made: for it will no longer be a matter of dire necessity that cotton cloth should be made a fraction of a farthing cheaper this year than last. It will be in our own choice whether we will work an extra half-hour-a-day more to obtain a clean home and green fields; nor will the starvation or misery of thousands follow some slight caprice in the market for wares not worth making at all. Of course (as I ought to have said before) there are many ornamental matters which will be made privately in people's leisure hours, as they could easily be: since it is not the making of a real work of art that takes so much ingenuity as the making of a machine for the making of a makeshift. And of course mere cheating and flunky centres like the horrible muck-heap in which we dwell (London, to wit) could be got rid of easier still; and a few pleasant villages on the side of the Thames might mark the place of that preposterous piece of folly once called London.

Now let us use the key to unlock the door of the education of the future. Our present education is purely commercial and political: we are none of us educated to be men, but some to be property-owners, and others to be property-servers. Again I demand the due results of revolution on the basis of non-ascetic simplicity of life. I think here also we must get rid of the fatal division-of-labour system. All people should learn how to swim, and to ride, and to sail a boat on sea or river; such things are not arts, they are merely bodily exercises, and should become habitual in the race; and also one or two elementary arts of life, as carpentry or smithying; and most should known how to shoe a horse and shear a sheep and reap a field and plough it (we should soon drop machinery in agriculture I believe when we were free). Then again there are things like cooking and baking, sewing, and the like, which can be taught to every sensible person in a few hours, and which everybody ought to have at his fingers' ends. All these elementary arts would be once again habitual, as also I suppose would be the arts of reading and writing; as also I suspect would the art of thinking, at present not taught in any school or university that I know of.

Well, armed with these habits and arts, life would lie before the citizen for him to enjoy; for whatever line he might like to take up for the exercise of his energies, he would find the community ready to help him with teaching, opportunities, and material. Nor for my part would I prescribe for him what he should do, being persuaded that the habits which would have given him the capacities of a man would stimulate him to use them; and that the process of the enjoyment of his life would be carried out, not at the expense of his fellow-citizens, but for their benefit. At present, you know, the gains held out as a stimulus to exertion, to all those who are not stimulated by the whip of the threat of death by starvation, are narrow, and are mainly the hope that the successfully energetic man shall be placed in a position where he shall not have to exercise his energies: the boredom of satiety, in short, is the crown of valiant exertion in civilization. But in a social condition of things, the gains that would lie before the exercise of one's energies would be various and wide indeed; nor do I in the least in the world believe that the possibility of mere personal use would, or indeed could, limit people's endeavour after them; since men would at last have recognized that it was their business to live, and would at once come to the conclusion that life without endeavour is *dull*. Now what direction that endeavour would take, of course I cannot tell you; I can only say that it would be set free from the sordid necessity to work at what doesn't please us, which is the besetting curse of civilization. The suggestion of a hope I may, however, make, which is of course personal – which is that perhaps mankind will regain their eyesight, which they have at present lost to a great extent. I am not here alluding to what I believe is also a fact, that the number of people of imperfect mechanical sight is increasing, but to what I suppose is connected with that fact, namely, that people have largely ceased to take in mental impressions through the eyes; whereas in times past the eyes were the great feeders of the fancy and imagination. Of course people use their eyes to prevent them from tumbling down stairs or from putting their forks to their noses instead of to their mouths, but there as a rule is an end of the use they are to people. I am in the habit when I go to an exhibition or a picture gallery of noticing their behaviour there; and as a rule I note that they seem very much bored, and their eyes wander vacantly over the various objects exhibited to them, and odd to say, a strange or unusual thing never attracts them, no doubt because it appeals to their minds chiefly through their eyes; whereas if they came across something which a printed label informs them is something familiar, they become interested and nudge each other. If, e.g., ordinary people go to our National Gallery, the thing which they want to see is the Blenheim Raphael, which, though well done, is a very dull picture, at least to anyone not an artist; and they do this because they have been told that the – h'm! the – the – well, the thief that owned it managed to squeeze an exorbitant sum of money out of the nation for it. While, when Holbein shows them the Danish princess of the sixteenth century yet living on the canvas, the demure half-smile not yet faded from her eyes; when Van Eyck opens a window for them into Bruges of the fourteenth century; when Botticelli shows them Heaven as it lived in the hearts of men before theology was dead, these things produce no impression on them, not so much even as to stimulate their curiosity and make them ask what 'tis all about; because these things were done to be looked at, and to make the eyes tell the mind tales of the past, the present, and the future.

Or again, in times past, when what is (I suppose as a joke) called the Educational Department at South Kensington was more or less mixed up with the Art Department, I have followed up a group through the wonders of the drift of the art of past days, and perceived that their eyes never steadied once on any of these things, but that they brightened up at once when they came across a glass case in which the constituent parts of an analysed beef-steak were neatly arranged and labelled, and that their eyes devoured little pin-ches of nothing in particular, with a trusting faith in the analyst which I confess I could not share, as it seemed to me that it would require a quite superhuman honesty in him not to snatch up a few pinches of road-dust or ashes and make them do duty for the recon-dite substances which his toil had brought to light in that familiar object. In literature you will find the same thing going on, and that those authors who appeal to our eyes to take in mental impressions are relegated by our most 'intellectual' critics to a second place at least: to pass by Homer and Beowulf and Chaucer, you will find the 'truly intellectual' man elevating mere rhetorical word-spinners and hunters of introspection above such masters of life as Scott and Dickens, who tell their tales to our senses and leave them alone to moralize the tale so told.

Now I have dwelt at some length on this matter of the eyesight, because to my mind it is the most obvious sign of the march of civi-lization towards the intellectual-paunch stage of existence which I have deprecated already; and also because I feel sure that no special claim need be made for the art and literature of the future: healthy bodily conditions, a sound and all round development of the senses, joined to the due social ethics which the destruction of all slavery will give us, will, I am convinced, as a matter of course give us the due art and literature, whatever that due may turn out to be. Only, if I may prophesy ever so little, I should say that both art and litera-ture, and especially art, will appeal to the senses directly, just as the art of the past has done. You see you will no longer be able to have novels relating the troubles of a middle-class couple in their struggle towards social uselessness, because the material for such literary treasures will have passed away. On the other hand the genuine tales of history will still be with us, and will, one might well hope, then be told in a cheerfuller strain than is now possible. Nor for my part can I doubt that art will appeal to the senses of men now grown healthy; which means that architecture and the kindred arts will again flourish amongst us as in the days before civilisation. Civilisation renders these arts impossible, because its politics and ethics force us to live in a grimy disorderly uncomfort-able world, a world that offends the senses at every turn: that ne-cessity reacts on the senses again, and forces us unconsciously to blunt their keenness. A man who notices the external forms of things much nowadays must suffer in South Lancashire or London, must live in a state of perpetual combat and anger; and he really must try to blunt his sensibility, or he will go mad, or kill some obnoxious person and be hanged for it; and this of course means that people will gradually get to be born without this inconvenient sensibility. On the other hand, let this irrational compulsion be removed from us, and the senses will grow again to their due and normal fulness and demand expression of the pleasure which their exercise gives us, which in short means art and literature at once sensuous and human.

Well, now I will try to draw these discursive remarks to a head, and will give you a more concise and complete idea of the society into which I would like to be reborn.

It is a society which does not know the meaning of the words rich and poor, or the rights of property, or law or legality, or nationality: a society which has no consciousness of being governed; in which equality of condition is a matter of course, and in which no man is rewarded for having served the community by having the power given him to injure it.

It is a society conscious of a wish to keep life simple, to forgo some of the power over nature won by past ages in order to be more human and less mechanical, and willing to sacrifice something to this end. It would be divided into small communities varying much within the limits allowed by due social ethics, but without rivalry between each other, looking with abhorrence at the idea of a holy race.

Being determined to be free, and therefore contented with a life not only simpler but even rougher than the life of slave-owners, division of labour would be habitually limited: men (and women too, of course) would do their work and take their pleasure in their own persons, and not vicariously: the social bond would be habitually and instinctively felt, so that there would be no need to be always asserting it by set forms: the family of blood-relationship would melt into that of the community and of humanity. The pleasures of such a society would be founded on the free exercise of the senses and passions of a healthy human animal, so far as this did not injure the other individuals of the community and so offend against social unity: no one would be ashamed of humanity or ask for anything better than its due development.

But from this healthy freedom would spring up the pleasures of intellectual development, which the men of civilization so foolishly try to separate from sensuous life, and to glorify at its expense. Men would follow knowledge and the creation of beauty for their own sakes, and not for the enslavement of their fellows, and they would be rewarded by finding their most necessary work grow in-

teresting and beautiful under their hands without their being conscious of it. The man who felt keenest the pleasure of lying on the
hill-side under a rushen hut among the sheep on a summer night,
would be no less fit for the enjoyment of the great communal hall
with all its splendours of arch and column, and vault and tracery.
Nor would he who took to heart the piping of the wind and
washing of the waves as he sat at the helm of the fishing-boat, be
deadened to the beauty of art-made music. It is workmen only and
not pedants who can produce real vigorous art.

And amidst this pleasing labour, and the rest that went with it,
would disappear from the earth's face all the traces of the past slavery. Being no longer driven to death by anxiety and fear, we should
have time to avoid disgracing the earth with filth and squalor, and
accidental ugliness would disappear along with that which was the
mere birth of fantastic perversity. The utterly base doctrine, as Carlyle has it, that this world is a cockney nightmare, would be known
no more.

But perhaps you may think that Society being thus happy and at
peace, its very success would lead it to corruption once more? Yes,
that might be if men were not watchful and valiant; but we have
begun by saying that they would be free, and free men are bound to
be responsible, and that means that they shall be watchful and
valiant. The world will be the world still, I do not deny it; but such
men as I have been thinking of will surely be fitter to meet its
troubles than the dwellers in our present muddle of authority and
unconscious revolt.

Or again, some may say such a condition of things might lead indeed to happiness but also to stagnation. Well, to my mind that
would be a contradiction in terms, if indeed we agree that happiness is caused by the pleasurable exercise of our faculties. And yet
suppose the worst, and that the world did rest after so many
troubles – where would be the harm? I remember, after having been ill
once, how pleasant it was to lie on my bed without pain or fever,
doing nothing but watching the sunbeams and listening to the
sounds of life outside; and might not the great world of men, if it
once deliver itself from the delirious struggle for life amidst dishonesty, rest for a little after the long fever and be none the worse for
it?

Anyhow, I am sure it would be the better for getting rid of its
fever, whatever came of it; and sure also that the simplicity of life I
have spoken of, which some would call stagnation, would give real

life to the great mass of mankind, and to them at least would be a well-spring of happiness. It would raise them at once to a higher level of life, until the world began to be peopled, not with common-place people, but with honest folk not sharply conscious of their superiority as 'intellectual' persons now are, but self-respecting and respecting the personality of others, because they would feel them-selves useful and happy, that is alive.

And as for the superior people, if such a world were not good enough for them I am sorry, but am driven to ask them how they manage to get on with the present one which is worse. I am afraid they would have to answer, We like it better because it *is* worse, and, therefore, relatively we are better.

Alas! my friends, these are the fools who are our masters now. The masters of fools then, you say? Yes, so it is; let us cease to be fools then, and they will be our masters no longer. Believe me, that will be worth trying for, whatever may come afterwards.

Take this for the last word of my dream of what is to be: the test of our being fools no longer will be that we shall no longer have masters.

1.3 SIDNEY WEBB: FABIAN COLLECTIVISM

The Fabian Society was founded in 1884 as an assorted group of middle-class ethical and social reformers, among whom was the idiosyncratic genius Bernard Shaw. It developed its distinctive non-Marxist doctrine of gradualist collectivism in the course of the 1880s, and this doctrine found its first mature expression in the celebrated *Fabian essays* of 1889. The key figure in this development of Fabian theory was Sidney Webb, a civil servant recruited to the Society by Shaw, and Webb's contribution to *Fabian essays* is a central document of classical Fabianism. Much of the argument of that essay was stated in rather more direct terms in Webb's account of *Socialism in England* (1890), from which this extract is taken.

'We are all Socialists now,' lately avowed Sir William Harcourt in the House of Commons, and the Prince of Wales recently made the same confession. Whatever may be the value of these vague dec-larations, it is certain that the progress of Socialism is just now the most marked characteristic of English thought.

At the same time, the influence of Socialism in our public life may very easily be overlooked by a casual observer, especially as it is still often ignored or misapprehended by public men themselves.

English politics are, by tradition, so exclusively an affair of the 'classes' that even the greatest movements in democratic thought are apt to escape the notice of those unaccustomed to watch the tendencies of the still largely inarticulate masses. The development of Socialistic institutions has, moreover, been so gradual, and has met with such universal acceptance, that the great majority of citizens are still quite unaware of the extent to which Individualist principles have been abandoned. The ordinary party politician, intent only upon the issues of the moment, will often deny that Socialism, as a vital political force, has any existence in England at all.

Few persons indeed, adequately realise the rapid progress of Democracy in England, whether political or social. We are getting beyond the time of Reform Bills. The changes now occurring are much less in the machinery of government than in the spirit by which that machinery is worked. Those unfamiliar with English political life are almost inevitably led to mistake the surviving forms of Feudalism, with corresponding social inequalities, for greater drawbacks and deductions from the political Democracy than they really are. It may confidently be asserted that the existence of an hereditary peerage offers less of an obstacle to genuine reform than that of the political 'rings and bosses,' so graphically portrayed by Mr Bryce. The English Conservative Party, moreover, by no means corresponds to the various conservative or reactionary elements in continental politics, but is itself constantly being 'permeated' by new ideas emanating from the other side. A party whose leaders carried the abolition of the Corn Laws (1846), most of the Factory Acts, household suffrage in the towns (1867), and Democratic local self-government in London and the rural districts (1888), cannot be said to be a mere party of reaction. The fact that all these measures were unwilling concessions to popular pressure only emphasises their democratic character.

Nor is it easy to realize the extent of the progress of the economic side of Democracy – that is to say, Socialism itself. Students have grown so accustomed to think of Socialism as a mere 'Utopia,' spun from the humanity-intoxicated brains of various Frenchmen of the beginning of the century, that they find great difficulty in recognising it in any other aspect. But on the part of the critics this is simple ignorance. Down to the present generation the aspirant after social reform, whether Socialist or Individualist, naturally embodied his ideas in a detailed plan of a new social order, from which all contemporary evils were eliminated. Just as Plato had his 'Republic,' Campanella his 'City of the Sun,' and Sir Thomas More his 'Utopia,' so Baboeuf had his 'Charter of Equality,' Cabet his 'Icaria,' St Simon his 'Industrial System,' and Fourier his ideal 'Phalanstery.' Robert Owen spent a fortune in pressing upon a stiff-necked generation a 'New Moral World'; and even Comte, superior as he was to many of the weaknesses of his time, must needs add a detailed 'Polity' to his 'Philosophy' of Positivism.

The leading feature of all these proposals (not excluding the last) was what may be called their 'statical' character. The ideal society was represented as a perfectly balanced equilibrium without need or possibility of future organic alteration. Now-a-days, owing mainly to the efforts of Comte, Darwin and Spencer, we can no longer think of the future society as an unchanging state. The social ideal from being statical has become dynamic. The necessity of the constant growth and development of the social organism has become axiomatic. No philosopher now looks for anything but the gradual passing of the old order into the new, without breach of continuity or abrupt general change of social tissue. The new becomes itself old, often before it is consciously recognised as new, and history shows us nothing but constant gradual evolution.

Most Socialists have learnt this lesson even better than their opponents, and find now their strongest argument therein. But the common criticism of Socialism has not yet noted the change, and continues to deal mainly with the obsolete Utopias of the pre-evolutionary age. Modern Socialists are still reproached with the domestic details of an imaginary 'Phalanstery,' or with the failure of 'Queenwood' or 'Icaria,' whereas they are now advocating the conscious adoption of principles of social organisation which advanced communities have already dimly and unconsciously found to be the inevitable outcome of Democracy and the Industrial Revolution.

A corresponding change has taken place in the stages by which it is expected that reforms will come. Two generations ago the social prophet, seeing the impossibility of at once converting the whole country, founded here and there small companies of the faithful, who immediately attempted to put in practice the complete ideal as held by their members. The gradual adoption of the ideal by the whole people was expected from the steady expansion of these isolated communities. But this expectation was not fulfilled, and although many of the societies attained, under favourable circumstances, a marked economic success, their success outside of the world was often only less fatal to the real progress of Socialism in the world than the complete failure of others.

Prophets, now-a-days, do not found a partial community which adopts the whole faith; they cause rather the partial adoption of their faith by the whole community. Incomplete reform is effected in the world of ordinary citizens, instead of complete reform outside of it. The gradual growth of Socialism is now seen to be by vertical instead of horizontal expansion. The endeavour is now not so much to disintegrate or supersede the existing social organisations, as to expand them. By this method not only is the social 'tradition' made use of in the social evolution, but also, though progress may be slow, failure is impossible. No nation having once nationalised or municipalised any industry has ever retraced its steps or reversed its action. No failure of any experiment in such 'collectivisation' is anywhere recorded.

Nor is there any special Socialist method of reform. It may suit the interested defenders of the existing order, or heated journalistic imaginations, to imagine that Socialism necessarily implies a sudden and forcible overthrow of police and government in a kind of tumultuous rising of the common people. The student of Socialism knows that it is not necessarily, or even usually, bound up with anything of the sort. It is a safe maxim that the character of a revolutionary movement in this respect depends mainly upon the nature of the repressing forces.

In Russia, for instance, whatever Socialist thought exists, is a portion of the so-called Nihilist movement. This is, itself, not Socialist in character, (either 'collectivist' or 'anarchist',) but seeks merely political and administrative reforms. The violent methods used by some of the Russian Nihilists are, however, not followed in countries enjoying greater political freedom. In Germany, in spite of considerable repression, Socialism is an exclusively Parliamentary force of the first magnitude. In France it is mainly a factor in Paris municipal politics. In England today the comparatively small avowed Socialist army obtains most of its influence by the unconscious permeation of all schools of thought. In all three countries the development of Socialistic institutions is gradual, persistent, and carried out by legislative enactments. Whatever may be the case in other countries, no one acquainted with English politics can reasonably fear that this feature will not continue. No student of society, whether Socialist or Individualist, can doubt that any important organic changes will necessarily be (1) Democratic, and thus acceptable to a majority of the people and prepared for in the minds of all; (2) gradual, and thus causing no dislocation, however rapid may be the rate of progress; (3) not regarded as immoral by the mass of people, and thus not subjectively demoralising to them;

and in this country, at any rate (4), constitutional and peaceful.

If Socialism is thus neither a Utopia nor a specially violent method of revolution, what, it may be asked, are its distinctive features? It is not easy to reply in a single sentence. The ideas denoted by Socialism represent the outcome of a gradual change of thought in economics, ethics and politics. The Socialist is distinguished from the Individualist, not so much by any special Shibboleth as by a complete difference as to the main principles of social organisation. The essential contribution of the century to sociology has been the supersession of the Individual by the Community as the starting point of social investigations. Socialism is the product of this development, arising with it from the contemporary industrial evolution. On the economic side, Socialism implies the collective administration of rent and interest, leaving to the individual only the wages of his labour, of hand or brain. On the political side, it involves the collective control over, and ultimate administration of, all the main instruments of wealth production. On the ethical side, it expresses the real recognition of fraternity, the universal obligation of personal service, and the subordination of individual ends to the common good.

These fundamental ideas of Socialism do not always find explicit expression in the programme of any one exponent. The character of the propaganda, like its practical demands upon the legislature, is necessarily conditioned by the particular circumstances of the locality and the time. Socialism suffers, too, like every other movement, from the imperfections of its advocates and adherents. Springing, as it does, from the existence of hideous social wrongs, and the unspeakable misery of tens of thousands of sufferers, we must not be surprised to find it frequently allied with bitterness, hatred and the wild justice of revenge. Long despised and rejected by nearly all the educated class, it is not to be wondered at that Socialism should find expression in forms and proposals often not consistent with science or with themselves. An easy triumph usually awaits those defenders of contemporary institutions who are satisfied with exposing the fallacies of any particular Socialist writer. An easy excuse for standing aloof is afforded to the 'philosophic Radical' or other 'superior person' by the cruder vagaries of badly organized Socialist bodies or uninstructed Socialist enthusiasts. The more candid student will endeavour to find out what it is, amid these fallacies and inconsistencies, that has secured the allegiance of millions and has been a beacon of hope to the workers for more than a generation. Worthy opponents will seek to deal with Socialism, not in its

weakest, but in its strongest aspects; and those who have fully realised the processes of social evolution will be prepared to find
Socialistic changes taking place under all those disguises by which
men love to persuade themselves that the existing order is strong
and 'endureth forever.' In England, especially, we shall find that
the progress of Socialism is to be sought mainly among those who
are unconscious of their Socialism, many of whom, indeed, still
proclaim their adherence to Individualism, Self-help and Laissez
Faire. But in any useful classification, position will not so much depend upon the label which a man gives to his opinions or actions as
upon their actual character. Not all those who are now coming forward to claim the name of Socialist can be admitted as such, whilst
many thousands have become Socialists without knowing it . . .

It may be summed up that the progress of Socialism in England
has hitherto been, and is still being accomplished, in four leading
directions, viz:

1. Constantly increasing restrictions upon the private ownership
of land and capital. (Factory Acts, &c.)

2. Gradual supersession of private industrial ventures by public
administration. (National Telegraphs, Municipal tramways, Paro-
chial schools.)

3. Progressive absorption by taxation of unearned incomes (rent
and interest), and 'rent of ability.' (Income tax, taxes on real property &c.)

4. The supplementing of private charity by public organisation,
aiming at raising the condition of the 'residuum.' (Public education, improved dwellings, &c.)

Philanthropic reformers will be surprised to find some of these
measures classed as socialistic. They, as well as many Socialists,
have been so accustomed to think of Socialism merely as an Ideal,
that they do not recognise the steps by which the Ideal is being
gradually realised. Wherever rent and interest are being absorbed
under public control for public purposes, wherever the collective
organisation of the community is being employed in place of individual effort, wherever, in the public interest, the free use of private land or capital is being further restrained, – there one more
step towards the complete realisation of the Socialist Ideal is being
taken. Society is reforming itself on Collectivist, nòt on Individualist principles, and although the advocates of each particular change
intend no further alteration, the result is nevertheless an increasing
social momentum in the same general direction . . .

The change in tone of English political leaders since 1880, is obvious and daily increasing, until it is not too much to assert that the Radical party, largely the creation of the Individualist Philosophers of seventy years ago, is now thoroughly permeated with Socialist ideas. The numerical increase of nominal Socialists is hindered by this very success. Those, who in Germany would naturally be enrolled as members of the Social Democratic party, in England still call themselves Liberals or Radicals, but demand such Socialist measures as the 'municipalisation' of urban land, the special taxation of rents and mining royalties, and the public provision of artisans' dwellings. This permeation is apparently destined to continue, and the avowed Socialist party in England will probably remain a comparatively small disentegrating and educational force, never itself exercising political power, but supplying ideas and principles of social reconstruction to each of the great political parties in turn, as the changing results of English politics bring them alternately into office . . .

Meanwhile a new conception of the State had arisen. From Comte, Darwin and Spencer the idea of the Social Organism was gradually filtering into men's minds, and unconsciously altering all their political theories and ideals. It has gradually become recognised that a Perfect City was something different from any number of good citizens, something to be tried by other tests and weighed in other balances. The lesson of Evolution, at first thought to be the apotheosis of anarchic individual competition, is now recognised to be quite the contrary. We have to learn, Professor Huxley tells us, to substitute consciously adapted co-ordination for internecine competition, if the Organism which will prove to be the 'Fittest to Survive,' is to be also the best. Even the Political Economists are learning this lesson, and the fundamental idea of a Social Organism paramount over and prior to the individual of each generation, is penetrating to their minds and appearing in their lectures, though it has not even yet affected to any great extent their more elaborate treatises . . .

This convergence has been facilitated by the fact that English Socialists are by no means blind worshippers of Karl Marx. Whilst recognising his valuable services to economic history, and as a stirrer of men's minds, a large number of English Socialist economists reject his special contributions to pure economics. His theory of value meets with little support in English economic circles, where that of Jevons is becoming increasingly dominant. Although the leaders of the two largest Socialist organisations have been strongly influenced by Marx, the rank and file of the Socialist party do not found their

Socialism on any special economic theories, but upon the patent results of individual ownership, as shown in the large payments for rent and interest. The great bulk of the unconscious Socialism of the English voter and statesman has been based merely upon empirical observation, and has certainly not been affected by any notion of 'surplus value' . . .

Our unconscious acceptance of this progressive Socialism is a striking testimony to the change which has come over the country of Godwin and Malthus. The 'practical man,' oblivious or contemptuous of any theory of the Social Organism or general principles of social organisation, has been forced by the necessities of the time, into an ever deepening collectivist channel. Socialism, of course, he still rejects and despises. The Individualist Town Councillor will walk along the municipal pavement, lit by municipal gas and cleansed by municipal brooms with municipal water, and seeing by the municipal clock in the municipal market, that he is too early to meet his children coming from the municipal school hard by the county lunatic asylum and municipal hospital, will use the national telegraph system to tell them not to walk through the municipal park but to come by the municipal tramway to meet him in the municipal reading room, by the municipal art gallery, museum and library, where he intends to consult some of the national publications in order to prepare his next speech in the municipal town-hall, in favour of the nationalisation of canals and the increase of the government control over the railway system. 'Socialism, sir,' he will say, 'don't waste the time of a practical man by your fantastic absurdities. Self-help, sir, individual self-help, that's what's made our city what it is.'

It is probable that in no other country are statesmen so ready as in England to carry out political proposals pressed upon them from below. Political platforms tend to be constructed, not so much out of abstract statements of rights and principles, as out of lists of new laws to be passed by the successful party. The English Constitution is admittedly deemed in need of perpetual legislative tinkering, and every Englishman, not excluding the most conservative, has his own pet list of necessary reforms. In the United States the popular cry seems to be mainly for good administration; in England it is undoubtedly for new laws. 'Measures, not men,' is still the English voter's motto.

This striking difference, in itself not without significance, leads to important consequences when public feeling is pressing in any political direction. The gradual 'socialising' of politics, out of which the parliamentary and municipal Socialism has sprung, is rendered possible by the fluidity of the English Constitution . . .

The steady growth of 'social compunction' among all classes will promote the same result. Just now (Dec. 1889) the tendency is strong in this direction, and it may perhaps carry us forward more rapidly than any politician yet foresees. The individual appropriation of rent and interest is becoming more and more discredited among the mass of the population who are practically unable to share in this income; and they are quickly coming to demand that social arrangements shall be deliberately based on what are essentially Socialist principles. The Christian is every day inclining to the feeling that his faith requires him to support the same demand; the Political Economist has ceased to resist, counselling merely circumspection and moderation; the Practical Reformer is driven by the impossibility of otherwise adequately dealing with social evils into the same direction, and the Statesman sees more and more clearly that this is the outcome of urban Democracy in advanced industrial communities, with their excessive development of city life. The industrial evolution, as usual, precedes and accompanies the political, and all social tendencies point to the same end. What the exact form and machinery may be, it is, of course, impossible to predict, nor how long each stage may last, but no student of English thought and politics can doubt that England is destined to become constantly more and more 'collectivist' as it advances in industrial complexity, in realised wealth, and in political democracy. The Individualism of the past is buried, and the immediate future is unmistakably with a progressive Socialism, the full extent of which no man can yet see.

1.4 EDWARD CARPENTER

Edward Carpenter, exponent of the simple life and critic of contemporary civilisation, is a minor prophet of early British socialism. Not belonging to any particular school or movement, he exercised a diffuse influence. Most influential was his long Whitmanesque prose-poem *Towards democracy* (1883), but this extract is from his *England's ideal* (1887).

At the bottom, and behind all the elaborations of economic science, theories of social progress, the changing forms of production, and class warfare, lies today the fact that the old ideals of society have become corrupt, and that this corruption has resulted in dishonesty of life. It is this dishonesty of personal life which is becoming the occasion of a new class-war, from whose fierce parturition-struggle will arise a new ideal – destined to sway human society for many a thousand years, and to give shape to the forms of its industrial, scientific, and artistic life . . .

The canker of effete gentility has eaten into the heart of this nation. Its noble men and women are turned into toy ladies and gentlemen; the eternal dignity of (voluntary) Poverty and Simplicity has been forgotten in an unworthy scramble for easy-chairs. Justice and Honesty have got themselves melted away into a miowling and watery philanthropy; the rule of honor between master and servant, and servant and master, between debtor and creditor, and buyer and seller, has been turned into a rule of dishonor, concealment, insincere patronage, and sharp bargains; and England lies done to death by her children who should have loved her.

As for you, working-men and working-women – in whom now, if anywhere, the hope of England lies – I appeal to you at any rate to cease from this ideal, I appeal to you to cease your part in this gentility business – to cease respecting people because they wear fine clothes and ornaments, and because they live in grand houses. You know you do these things, or pretend to do them, and to do either is foolish. We have had ducking and fore-lock pulling enough. It is time for *you* to assert the dignity of human labour . . .

Be arrogant rather than humble, rash rather than stupidly contented; but, best of all, be firm, helpful towards each other, forgetful of differences, scrupulously honest in yourselves, and charitable even to your enemies, but determined that *nothing* shall move you from the purpose you have set before you – the righteous distribution in society of the fruits of your own and other men's labour, the return to Honesty as the sole possible basis of national life and national safety, and the redemption of England from the curse which rests upon her.

1.5 ROBERT BLATCHFORD

With the formation of the Independent Labour Party in 1893, Robert Blatchford emerged as one of the new movement's most effective propagandists. Editor of the *Clarion*, his robust style won a large working-class audience for socialist ideas. Blatchford's *Merrie England* (1893), addressed to 'John Smith, of Oldham, a hard-headed workman, fond of facts', became British socialism's best seller. This is a sample.

So now let me tell you roughly what I suggest as an improvement on things as they now are.

First of all, I would restrict our mines, furnaces, chemical works, and factories to the number actually needed for the supply of our own people. Then I would stop the smoke nuisance by developing water power and electricity. Then I would set men to work to grow wheat and fruit and rear cattle and poultry for our own use. Then I would develop the fisheries and construct great fish-breeding lakes and harbours.

In order to achieve these ends I would make all the land, mills, mines, factories, works, shops, ships, and railways the property of the people.

I would have the towns rebuilt with wide streets, with detached houses, with gardens and fountains and avenues of trees. I would make the railways, the carriage of letters, and the transit of goods as free as the roads and bridges.

I would make the houses loftier and larger, and clear them of all useless furniture. I would institute public dining halls, public baths, public wash-houses on the best plans, and so set free the hands of those slaves – our English women.

I would have public parks, public theatres, music halls, gymnasiums, football and cricket fields, public halls and public gardens for recreation and music and refreshment. I would have all our children fed and clothed and educated at the cost of the State. I would have them all taught to play and to sing. I would have them all trained to athletics and to arms. I would have public halls of science. I would have the people become their own artists, actors, musicians, soldiers, and police. Then, by degrees, I would make all these things *free*. So that clothing, lodging, fuel, food, amusement, intercourse, education, and all the requirements for a perfect human life should be produced and distributed and enjoyed by the people without the use of money.

1.6 WILLIAM MORRIS AND BELFORT BAX

Belfort Bax, who accompanied Morris into the Socialist League, was a philosopher influenced by the German philosophical tradition and who therefore had a special role in the presentation of aspects of Marxism to British socialists. Like Morris, Bax was concerned with the ethical revaluation and harmony to be achieved through socialism and this influenced their presentation of scientific socialism, as in this extract from their collaborative work on *Socialism: its growth and outcome* (1893).

As regards the future form of the moral consciousness, we may safely predict that it will be in a sense a return on a higher level to the ethics of the older world, with the difference that the limitation of scope to the kinship group in its narrower sense, which was one of the causes of the dissolution of ancient society, will disappear, and the identification of individual with social interests will be so complete that any divorce between the two will be inconceivable to the average man.

It will be noticed that we have above been speaking of religion and morality as distinct from one another. But the religion of Socialism will be but the ordinary ethics carried into a higher atmosphere, and will only differ from them in *degree* of conscious responsibility to one's fellows. Socialistic Ethics would be the guide of our daily habit of life; socialistic religion would be that higher form of conscience that would impel us to actions on behalf of a future of the race, such as no man could command in his ordinary moods.

1.7 BERNARD SHAW

The erratic genius of Bernard Shaw, man of letters and Irish wit, was influential in shaping the developing doctrine of the Fabian Society, of which he was a leading member. One of his special tasks, as he saw it, was to demonstrate the superiority of Fabian socialism over other socialist traditions of the kind represented here. This extract is from Shaw's essay on 'The illustrations of socialism' (in *Forecasts of the coming century* (1897), ed. Edward Carpenter).

Now, therefore, if I say flatly that Socialism as it appears to ninety-nine out of every hundred of the ardent young Socialists who will read this book, is an illusion, I do not say that there is no reality behind the illusion, not that the reality will not be much better than the illusion. Only, I do say, very emphatically, that if the Socialist future were presented in its reality to those who are devoting all the energy they have to spare after their day's work, and all the enthusiasm of which they are capable, to 'the Cause', many of them would not lift a finger for it, and would even disparage and loathe it as a miserably prosaic 'bourgeois' development and extension of the middle class respectability of today. When any part of Socialism presents itself in the raw reality of a concrete proposal, capable of being adopted by a real Government, and carried out by a real Executive, the professed Socialists are the last people in the country who can be depended on to support it. At best, they will disparage it as 'a palliative', and assure the public that it will do no good unless the capitalist system is entirely abolished as well. At worst, they will violently denounce it, and brand its advocates as

frauds, traitors, and so on. This natural antagonism between the
enthusiasts who conceive Socialism and the statesmen who have
to reduce it to legislative and administrative measures, is inevitable, and must be put up with. But it need not be put with
silently . . .

I myself am firmly persuaded that Socialism will not prove worth
carrying out in its integrity – that long before it has reached every
corner of the political and industrial organisation, it will have so
completely relieved the pressure to which it owes its force that it
will recede before the next great movement in social development,
leaving relics of untouched Individualist Liberalism in all directions
among the relics of feudalism which Liberalism itself has left. I believe that its dissolution of the petty autocracies and oligarchies of
private landlordism and capitalism will enormously stimulate
genuine individual enterprise instead of suppressing it: and I
strongly suspect that Socialist States will connive at highly undemocratic ways of leaving comparatively large resources in the hands
of certain persons, who will thereby become obnoxious as a privileged class to the consistent levellers. If I am right, Socialism at
its height will be as different from the ideal of the 'Anti-State Communists' of the Socialist League in 1885 . . . as current Christianity
is from the ideal of the apostles and of Tolstoi . . .

It is in such ways that the will of the world accomplishes itself.
Out of the illusion of 'the abolition of the wage system' we shall get
steady wages for everybody, and finally discredit all other sources
of income as disreputable. By the illusion of the downfall of Capitalism we shall turn whole nations into Joint Stock Companies; and
our determination to annihilate the *bourgeoisie* will end in making
every workman a *bourgeois gentilhomme*. By the illusion of Democracy, or government by everybody, we shall establish the most
powerful bureaucracy ever known on the face of the earth . . .

Part two
1900–1925

2.1 RAMSAY MACDONALD: EVOLUTIONARY SOCIALISM

James Ramsay MacDonald began life as the illegitimate son of a
Scottish agricultural labourer and became Labour's first Prime
Minister. Remembered best for his 'betrayal' of Labour in the economic
crisis of 1931, MacDonald was nevertheless a leading figure in the early
development of Labour's political organisation and in the elaboration of
its distinctive ideology of evolutionary socialism. His series of socialist
textbooks sought to make this tradition respectable and to distinguish it
from other socialist traditions. One of these books was *Socialism and
society*, from which the following section is taken. First published in
1905, its many editions provided a key text for British socialists of the
period.

What then are the forces in present-day Society which Socialists
should regard as making for Socialism?

The Marxian answer is that a war of classes is going on which
one's eyes can see and one's ears hear. On the one hand is the exploiter, the person who accumulates surplus value; on the other,
the exploited, the person who sells his labour power for a price
which tends to sink to a bare subsistence level. The opposition between these two classes grows in intensity. It will continue to grow
until the workers become class conscious, seize political power, and
establish the Socialist state . . .

Such a view is both inaccurate as to the facts it assumes and misleading as a guide for action.

In the first place, it is not true that there are only two great economic classes in the community – the assumption which is constantly made by those who hold to the class war explanation of progress.
Marx was so anxious to separate himself from 'bourgeoisie' economists that he would on no account recognise the conflicting in-

terests of the receivers of rent and of profits. Some of his followers without allowing for the admission in their systems, concede the antagonism . . .

But further, any idea which assumes that the interests of the proletariat are so simply opposed to those of the bourgeoisie as to make the proletariat feel an economic oneness is purely formal and artificial. It is a unification arrived at only by overlooking many differences and oppositions, which have been growing for some time rather than diminishing. The economic structure of Society is simplified out of all recognition when it is described as a contest between two economic classes, and the political problems of democracy are still more distorted under the guise of simplification when they are stated as being nothing more than an effort to give political form to this economic antagonism. The bourgeoisie is not united either for economic or political purposes, the proletariat is in the same position. For, just as in the earlier years of the Factory System, the line between workman and employer was not clearly drawn, and men could reasonably hope that, by saving and by procuring credit, they could become masters, today there is still a goodly number of workmen who cross the line and become employers or employing managers; whilst the great thrift movements, the Friendly Societies, the Building Societies, the Co-operative Societies, connect working class interests to the existing state of things. In addition, there are considerable classes of workers in the community whose immediate interests are bound up with the present distribution of wealth, and who, obedient to class interests, would range themselves on the side of the *status quo*.

Of course it may be said that all these sections, in refusing to help on the change towards Socialism, are making a mistake from the point of view of their own interests, and that if they were properly enlightened they would see that they belong to an exploited class, one and indivisible. That may be true, but a mode of action which is ineffective until men are 'fully enlightened' is a chimera. Moreover, it is equally true that if the capitalist were fully enlightened, he too would embrace Socialism on account of the great blessings which it would bring to him. Thus all that the class war means, when used to indicate the opposing armies whose combat is used to usher in the reign of Socialism, is that an enlightened proletariat, not blinded by its immediate interests but guided by its permanent ones, will be Socialist. But so also will a similarly enlightened bourgeoisie. Hence the value of the class war as an uncompromising statement of hard economic fact becomes a mere semblance. It is nothing but a grandiloquent and aggressive figure of speech.

It is an indisputable fact that the wage earner and the wage payer have interests which are antagonistic, and in the nature of things cannot be reconciled. The supposed identity of interest between capital and labour, which is assumed to be proved by the discovery that unless capital pays high wages it will not be able to command efficient labour, is no identity of interest at all. The efficient labour which high wages produce is still bought and sold by capital, is still employed or rejected as it suits the convenience of capital, is still underpaid to enable capital to accumulate high dividends, is still treated, not as something possessing rights of its own, but as something which ministers to the interests of others. This opposition may be expressed as a class war. But it is only one of the many oppositions tending to modify social organisation, and it is by no means the most active or most certain in improving that organisation.

There is, for instance, the opposition between consumer and producer. This opposition is peculiarly complex, because a man is a producer one hour and a consumer the next. The most valid objection that can be taken to Trade Unionism (if it can be substantiated) is that it sacrifices the interests of the consumer to those of the producer ... In other words, trade rivalry is as real as, and more forceful as an impulse of the day, than class rivalry ...

The conflict of economic interest between the consumer demanding cheapness and the producer desiring to sell the use of his labour or the use of his capital at the highest rates, is an economic conflict which must not be overlooked or smoothed away in a formal generalisation. And it must be emphasised that the opposition is not one whit more unreal because the same man may belong at the same time to both the opposing classes.

Certain modern developments are tending to break up into well defined economic sections this 'uniform' proletariat class. Of these the Co-operative and Building Societies are the most important. In the first of those movements, the wage earner becomes an employer –or, as it presents itself more familiarly to him, he is a receiver of dividends which, in part, are profits from other people's labour. All day, at his work in the factory or mine, he thinks of himself as the victim of the exploiter, as the loyal trade unionist, as the wage earner. But he comes home in the evening, washes himself, puts a better coat on his back, goes to his Co-operative Committee and immediately undergoes a fundamental change. Psychologically, he is a different man. He is no longer a wage earner and a trade unionist, but a capitalist employer who has been known to join in an anathema against labour combinations.

This does not mean that wealth is being better distributed, but rather that the psychological basis of class is being undermined . . . But the point is best illustrated by certain recent developments of co-partnership, which as an industrial theory is admirable, but as a sociological influence may be most reprehensible . . .

By the second of these organisations – Building Societies – the interests of the working classes become identified with those of the landowning classes, and are opposed to every attempt of the community to enter into possession of the unearned increments on land.

There is also another aspect to this. The interests injured by our present social state are not merely those of the wage earners. Considerable classes of people depend on the wage earners and of these the small shop-keeper is a type. His ambitions and sympathy, however, unite him with the *petite bourgeoisie* and divorce him from his economic supporters – the working classes – and thus rebuke the theorists who see in social motive little more than economic motive. Then, there are those whose comfort and success under existing conditions are but precarious, the bankrupts, the struggling business people, those engaged in industries which are passing under the control of trusts. All those are in economic positions which expose them to the allurement of the Socialist ideal. But they are possessed by a pathetic desire to attach themselves to the classes which rest in economic calm and bask in a blaze of social sunshine above the tempests and the shadows in which the lower beings live. From the depths to which they are driven they cast an adoring eye upon those 'above' them, and from the midst of their ruin they bow the knee to whatever bears the stamp of respectability.

Class, in the sense in which the Marxians use it, is an economic abstraction, an academic generalisation.

Having discovered what are the facts, we can now turn to consider what is the idea which is in reality expressed by those who use the word class in this connection, and what is its value as a motive force making for social change. When we appeal to class interests what do we do in reality? A man's class interests cannot appear to him to be anything else than his personal interests – not his interests as a member of the wage earning class, not his interests as a citizen, not his interests as a member of the community, but his individual interests from day to day. There is no principle of social reconstruction in this feeling. There is the motive of a scramble, or of class defence and preservation, the motive to secure big wages, short hours and favourable conditions of work. But that is all. The tug of the class war is across not upwards. There is no constructive value in a class war.

The best expression of a class war is Trade Unionism. It is created on the assumption and experience that capital will do its utmost to exploit labour, and that labour ought to do its best to prevent capital from succeeding. The position is a simple and frank recognition of existing industrial fact. It concerns itself with no opposition except that between capital and labour, no union of interests except the interests of wage earning, no field of activity wider than the factory. It leads nowhere because it has no ideal goal; its only results can be the bondage of one side or the other. Here is the pure example of the class war. Nay, more, it is *the* class war . . .

Convey it in what spirit we may, an appeal to class interest is an appeal to personal interest. Socialist propaganda carried on as a class war suggests none of those ideals of moral citizenship with which Socialist literature abounds – 'each for all, and all for each', 'service to the community is the sole right of property', and so on. It is an appeal to individualism, and results in getting men to accept Socialist formulae without becoming Socialists. It springs from a time in the evolution of the Labour Movement when the narrow creed of the old Trade Unionism was the widest revelation that nature had yet made to men striving to protect themselves against the encroachment of capitalist power. In other words, the 'class war' idea belongs to the pre-Socialist and pre-scientific phase of the Labour Movement.

I am aware that the Marxian argues that this class struggle is the last in history, and that when the proletariat have been emancipated, the epochs of struggle end. The argument is but a vain assumption. The emancipation of the proletariat will of itself be the signal for new struggles of economic sections with apparently opposing interests, and so long as these oppositions are made the main reason for social change, each triumph can only lead to other battles, again and again renewed. It is not the emancipation of the numerical majority, or of a class so big as to be 'no class but the nation', which matters. What matters is the character of the motive power which effected the emancipation. If that power is the conflict of interests it will reappear in the new regime, and if it finds no complete class to infuriate, it will enter class sub-sections, which will then be prepared to fly at each others' throats. The assumption that by a class triumph Society is to emerge from the epoch of class conflict and sail gaily away upon the calm waters of fraternity, can be held only by those who have not ceased to believe in the magical and the irrational.

The antagonisms in Society which result in organic change of a progressive nature are not merely economic. They are also intellectual and moral. Man is moved by his head as well as by his pocket, by the growth of social instinct as well as by cupidity. The richest possession of any man is an approving conscience. People who themselves have no quarrel with existing economic arrangements, must measure the achievements of existing Society by standards of right and wrong, must enter its dark corners and sojourn amongst its waste places, its wrecks and its ruins, and they will turn in horror and weariness from the spectacle and begin preparing for a new order of things. Everybody does not pile up riches on his inner lights so as to smother them. Even if we regard economics as the mainspring by which history moves, that does not prevent us from recognising that only by a combination of intellectual guidance and economic needs does historical change become one and the same thing with progress.

The scheme upon which humanity evolves to higher and more humane stages of existence is either rational or it is not. If it is not, all organised attempts to hasten reform and make it effective – Socialism included – are waste effort. If it is rational, then progress becomes a matter of intellectual conviction, and man, seeking intellectual peace as well as economic security, will have to choose which he is to pursue. Even supposing he is a wage earner and his pursuit of the means of life brings him into conflict with the existing state of Society, his success will not depend upon the richness of his experience of poverty, but upon the meaning he places upon his experience and the methods he adopts to place himself in different conditions. Economic needs may give volume and weight to the demand for change, but reason and intelligence, the maturing of the social mind, ideals of social justice grasped so firmly that they have become real existence for those who hold them, give that demand a shape, a policy, a direction. Socialism must, therefore, recognise the intellectual as well as the economic movement. And if it over-emphasises either side, let it be the former . . .

Not only, therefore, is it incumbent upon Socialism to recognise the existence of an intellectual motive, it must place that motive above the economic, because without it the economic struggle would be devoid of any constructive value; it would be a mere tug-of-war; it would never bring us to Socialism. The economic motive must be led by the light of reason or morality – as, indeed, it has always been when it is a factor in progress.

This line of thought appears to overlook the article in the Marxian creed that Socialism is inevitable. But the industrial and economic inevitability of Socialism is a mere fancy. It is inevitable only if intelligence makes it so. It is inevitable only if we are to develop on rational lines; it is inevitable, not because men are exploited or because the fabric of capitalism must collapse under its own weight, but because men are rational. It is the action of reason alone which makes our evils a sure cause of progress and not the possible beginning of final deterioration. Intelligence and morality indicate the goal by which the struggle to escape the existing purgatory is guided. Human evolution is a stretching out, not a being pushed forward. Acorns produce oaks, grubs grow into beetles, tadpoles into frogs, but slums, industrial crises, poverty, trusts, do not in the same way grow into Socialism. In the struggle for life which has taken place in the world of nature since life began, many species have been exterminated, many evolutions have never been completed. Arrested development is as conspicuous in nature as finished processes . . .

In order, therefore, that the social organism may perfect itself, there must be the will for perfection and the definite idea as to what changes are required. The life of the organism is continued through change, and the organism itself is ever in a state of reorganisation. Nation after nation has risen and fallen, others have risen and attained to a certain civilization and there have stuck. But stagnation is impossible for our own Western peoples. They may fall; political combinations may crush them; the canker of poverty may make them degenerate. But if they are to continue to grow and to adapt themselves to new circumstances, if they are to continue to improve, it must be by the organisation of opinion and the operations of a constructive genius which sees a stage ahead and leads the people so that they attain to it. The Socialist appeal, therefore, is to all who believe in social evolution, who agree that the problem which Society has now to solve is that of the distribution of wealth, who trust in democracy, who regard the State not as antagonistic to but as an aspect of, individuality, and who are groping onwards with the co-operative faith guiding them. That appeal may find some people in poverty, and they may follow because it offers them economic security, but it will find others in wealth, and they will follow because it brings order where there is now chaos, organisation where there is now confusion, law where there is now anarchy, justice where there is now injustice.

Socialism marks the growth of Society, not the uprising of a class. The consciousness which it seeks to quicken is not one of economic class solidarity, but one of social unity and growth towards organic wholeness. The watchword of Socialism, therefore, is not class consciousness but community consciousness.

We can now see to what combination of interests and convictions we must appeal, and how we must direct that appeal, so as to create the order of the Socialist State out of the chaos of the present day.

I reject what seems to me to be the unsatisfactory expression of a class war, because class consciousness leads nowhere, and a class struggle may or may not be intelligent. A 'class war' describes only a part of the condition which Society presents to our eyes today. But still, we turn our hopes first of all to the wage earners. They are the most certainly doomed victims of the present chaos; they suffer most from the inability of the present system to provide employment, wages, life; they are least buoyed up by elusive hopes that a lucky turn of the wheel of fortune may pitch them up on the backs of others; they are the helpless spills tossing on the troubled waters of present day strife; their attempts to share in the benefits of an efficient method of production result in little but turmoil, hunger and poverty; and above all, their needs have now become the chief concern of Society, because in fulness of time social organisation is being tested by its human results, and because the economic enfranchisement of the people naturally treads upon the heels of their political emancipation.

And it is of special note for the moment that they have been subject recently to rebuffs and attacks in the Press, the Courts of Law and Parliament, and thus have been taught the necessity of political unity and independent organisation. They have given us the Labour Party in consequence. The politics of an enlightened democracy is of necessity social, and is aimed at ending experiences of unemployment, old age pauperism, and so on. Hence, as one of the laws of evolution is, that need creates organs, redistributes and organises functions and changes biological types, working class

policy must be directed towards the organisation and the development of the organs and functions of mutual aid in Society. The
political policy of the Labour Party might well be described as an
attempt to give mutual aid shape and form in our national life. So
soon as a serious attempt has been made to frame a policy directed
to such ends, it will be found that monopoly in land and the use of
industrial capital for individual profit are the sources of the experiences which Society now seeks to shun, and they must consequently be supplanted by public ownership and production for use, before labour can enter into enjoyment of the blessings which an
efficient method of wealth production would make possible.
Labour has but one intelligent road of advance – that of economic
and industrial reconstruction – that of Socialism.

Among the wage earners, therefore, we must expect to find in
fullest development, and in forms most political and effective for
organic change, those vital and vitalising disturbances which indicate active life pushing out to higher forms of organisation. But
those disturbances, as has been shown, are not purely economic,
and are not therefore confined to wage earners, and consequently in
order to gather together the forces making for Socialism, the basis
of the movement must be such that everyone sharing in the disturbed promptings must be included.

All barrier phrases and sectional dogmas must be removed from
Socialism. The experiments in factory legislation, in public health
regulations, in education, in municipalisation, are pointing out to
men of all classes the desirability of going yet further along the road
which leads to Socialism, and are forming in the minds of men of
all classes a conception of Society, of the community and the individual, formed on Socialist principles. When we think systematically of the scattered fragments of reform promised by the political
parties, we see that they are but the foreshadowing of Socialism;
when the tendencies begun by scores of experiments – factory laws,
public health laws, municipalisation – are followed out, joined
together, systematised, Socialism is the result. This completeness of
organisation, this idea of national and communal growth, this state
of business efficiency, nothing short of it and nothing which is sectional in it, should be laid down as the basis of Socialism. And the
political movement which is to express and ultimately satisfy, this
need for the organic unity of Society, must be a movement of the
whole of Society and not of one of its sections – the working classes.
As the brain moves obedient to the grossest as well as the purest
prompting of the needs of the living thing, so must the political

organ in Society be subject to the purest prompting of moral intelligence as well as the grosser prompting of economic need; but both must be united if a more perfect form of Society is to be created.

Economic hardships are the flints on the road, but these flints may develop on us the hoofs of the beast, or may compel us to use our intelligence to find smoother paths. Socialism is the latter alternative.

2.2 G. D. H. COLE: GUILD SOCIALISM

G. D. H. Cole came to prominence when, as a young Oxford academic, he led an attack on Fabian collectivism in the name of a doctrine of participatory democracy and workers' control known as Guild Socialism. Cole did not invent Guild Socialism, but he did become its leading advocate and theorist in the decade after 1914. Subsequently, he went on to assume a role of intellectual leadership, along with R. H. Tawney and Harold Laski, within British socialism during the inter-war and immediate post-war periods. An immensely prolific writer, Cole devoted many books to Guild Socialism. One of these was *Self-Government in Industry* (1917), which contains a vigorous and polemical statement of his general argument and from which the following chapter is taken.

No movement can be dangerous unless it is a movement of ideas. Often as those whose ideals are high have failed because they have not kept their powder dry, it is certain that no amount of dry powder will make a revolution succeed without ideals. Constructive idealism is not only the driving force of every great uprising; it is also the bulwark against reaction.

If, then, Trade Unionism is to be the revolutionary power of the future, it will become so only by virtue of the idealism that inspires it. While it remains merely materialistic, it will not stand a dog's chance of changing the capitalist system into something better. Socialists, therefore, when they put their trust in organised Labour, are expressing their belief that Trade Unionism means something more than the desire of its members for greater material comfort . . .

It was not unnatural . . . that the early Socialists, including most of the prominent members of the old Social Democratic Federation, regarded the Unions as too hopelessly reactionary to be of any assistance in achieving the Socialist Commonwealth. The result of this natural mistake was, however, none the less disastrous. English Socialism, as it grew up, remained a doctrine almost wholly political in character: on the industrial side, its last word concerning the future organisation of production was nationalisation . . .

Human nature, however, came to the rescue. While the recognised leaders of Trade Unionism in too many cases frittered away their strength in politics – which, necessary as it may be, is not their job – the rank and file were being slowly fired by the new idealism which the Socialists had failed to understand. Half-unconsciously, the revolt against despotism in the workshop began to take form, and the workers began to realise that there could be no end to their subordination until they themselves were masters of their own industries. The conduct of the nationalised services, too, made them feel that the management of industry by State departments, though, generally extended, it might result in a fairer distribution of income, could never by itself answer their demand for industrial freedom. Syndicalism, or at any rate doctrines tinged with Syndicalism, began to take root, and, when the industrial unrest took form, it was found to be not merely a demand for higher wages, but an insurgence against tyranny and an aspiration towards industrial self-government.

This new spirit grew up within the Trade Unions, and to a great extent outside Socialism, simply because Socialists had no imagination. But, growing up in this way, it was inevitably one-sided and incomplete. It was a purely industrial doctrine, when the need was for a doctrine at once industrial and political. It is the business of Socialists today to achieve what should have been achieved at the time of the Dock Strike twenty-five years ago, and to make a synthesis of the twin idealisms of Socialism and Trade Unionism. The working out of the new Socialism should be the main business of all those who know the value of ideals, and desire to bring about a social revolt imbued with constructive idealism.

In the Society of today the State is a coercive power, existing for the protection of private property, and merely reflecting, in its subservience to Capitalism, the economic class-structure of the modern world. The Trade Unions are today merely associations of wage-earners, combining in face of exploitation to make the conditions of their servitude less burdensome. Out of these two – out of the Capitalist State and the Trade Union of wage-earners – what vision of the future Society can we Socialists conjure up?

Realising rightly that the structure of our industrial Society finds its natural and inevitable expression in the class-struggle, and preoccupied ceaselessly with the demands of our everyday warfare with Capitalism, we are too apt, despite our will to regenerate Society, to regard the present characteristics of the State and the Unions as fixed and unalterable. Some regard the State as essentially the expression of Capitalism, and hold that with the rise of the worker to power, the State and all its functions will disappear automatically. This is Anarchism, to which one kind of Syndicalism approximates. Others, again, regard the Trade Union as essentially a bargaining body which, with the passing of Capitalism, will have fulfilled its purpose, and will at once cease to exist or become of very minor importance. This is the attitude of pure State Socialism – or collectivist theory, as it has been commonly misunderstood, both in Great Britain and abroad.

Both these views rest on false assumptions. One side presupposes that the State must be always much as it is today; the other assumes that its narrow conception of the function of the Trade Union under Capitalism includes all the functions the Unions ever could, or ought to, assume. Both views are one-sided in that they accept the possibility of transforming one of the two bodies in question, and deny the possibility of transforming the other. But nothing is more certain than that both State and Trade Union, if they are to form the foundation of a worthy Society, must be radically altered and penetrated by a new spirit.

A stable community, recognising the rights and personality of all sections of consumers and producers alike, can only be secured if both the State and the Trade Unions take on new functions, and are invested with control in their respective spheres. Collectivism which is not supplemented by strong Trade Unions will be merely State bureaucracy on a colossal scale; Trade Unions not confronted by a strong and democratised State might well be no less tyrannous than a supreme State unchecked by any complementary association.

The proper sphere of the industrial organisation is the control of production and of the producer's side of exchange: its function is industrial in the widest sense, and includes such matters as directly concern the producer as a producer – in his work, the most important and serviceable part of his daily life. It has no claim to decide 'political' questions: for its right rests upon the fact that it stands for the producer, and that producers ought to exercise direct control over production.

The proper sphere of the State in relation to industry is the expression of those common needs and desires which belong to men as consumers or users of the products of industry. It has no claim to decide producers' questions or to exercise direct control over production; for its right rests upon the fact that it stands for the consumers, and that the consumers ought to control the division of the national product, or the division of income in the community.

Industry, in the widest sense, is a matter of both production and use. The product has to be produced, and it has to be determined who shall have the right to consume it. On the one hand, the decision of the character and use of the product is clearly a matter primarily for the user; on the other, the conditions under which work is carried on so vitally and directly concern the various sections of organised producers that they cannot afford to let the control of those conditions remain in the hands of outsiders. The old Collectivist claimed everything for the democratic community, and maintained that the workers would find their grievances adequately ventilated and their interests thoroughly safeguarded by means of a reformed Parliament under democratic control. He looked forward to a future Society in which the State and the Municipalities would employ all the workers much as they now employ men in the post office, the Government dockyards, or on the tramways, with the difference that the goodwill of the whole body of consumers would secure for the worker decent wages, hours and conditions of labour. The new Syndicalist claims everything for the organised workers; he would have them so organised as to secure the monopoly of their labour, and supplement this first principle of economic power by the provision of economic resource, and then he would have them, by direct action, oust the Capitalist from the control of industry, and enter themselves into complete possession of the means of production and distribution.

There is in this more than a clash of policies; there is a clash of fundamental ideas. The Collectivist, immersed in the daily struggle of the worker for a living wage, has thought only of distribution. High wages under State control have been the sum of his ambition; he has dismissed, as artists, dreamers, or idealists, those who, like William Morris, have contended that no less fundamental is the question of production – the problem of giving to the workers responsibility and control, in short, freedom to express their personality in the work which is their way of serving the community. The problem of Socialist theory in the present is the reconciliation of these two points of view; for either, alone, is impotent to form the framework of a noble ideal. Political democracy must be completed by democracy in the workshop; industrial democracy must realise that, in denying the State, it is falling back into a tyranny of industrialism. If, instead of condemning Syndicalism unheard, the Socialist would endeavour to grasp this, its central idea, and harmonise it with his own ideal of political justice, Collectivism and Syndicalism would stand forth as, in essentials, not opposing forces, but indispensable and complementary ideas.

A close analysis of the Syndicalist demand points the way to the only real solution. That absolute ownership of the means of production by the Unions to which some Syndicalists look forward is but a perversion and exaggeration of a just demand. The workers ought to control the normal conduct of industry; but they ought not to regulate the price of commodities at will, to dictate to the consumer what he shall consume, or, in short, to exploit the community as the individual profiteer exploits it today.

What, then, is the solution? Surely it lies in a division of functions between the State as the representative of the organised consumers and the Trade Unions, or bodies arising out of them through industrial Unionism, as the representatives of the organised producers.

These bodies we call National Guilds, in order both to link them up with the tradition of the Middle Ages and to distinguish them from that tradition. We, who call ourselves National Guildsmen, look forward to a community in which production will be organised through democratic associations of all the workers in each industry, linked up in a body representing all workers in all industries. On the other hand, we look forward to a democratisation of the State and of local government, and to a sharing of industrial control between producers and consumers. The State should own the means of production: the Guild should control the work of production. In some such partnership as this, and neither in pure Collectivism nor in pure Syndicalism, lies the solution of the problem of industrial control.

Naturally, such a suggestion needs far more elaborate working out than can be given here, and, in particular, much must be left for decision in the future as the practical problems arise. We cannot hope to work out a full and definite scheme of partnership in advance; but we have everything to gain by realising, even in broad outline, what kind of Society we actually desire to create. We need at the same time to satisfy the producers' demand for responsibility and self-government, and to meet the consumers' just claim to an equitable division of the national income, and to a full provision of the goods and services which he justly requires.

Some sort of partnership, then, must come about; but there is a notable tendency nowadays for persons to adopt the phrase without intending to bring any effective partnership into being. The partnership, to be worth anything, must be a partnership of equals, not the revocable concession of a benignant and superior State, and, to make it real, the Guilds must be in a position to bargain on equal terms with the State. The conditions upon which the producers consent to serve, and the community to accept their service, must be determined by negotiation between the Guilds and the State. The Guild must preserve the right and the economic resource to withdraw its labour; the State must rely, to check unjust demands, on its equal voice in the decision of points of difference, and on the organised opinion of the community as a whole. As a last resort the preservation of equality between the two types of organisation involves the possibility of a deadlock; but it is almost impossible to imagine such a deadlock arising in an equalitarian Society.

I have stated my ideal very baldly, because it has already been stated well and fully elsewhere, and I do not desire to go over again the ground which others have covered. I must, however, state briefly the fundamental moral case both against Socialism as it is usually conceived and in favour of the ideal for which I am contending.

What, I want to ask, is the fundamental evil in our modern Society which we should set out to abolish?

There are two possible answers to that question, and I am sure that very many well-meaning people would make the wrong one. They would answer POVERTY, when they ought to answer SLAVERY. Face to face every day with the shameful contrasts of riches and destitution, high dividends and low wages, and painfully conscious of the futility of trying to adjust the balance by means of charity, private or public, they would answer unhesitatingly that they stand for the ABOLITION OF POVERTY.

Well and good! On that issue every Socialist is with them. But their answer to my question is none the less wrong.

Poverty is the symptom: slavery the disease. The extremes of riches and destitution follow inevitably upon the extremes of license and bondage. The many are not enslaved because they are poor, they are poor because they are enslaved. Yet Socialists have all too often fixed their eyes upon the material misery of the poor without realising that it rests upon the spiritual degradation of the slave . . .

Inspired by the idea that poverty is the root evil, Socialists have tried to heal the ills of Society by an attempt to redistribute income. In this attempt, it will be admitted that they have hitherto met with no success. The gulf between rich and poor has not grown an inch narrower; it has even appreciably widened. It is the conviction of Guild-Socialists that the gulf will never be bridged, as long as the social problem is regarded as pre-eminently a question of distribution.

Idle rich and unemployed poor apart, every individual has two functions in the economic sphere – he is both a producer and a consumer of goods and services. Socialists, in seeking a basis on which to build their ideal Society, have alternated between these two aspects of human activity. The Fourierists, the Christian Socialists and the Communists, with their ideals of the phalang- stery, the self-governing workshop, and the free Commune, built – and built imperfectly – upon man the producer. Collectivism, on the other hand, which includes most modern schools of Socialism, builds upon man the consumer. It is our business to decide which, if either, of them is right.

It is the pride of the practical social reformer that he deals with 'the average man in his average moments'. He repudiates, as high- falutin nonsense, every attempt to erect a new social order on a basis of idealism; he is vigilantly distrustful of human nature, hu- man initiative and human freedom; and he finds his ideal in a pater- nal governmentalism tempered by a preferably not too real demo- cratic control. To minds of such a temper, Collectivism has an irresistible appeal. The idea that the State is not only supreme in the last resort, but also a capable jack of all trades, offers to the bureaucrat a wide field for petty tyranny. In the State of today, in which democratic control through Parliament is little better than a farce, the Collectivist State would be the Earthly Paradise of bureaucracy.

The Socialist in most cases admits this, but declares that it could be corrected if Parliament were democratised. The 'conquest of political power' becomes the Alpha and Omega of his political method: all his cheques are postdated to the Greek Kalends of the first Socialist Government. Is, then, his ideal of the democratic con- trol of industry through Parliament an ideal worthy of the energy which is expended in its furtherance?

The crying need of our days is the need for freedom. Machinery and Capitalism between them have made the worker a mere serf, with no interest in the product of his own labour beyond the in- adequate wage which he secures by it. The Collectivist State would only make his position better by securing him a better wage, even if we assume that Collectivism can ever acquire the driving power to put its ideas into practice: in other respects it would leave the work- er essentially as he is now – a wage slave, subject to the will of a master imposed on him from without. However democratically minded Parliament might be, it would none the less remain, for the worker in any industry, a purely external force, imposing its commands from outside and from above. The postal workers are no more free while the Post Office is managed by a State department than Trade Unionists would be free if their Executive Committees were appointed by His Majesty's Minister of Labour . . .

The Collectivist is prepared to recognise Trade Unionism under a Collectivist regime. But he is not prepared to trust Trade Unionism, or to entrust it with the conduct of industry. He does not believe in industrial self-government; his 'industrial democracy' embodies only the right of the workers to manage their Trade Unions, and not their right to control industry. The National Guildsman, on the other hand, bases his social philosophy on the idea of function. In the industrial sphere, he desires not the recognition of Trade Unions by a Collectivist State, but the recognition of a democratic State by National Guilds controlling industry in the common interest . . .

This idea of the control of industry, which was forced to the front by the coming of Syndicalism in its French and American forms, is not new, but is a revival of the first ideas of working-class combinations. It represents a return, after a long sojourn in the wilderness of materialism and reform, to the idealism of the early revolutionaries. But this time the idealism is clothed not only with a fundamentally right philosophy, but also with a practical policy. The new revolutionaries know that only by means of Trade Unionism can Capitalism be transformed and they know also by what methods the revolution can be accomplished. They aim at the consolidation of Trade Union forces, because beyond the Trade Union lies the Guild.

Out of the Trade Unionism of today must rise a Greater Unionism, in which craft shall be no longer divided from craft, nor industry from industry. Industrial Unionism lies next on the road to freedom, and Industrial Unionism means not 'One Industry, One Union, One Card,' but the linking-up of all industries into one great army of labour.

But even this great army will achieve no final victory in the war that really matters unless it has behind it the driving force of a great constructive idea. This idea Guild Socialism fully supplies. The workers cannot be free unless industry is managed and organised by the workers themselves in the interests of the whole community. The Trade Union, which has been till now a bargaining force, disputing with the employer about the conditions of labour, must become a controlling force, an industrial republic. In short, out of the bargaining Trade Union must grow the producing Guild.

In the Middle Ages, before the dark ages of Capitalism descended on the world, industry was organised in guilds. Each town was then more or less isolated and self-sufficient, and within each town was a system of guilds, each carrying on production in its own trade. These guilds were indeed associations of small masters, but in the period when the guilds flourished there was no hard-and-fast line between master and man, and the journeyman in due course normally became a master. The mediaeval guilds, existing in an undemocratic society, were indeed themselves always to some extent undemocratic; and, as Capitalism began to take root, inequality grew more marked and the guild system gradually dissolved. Our age has its own needs; and the guilds which Guild Socialists desire to see established will be in many ways unlike those of the mediaeval period; but both are alike in this, that they involve the control of industry by the workers themselves . . .

I have dwelt . . . upon the Socialism of William Morris because I feel that he, more than any other prophet of revolution, is of the same blood as National Guildsmen. Freedom for self-expression, freedom at work as well as at leisure, freedom to serve as well as to enjoy – that is the guiding principle of his work and of his life. That, too, is the guiding principle of National Guilds. We can only destroy the tyranny of machinery – which is not the same as destroying machinery itself – by giving into the hands of the workers the control of their life and work, by freeing them to choose whether they will make well or ill, whether they will do the work of slaves or of free men. All our efforts must be turned in that direction: in our immediate measures we must strive to pave the way for the coming free alliance of producers and consumers.

This is indeed a doctrine directly in opposition to the political tendencies of our time. For today we are moving at a headlong pace in the direction of a 'national' control of the lives of men which is in fact national only in the sense that it serves the interests of the dominant class in the nation. Already many of the Socialists who have been the most enthusiastic advocates of State action are standing aghast at the application of their principles to an undemocratic Society. The greatest of all dangers is the 'Selfridge' State, so loudly heralded these twenty years by Mr 'Callisthenes' Webb. The workers must be free and self-governing in the industrial sphere, or all their struggle for emancipation will have been in vain. If we had to choose between Syndicalism and Collectivism, it would be the duty and impulse of every good man to choose Syndicalism, despite the dangers it involves. For Syndicalism at least aims high, even though it fails to ensure that production shall actually be carried on, as it desires, in the general interest. Syndicalism is the infirmity of noble minds: Collectivism is at best only the sordid dream of a business man with a conscience. Fortunately, we have not to choose between these two: for in the Guild idea Socialism and Syndicalism are reconciled. To it Collectivism will yield if only all lovers of freedom will rally round the banner, for it has a message for them especially such as no other school of Socialism has had. Out of the Trade Union shall grow the Guild; and in the Guild alone is freedom for the worker and a release from the ever-present tyranny of modern industrialism.

2.3 R. H. TAWNEY: SOCIAL PURPOSE

As economic historian, social theorist and pioneer of the workers' adult education movement, R. H. Tawney exercised a profound influence on a whole generation of British socialists. In such books as *The acquisitive society* (1921), *Religion and the rise of capitalism* (1926) and *Equality* (1931), Tawney's religious outlook combined with his historical approach to produce (in elegant prose) an indictment of capitalist values and an advocacy of socialist ones. The following extract is taken from his Fabian pamphlet *The sickness of an acquisitive society* (1920), which formed the basis of his subsequent book of similar title, and in which he contrasts an 'acquisitive' society with a 'functional' one in terms of their social purpose.

It is a commonplace that the characteristic virtue of Englishmen is their power of sustained practical activity, and their characteristic vice an inability to test the quality of that activity by reference to principles. They are incurious as to theory, take fundamentals for granted, and are more interested in the state of the roads than in their place on the map. And it might fairly be argued that in ordinary times that combination of intellectual tameness with practical energy is sufficiently serviceable to explain, if not to justify, the equanimity with which its possessors bear the criticism of more mentally adventurous nations. It is the mood of those who have made their bargain with fate and are content to take what it offers without re-opening the deal. It leaves the mind free to concentrate undisturbed upon profitable activities, because it is not distracted by a taste for unprofitable speculations. Most generations, it might be said, walk in a path which they neither make nor discover, but accept; the main thing is that they should march. The blinkers worn by Englishmen enable them to trot all the more steadily along the beaten road, without being disturbed by curiosity as to their destination.

But if the medicine of the constitution ought not to be made its daily food, neither can its daily food be made its medicine. There are times which are not ordinary, and in such times it is not enough to follow the road. It is necessary to know where it leads, and, if it leads nowhere, to follow another. The search for another involves reflection, which is uncongenial to the bustling people who describe themselves as practical, because they take things as they are and leave them as they are. But the practical thing for a traveller who is uncertain of his path is not to proceed with the utmost rapidity in the wrong direction: it is to consider how to find the right one. And the practical thing for a nation which has stumbled upon one of the turning-points of history is not to behave as though nothing very important were involved, as if it did not matter whether it turned to the right or to the left, went up hill or down dale, provided that it continued doing with a little more energy what it has done hitherto; but to consider whether what it has done hitherto is wise, and, if it is not wise, to alter it. When the broken ends of its industry, its politics, its social organization, have to be pieced together after a catastrophe, it must make a decision; for it makes a decision even if it refuses to decide. If it is to make a decision which will wear, it must travel beyond the philosophy momentarily in favour with the proprietors of its newspapers. Unless it is to move with the energetic futility of a squirrel in a revolving cage, it must have a clear apprehension both of the deficiency of what is, and of the character of what ought to be. And to obtain this apprehension it must appeal to some standard more stable than the momentary exigencies of its commerce or industry or social life, and judge them by it. It must, in short, have recourse to Principles.

Such considerations are, perhaps, not altogether irrelevant at a time when facts have forced upon Englishmen the reconsideration of their social institutions which no appeal to theory could induce them to undertake. An appeal to principles is the condition of any considerable reconstruction of society, because social institutions are the visible expression of the scale of moral values which rules the minds of individuals, and it is impossible to alter institutions without altering that moral valuation. Parliament, industrial organizations, the whole complex machinery through which society expresses itself, is a mill which grinds only what is put into it, and when nothing is put into it grinds air. There are many, of course, who desire no alteration, and who, when it is attempted, will oppose it. They have found the existing economic order profitable in the past. They desire only such changes as will ensure that it is equally profitable in the future . . .

There are others, however, who are conscious of the desire for a new social order, but who yet do not grasp the implications of their own desire. Men may genuinely sympathise with the demand for a radical change. They may be conscious of social evils and sincerely anxious to remove them. They may set up a new department, and appoint new officials, and invent a new name to express their resolution to effect something more drastic than reform, and less disturbing than revolution. But unless they will take the pains, not only to act, but to reflect, they end by effecting nothing. For they deliver themselves bound to those who think they are practical, because they take their philosophy so much for granted as to be unconscious of its implications, and directly they try to act, that philosophy re-asserts itself, and serves as an overruling force which presses their action more deeply into the old channels . . . When they desire to place their economic life on a better foundation, they repeat, like parrots, the word 'Productivity', because that is the word that rises first in their minds: regardless of the fact that productivity is the foundation on which it is based already, that increased productivity is the one characteristic achievement of the age before the war, as religion was of the middle ages or art of classical Athens, and that it is precisely in the century which has seen the greatest increase in productivity since the fall of the Roman Empire that economic discontent has been most acute. When they are touched by social compunction, they can think of nothing more original than the diminution of poverty, because poverty, being the opposite of the riches which they value most, seems to them the most terrible of human afflictions, and they do not understand that poverty is a symptom and a consequence of social disorder, while the disorder itself is something at once more fundamental and more incorrigible, and that the quality in their social life which causes it to demoralize a few by excessive riches, is also the quality which causes it to demoralize many by excessive poverty . . .

Yet all the time the principles upon which industry should be based are simple, however difficult it may be to apply them; and if they are overlooked it is not because they are difficult, but because they are elementary. They are simple because industry is simple. An industry, when all is said, is, in its essence, nothing more mysterious than a body of men associated, in various degrees of competition and co-operation, to win their living by providing the community with some service which it requires. Organize it as you will, let it be a group of craftsmen labouring with hammer and chisel, or peasants ploughing their own fields, or armies of mechanics of a hundred different trades constructing ships which are miracles of complexity with machines which are the climax of centuries of invention, its function is service, its method is association. Because its function is service, an industry as a whole has rights and duties towards the community, the abrogation of which involves privilege. Because its method is association, the different parties within it have rights and duties towards each other; and the neglect or perversion of these involves oppression.

The conditions of a right organization of industry are, therefore, permanent, unchanging, and capable of being apprehended by the most elementary intelligence, provided it will read the nature of its countrymen in the large outlines of history, not in the bloodless abstractions of experts. The first is that it should be subordinated to the community in such a way as to render the best service technically possible, that those who render that service faithfully should be honourably paid, and those who render no service should not be paid at all, because it is of the essence of a function that it should find its meaning in the satisfaction not of itself, but of the end which it serves. The second is that its direction and government should be in the hands of persons who are responsible to those who are directed and governed, because it is the condition of economic freedom that men should not be ruled by an authority which they cannot control. The industrial problem, in fact, is a problem of right, not merely of material misery, and because it is a problem of right it is most acute among those sections of the working classes whose material misery is least. It is a question, first of Function, and secondly of Freedom.

A function may be defined as an activity which embodies and expresses the idea of social purpose. The essence of it is that the agent does not perform it merely for personal gain or to gratify himself, but recognizes that he is responsible for its discharge to some higher authority. The purpose of industry is obvious. It is to supply man with things which are necessary, useful or beautiful, and thus to bring life to body or spirit. In so far as it is governed by this end, it is among the most important of human activities. In so far as it is diverted from it, it may be harmless, amusing, or even exhilarating to those who carry it on, but it possesses no more social significance than the orderly business of ants and bees, the strutting of peacocks, or the struggles of carnivorous animals over carrion. Men have normally appreciated this fact, however unwilling or unable they may have been to act upon it; and therefore from time to time, in so far as they have been able to control the forces of violence and greed, they have adopted various expedients for emphasizing the social quality of economic activity. It is not easy, however, to emphasize it effectively, because to do so requires a constant effort of will, against which egotistical instincts are in rebellion, and because, if that will is to prevail, it must be embodied in some social and political organization, which may itself become so arbitrary, tyrannical and corrupt as to thwart the performance of function instead of promoting it. When this process of degeneration has gone far, as in most European countries it had by the middle of the eighteenth century, the indispensable thing is to break the dead organization up and to clear the ground. In the course of doing so, the individual is emancipated and his rights are enlarged; but the idea of social purpose is discredited by the discredit justly attaching to the obsolete order in which it is embodied.

It is not surprising, therefore, that in the new industrial societies which arose on the ruins of the old regime the dominant note should have been the insistence upon individual rights, irrespective of any social purpose to which their exercise contributed . . .

This doctrine has been qualified in practice by particular limitations to avert particular evils and to meet exceptional emergencies. But it is limited in special cases precisely because its general validity is regarded as beyond controversy, and, up to the eve of the present war, it was the working faith of modern economic civilization. What it implies is, that the foundation of society is found, not in functions, but in rights; that rights are not deducible from the discharge of functions, so that the acquisition of wealth and the enjoyment of property are contingent upon the performances of services, but that the individual enters the world equipped with rights to the free disposal of his property and the pursuit of his economic self-interest, and that these rights are anterior to, and independent of, any service which he may render. True, the service of society will, in fact, it is assumed, result from their exercise. But it is not the primary motive and criterion of industry, but a secondary consequence, which emerges incidentally through the exercise of rights, a consequence which is attained, indeed, in practice, but which is attained without being sought. It is not the end at which economic activity aims, or the standard by which it is judged, but a bye-product, as coal-tar is a bye-product of the manufacture of gas;

whether that bye-product appears or not, it is not proposed that the rights themselves should be abdicated. For they are regarded, not as a conditional trust, but as a property, which may, indeed, give way to the special exigencies of extraordinary emergencies, but which resumes its sway when the emergency is over, and in normal times is above discussion . . .

A society which aimed at making the acquisition of wealth contingent upon the discharge of social obligations, which sought to proportion remuneration to service and denied it to those by whom no service was performed, which inquired first not what men possess but what they can make or create or achieve, might be called a Functional Society, because in such a society the main subject of social emphasis would be the performance of functions. But such a society does not exist, even as a remote ideal, in the modern world, though something like it has hung, an unrealized theory, before men's minds in the past. Modern societies aim at protecting economic rights, while leaving economic functions, except in moments of abnormal emergency, to fulfil themselves. The motive which gives colour and quality to their public institutions, to their policy and political thought, is not the attempt to secure the fulfilment of tasks undertaken for the public service, but to increase the opportunities open to individuals of attaining the objects which they conceive to be advantageous to themselves. If asked the end or criterion of social organization, they would give an answer reminiscent of the formula the greatest happiness of the greatest number. But to say that the end of social institutions is happiness, is to say that they have no common end at all. For happiness is individual, and to make happiness the object of society is to resolve society itself into the ambitions of numberless individuals, each directed towards the attainment of some personal purpose.

Such societies may be called Acquisitive Societies, because their whole tendency and interest and preoccupation is to promote the acquisition of wealth. The appeal of this conception must be powerful for it has laid the whole modern world under its spell. Since England first revealed the possibilities of industrialism, it has gone from strength to strength, and as industrial civilization invades countries hitherto remote from it, as Russia and Japan and India and China are drawn into its orbit, each decade sees a fresh extension of its influence. The secret of its triumph is obvious. It is an invitation to men to use the powers with which they have been endowed by nature or society, by skill or energy or relentless egotism or mere good fortune, without enquiring whether there is any prin-

ciple by which their exercise should be limited. It assumes the social organization which determines the opportunities which different classes shall in fact possess, and concentrates attention upon
the rights of those who possess or can acquire power to make the
fullest use of it for their own self-advancement. By fixing men's
minds, not upon the discharge of social obligations, which restricts
their energy, because it defines the goal to which it should be
directed, but upon the exercise of the right to pursue their own
self-interest, it offers unlimited scope for the acquisition of riches,
and therefore gives free play to one of the most powerful of human
instincts. To the strong it promises unfettered freedom for the exercise of their strength; to the weak the hope that they too one day
may be strong. Before the eyes of both it suspends a golden prize,
which not all can attain, but for which each may strive, the en-
chanting vision of infinite expansion. It assures men that there are
no ends other than their ends, no law other than their desires, no
limit other than that which they think advisable. Thus it makes the
individual the centre of his own universe, and dissolves moral principles into a choice of expediences. And it immensely simplifies the
problems of social life in complex communities. For it relieves
them of the necessity of discriminating between different types of
economic activity and different sources of wealth, between enterprise and avarice, energy and unscrupulous greed, property which
is legitimate and property which is theft, the just enjoyment of the
fruits of labour and the idle parasitism of birth or fortune, because
it treats all economic activities as standing upon the same level,
and suggests that excess or defect, waste or superfluity, require no
conscious effort of the social will to avert them, but are corrected
almost automatically by the mechanical play of economic forces.

Under the impulse of such ideas men do not become religious or
wise or artistic; for religion and wisdom and art imply the acceptance of limitations. But they become powerful and rich. They in-
herit the earth and change the face of nature if they do not possess
their own souls; and they have that appearance of freedom which
consists in the absence of obstacles between opportunities for self-
advancement and those whom birth or wealth or talent or good fortune has placed in a position to seize them. It is not difficult either
for individuals or for societies to achieve their object, if that object
be sufficiently limited and immediate, and if they are not distracted
from its pursuit by other considerations. The temper which dedi-
cates itself to the cultivation of opportunities, and leaves obligations
to take care of themselves, is set upon an object which is at once

simple and practicable. The eighteenth century defined it. The twentieth century has very largely attained it. Or, if it has not attained it, it has at least grasped the possibilities of its attainment . . .

Such happiness is not remote from achievement. In the course of achieving it, however, the world has been confronted by a group of unexpected consequences, which are the cause of its *malaise*, as the obstruction of economic opportunity was the cause of social *malaise* in the eighteenth century. And these consequences are not, as is often suggested, accidental mal-adjustments, but flow naturally from its dominant principle: so that there is a sense in which the cause of its perplexity is not its failure, but the quality of its success, and its light itself a kind of darkness. The will to economic power, if it is sufficiently single-minded, brings riches. But if it is single-minded it destroys the moral restraints which ought to condition the pursuit of riches, and therefore also makes the pursuit of riches meaningless. For what gives meaning to economic activity, as to any other activity is, as we have said, the purpose to which it is directed. But the faith upon which our economic civilization reposes, the faith that riches are not a means but an end, implies that all economic activity is equally estimable, whether it is subordinated to a social purpose or not. Hence it divorces gain from service, and justifies rewards for which no function is performed, or which are out of all proportion to it. Wealth in modern societies is distributed according to opportunity; and while opportunity depends partly upon talent and energy, it depends still more upon birth, social position, access to education and inherited wealth; in a word, upon property. For talent and energy can create opportunity. But property need only wait for it. It is the sleeping partner who draws the dividends which the firm produces, the residuary legatee who always claims his share in the estate . . .

The rejection of the idea of purpose involves another consequence which every one laments, but which no one can prevent, except by abandoning the belief that the free exercise of rights is the main interest of society and the discharge of obligations a secondary and incidental consequence which may be left to take care of itself. It is that social life is turned into a scene of fierce antagonisms, and that a considerable part of industry is carried on in the intervals of a disguised social war. The idea that industrial peace can be secured merely by the exercise of tact and forbearance is based on the idea that there is a fundamental identity of interest between the different groups engaged in it, which is occasionally interrupted by regrettable misunderstandings. Both the one idea and the other are an illusion. The disputes which matter are not caused by a misunderstanding of identity of interests, but by a better understanding of diversity of interests. Though a formal declaration of war is an episode, the conditions which issue in a declaration of war are permanent; and what makes them permanent is the conception of industry which also makes inequality and functionless incomes permanent. It is the denial that industry has any end or purpose other than the satisfaction of those engaged in it. That motive produces industrial warfare, not as a regrettable incident, but as an inevitable result. It produces industrial war, because its teaching is that each individual or group has a right to what they can get, and denies that there is any principle, other than the mechanism of the market, which determines what they ought to get. For, since the income available for distribution is limited, and since, therefore, when certain limits have been passed, what one group gains another group must lose, it is evident that if the relative incomes of different groups are not to be determined by their functions, there is no method other than mutual self-assertion which is left to determine them. Self-interest indeed, may cause them to refrain from using their full strength to enforce their claims, and, in so far as this happens, peace is secured in industry, as men have attempted to secure it in international affairs, by a balance of power. But the maintenance of such a peace is contingent upon the estimate of the parties to it that they have more to lose than to gain by an overt struggle, and is not the result of their acceptance of any standard of remuneration as an equitable settlement of their claims. Hence it is precarious, insincere and short. It is without finality, because there can be no finality in the mere addition of increments of income, any more than in the gratification of any other desire for material goods. When demands are conceded the old struggle recommences upon a new level, and will always recommence as long as men seek to end it merely by increasing remuneration, not by finding a principle upon which all remuneration, whether large or small, should be based.

Such a principle is offered by the idea of function, because its application would eliminate the surpluses which are the subject of contention, and would make it evident that remuneration is based upon service, not upon chance or privilege or the power to use opportunities to drive a hard bargain. But the idea of function is incompatible with the doctrine that every person and organization have an unlimited right to exploit their economic opportunities as fully as they please, which is the working faith of modern industry;

and since it is not accepted, men resign themselves to the settlement of the issue by force, or propose that the state should supersede the force of private association by the use of its force, as though the absence of a principle could be compensated by a new kind of machinery. Yet all the time the true cause of industrial warfare is as simple as the true cause of international warfare. It is that if men recognise no law superior to their desires, then they must fight when their desires collide. For though groups or nations which are at issue with each other may be willing to submit to a principle which is superior to them both, there is no reason why they should submit to each other. Hence the idea, which is popular with rich men, that industrial disputes would disappear if only the output of wealth were doubled, and every one were twice as well off, not only is refuted by all practical experience, but is in its very nature founded upon an illusion . . .

So here, again, the prevalent insistence upon rights, and prevalent neglect of functions, brings men into a vicious circle which they cannot escape, without escaping from the false philosophy which dominates them. But it does something more. It makes that philosophy itself seem plausible and exhilarating, and a rule not only for industry, in which it had its birth, but for politics and culture and religion and the whole compass of social life. The possibility that one aspect of human life may be so exaggerated as to overshadow, and in time to atrophy, every other, has been made familiar to Englishmen by the example of 'Prussian militarism'. Militarism is the characteristic, not of an army, but of a society. Its essence is not any particular quality or scale of military preparation, but a state of mind, which, in its concentration on one particular element in social life, ends finally by exalting it until it becomes the arbiter of all the rest. The purpose for which military forces exist is forgotten. They are thought to stand by their own right and to need no justification. Instead of being regarded as an instrument which is necessary in an imperfect world, they are elevated into an object of superstitious veneration, as though the world would be a poor insipid place without them, so that political institutions and social arrangements and intellect and morality and religion are crushed into a mould made to fit one activity, which in a sane society is a subordinate activity, like the police, or the maintenance of prisons, or the cleansing of sewers, but which in a militarist state is a kind of mystical epitome of society itself.

Militarism, as Englishmen see plainly enough, is fetish worship. It is the prostration of men's souls before, and the laceration of their bodies to appease, an idol. What they do not see is that their reverence for economic activity and industry and what is called business is also fetish worship, and that in their devotion to that idol they torture themselves as needlessly and indulge in the same meaningless antics as the Prussians did in their worship of militarism. For what the military tradition and spirit have done for Prussia, with the result of creating militarism, the commercial tradition and spirit have done for England, with the result of creating industrialism. Industrialism is no more a necessary characteristic of an economically developed society than militarism is a necessary characteristic of a nation which maintains military forces. It is no more the result of applying science to industry, than militarism is the result of the application of science to war, and the idea that it is something inevitable in a community which uses coal and iron and machinery, so far from being the truth, is itself a product of the perversion of mind which industrialism produces. Men may use what mechanical instruments they please and be none the worse for their use. What kills their souls is when they allow their instruments to use them. The essence of industrialism, in short, is not any particular method of industry, but a particular estimate of the importance of industry, which results in it being thought the only thing that is important at all, so that it is elevated from the subordinate place which it should occupy among human interests and activities into being the standard by which all other interests and activities are judged.

When a Cabinet Minister declares that the greatness of this country depends upon the volume of its exports, so that France, which exports comparatively little, and Elizabethan England, which exported next to nothing, are presumably to be pitied as altogether inferior civilizations, that is Industrialism. It is the confusion of one minor department of life with the whole of life. When manufacturers cry and cut themselves with knives, because it is proposed that boys and girls of fourteen shall attend school for eight hours a week, and the President of the Board of Education is so gravely impressed by their apprehensions, that he at once allows the hours to be reduced to seven, that is Industrialism. It is fetish worship. When the Government obtains money for a war, which costs £7,000,000 a day, by closing the Museums, which cost £20,000 a year, that is Industrialism. It is contempt for all interests which do not contribute obviously to economic activity. When the Press clamours that the one thing needed to make this island an Arcadia is productivity, and more productivity, and yet more productivity, that is Industrialism. It is the confusion of means with ends. Men will always confuse means with ends if they are without any clear conception that it is the ends, not the means, which matter – if they allow their minds to slip from the fact that it is the social purpose of industry which gives it meaning and makes it worth while to carry it on at all. And when they do that, they will turn their whole world upside down, because they do not see the poles upon which it ought to move. So when, like England, they are thoroughly industrialized, they behave like Germany, which was thoroughly militarized. They talk as though man existed for industry, instead of industry existing for man, as the Prussians talked of man existing for war. They resent any activity which is not coloured by the predominant interest, because it seems a rival to it. So they destroy religion and art and morality, which cannot exist unless they are disinterested; and having destroyed these, which are the end, for the sake of industry, which is a means, they make their industry itself what they make their cities, a desert of unnatural dreariness, which only forgetfulness can make endurable, and which only excitement can enable them to forget . . .

Thus, as long as men move on this plane, there is no solution. They can obtain peace only by surrendering the claim to the unfettered exercise of their rights, which is the cause of war. What we have been witnessing, in short, during the past five years, both in international affairs and in industry, is the breakdown of the organization of society on the basis of rights divorced from obligations. Sooner or later the collapse was inevitable, because the basis was too narrow. For a right is simply a power which is secured by legal sanctions, 'a capacity', as the lawyers define it, 'residing in one man, of controlling, with the assistance of the State, the action of others', and a right should not be absolute for the same reason that a power should not be absolute. No doubt it is better that individuals should have absolute rights than that the State or the Government should have them; and it was the reaction against the abuses of absolute power by the State which led in the eighteenth century to the declaration of the absolute right of individuals. The most obvious defence against the assertion of one extreme was the assertion of the other. Because Governments and the relics of feudalism had encroached upon the property of individuals it was affirmed that the right of property was absolute; because they had strangled enterprise, it was affirmed that every man had a natural right to conduct his business as he pleased. But, in reality, both the one assertion and the other are false, and, if applied to practice, must lead to disaster. The State has no absolute rights; they are limited by its commission. The individual has no absolute rights; they are relative to the function which he performs in the community of which he is a member, because, unless they are so limited, the consequences must be something in the nature of private war. All rights, in short, are conditional and derivative, because all power should be conditional and derivative. They are derived from the end or purpose of the society in which they exist. They are conditional on being used to contribute to the attainment of that end, not to thwart it. And this means in practice that, if society is to be healthy, men must regard themselves not as the owners of rights, but as trustees for the discharge of functions and the instruments of a social purpose . . .

So the organisation of society on the basis of function, instead of on that of rights, implies three things. It means, first, that proprietary rights shall be maintained when they are accompanied by the performance of service and abolished when they are not. It means, second, that the producers shall stand in a direct relation to the community for whom production is carried on, so that their responsibility to it may be obvious and unmistakable, not lost, as at present, through their immediate subordination to shareholders whose interest is not service but gain. It means, in the third place, that the obligation for the maintenance of the service shall rest upon the professional organisation of those who perform it, and that, subject to the supervision and criticism of the consumers, those organisations shall exercise so much voice in the government of industry as may be needed to secure that the obligation is discharged. It is obvious, indeed, that no change of system or machinery can avert those causes of social *malaise* which consist in the egotism, greed, or quarrelsomeness of human nature. What it can do is to create an environment in which those are not the qualities which are encouraged. It cannot secure that men live up to their principles. What it can do is to establish their social order upon principles to which, if they please, they can live up and not live down. It cannot control their actions. It can offer them an end on which to fix their minds. And, as their minds are, so, in the long run and with exceptions, their practical activity will be.

The first condition of the right organisation of industry is, then, the intellectual conversion which, in their distrust of principles, Englishmen are disposed to place last or to omit altogether. It is that emphasis should be transferred from the opportunities which it offers individuals to the social functions which it performs; that they should be clear as to its end and should judge it by reference to that end, not by incidental consequences which are foreign to it, however brilliant or alluring those consequences may be. What gives its meaning to any activity which is not purely automatic is its purpose. It is because the purpose of industry, which is the conquest of nature for the service of man, is neither adequately expressed in its organisation nor present to the minds of those engaged in it, because it is not regarded as a function but as an opportunity for personal gain or advancement or display, that the economic life of modern societies is in a perpetual state of morbid irritation. If the conditions which produce the unnatural tension are to be removed, it can only be effected by the growth of a habit of mind which will approach questions of economic organisation from the standpoint of the purpose which it exists to serve, and which will apply to it something of the spirit expressed by Bacon when he said that the work of a man ought to be carried on 'for the glory of God and the relief of men's estate'.

Viewed from that angle issues which are insoluble when treated on the basis of rights may be found more susceptible of reasonable treatment. For a purpose is, in the first place, a principle of limitation. It determines the end for which, and therefore the limits within which, an activity is to be carried on. It divides what is worth doing from what is not, and settles the scale upon which what is worth doing ought to be done. It is, in the second place, a principle of unity, because it supplies a common end to which efforts can be directed, and submits interests, which would otherwise conflict, to the judgement of an over-ruling object. It is, in the third place, a principle of apportionment or distribution. It assigns to the different parties of groups engaged in a common undertaking the place which they are to occupy in carrying it out. Thus it establishes order, not upon chance or power, but upon a principle, and bases remuneration not upon what men can with good fortune snatch for themselves nor upon what, if unlucky, they can be induced to accept, but upon what is appropriate to their function, no more and no less, so that those who perform no function receive no payment, and those who contribute to the common end receive honourable payment for honourable service . . .

The famous lines in which Piccarda explains to Dante the order of Paradise are a description of a complex and multiform society which is united by overmastering devotion to a common end. By that end all stations are assigned and all activities are valued. The parts derive their quality from their place in the system, and are so permeated by the unity which they express that they themselves are glad to be forgotten, as the ribs of an arch carry the eye from the floor from which they spring to the vault in which they meet and interlace. Such a combination of unity and diversity is possible only to a society which subordinates its activities to the principle of purpose. For what that principle offers is not merely a standard for determining the relations of different classes and groups of producers, but a scale of moral values.

Above all, it assigns to economic activity itself its proper place as the servant, not the master, of society. The burden of our civilisation is not merely, as many suppose, that the product of industry is ill-distributed, or its conduct tyrannical, or its operation interrupted by embittered disagreements. It is that industry itself has come to hold a position of exclusive predominance among human interests, which no single interest, and least of all the provision of the material means of existence, is fit to occupy. Like a hypochondriac who is so absorbed in the processes of his own digestion that he goes to his grave before he has begun to live, industrialised communities neglect the very objects for which it is worth while to acquire riches in their feverish preoccupation with the means by which riches are acquired. That obsession by economic issues is as local and transitory as it is repulsive and disturbing. To future generations it will appear as pitiable as the obsession of the seventeenth century by religious quarrels appears today; indeed, it is less rational since the object with which it is concerned is less important. And it is a poison which inflames every wound and turns each trivial scratch into a malignant ulcer. Society will not solve the particular problems of industry which afflict it, until that poison is expelled, and it has learned to see industry itself in the right perspective. If it is to do that, it must rearrange its scale of values. It must regard economic interests as one element in life, not as the whole of life. It must persuade its members to renounce the opportunity of gains which accrue without any corresponding service, because the struggle for them keeps the whole community in a fever. It must so organize industry that the instrumental character of economic activity is emphasised by its subordination to the social purpose for which it is carried on.

2.4 KEIR HARDIE

James Keir Hardie was the leading figure in the Independent Labour Party and the personification of the ILP tradition of ethical socialism.

Not a serious theorist, Hardie described his book *From serfdom to socialism* (1907), from which this extract comes, as 'a brief unadorned statement of the case for Socialism, easily understandable by plain folk'.

If, as Herbert Spencer said, life means internal correspondence to external environment, then Socialism or decay are the alternatives we have to face. What we have at present is an altruistic spirit struggling against an individualistic environment. The change which the Socialist seeks is to make the material environment correspond to the ethical spirit. Progress cannot for ever be confined by the cerements of a dead past. Unless the Social quagmire of Poverty can be cleansed, its foul miasma will poison the blood of the body politic and produce decay and death.

We have seen how in our own country the boundaries of freedom have been widening with the progress of the ages. The slave of a thousand years ago, with no more right than the swine he tended, has fought his way upward through Serfdom to Citizenship. The modern workman is theoretically the equal in the eye of the law of every other class. His vote carries equal weight in the ballot box with that of the millionaire who employs him; he is as free to worship when and how he pleases as the noblest baron; his rights are in all respects the same as theirs. Combination and energy have raised him to where he now stands. But his task is not yet finished; the long drawn out struggle is not yet over. There is one more battle to be fought, one more fortress to be assailed ere he stands within the charmed circle of perfect equality. He has yet to overcome property and win economic freedom. When he has made property his servant, not his master, he will literally have put all his enemies under his feet . . .

To dogmatise about the form which the Socialist State shall take is to play the fool. That is a matter with which we have nothing whatever to do. It belongs to the future, and is a matter which posterity alone can decide. The most we can hope to do is to make the coming of Socialism possible in the full assurance that it will shape itself aright when it does come. We have seen how mankind when left free has always and in all parts of the world naturally turned to Communism. That it will do so again is the most likely forecast of the future which can be made, and the great industrial organisations, the Trades Unions, the Co-operative Movement, the Friendly Orders, the Socialist Organisations and the Labour Party are each and all developing the feeling of solidarity and of mutual aid which will make the inauguration of Communism a comparatively easy task as the natural successor to State Socialism.

2.5 H. G. WELLS

Novelist, visionary and social critic, H. G. Wells launched himself upon the Fabian Society in the first decade of the century and sought to reconstruct both the Society and its doctrine. In a series of bold sketches he presented socialism as a rational, planned and scientific social order, as in this extract from his *New worlds for old* (1908).

The fundamental idea upon which Socialism rests is the same fundamental idea as that upon which all real scientific work is carried on. It is the denial that chance impulse and individual will and happening constitute the only possible methods by which things may be done in the world. It is an assertion that things are in their nature orderly, that things may be computed, may be calculated upon and foreseen. In the spirit of this belief Science aims at a systematic knowledge of material things. 'Knowledge is power', knowledge that is frankly and truly exchanged – that is the primary assumption of the *New Atlantis* which created the Royal Society and the organisation of research. The Socialist has just that same faith in the order, the knowableness of things and the power of men in co-operation to overcome chance; but to him, dealing as he does with the social affairs of men, it takes the form not of schemes for collective research but for collective action and the creation of a comprehensive design for all the social activities of man. While Science gathers knowledge, Socialism in an entirely harmonious spirit criticises and develops a general plan of social life. Each seeks to replace disorder by order . . .

Now the Socialist, inspired by this conception of a possible frank and comprehensive social order to which mean and narrow ends must be sacrificed, attacks and criticises the existing order of things at a great number of points and in a great variety of phraseology. At all points, however, you will find upon analysis that his criticism amounts to a declaration that there is wanting a sufficiency of CONSTRUCTIVE DESIGN. That in the last resort is what he always comes to.

He wants a complete organisation for all those human affairs that are of collective importance. He says, to take instances almost haphazard, that our ways of manufacturing a great multitude of necessary things, of getting and distributing food, of conducting all sorts of business, of begetting and rearing children, of permitting diseases to engender and spread are chaotic and undisciplined, so badly done that here is enormous hardship, and there enormous waste, here excess and degeneration, and there privation and death. He declares that for these collective purposes, in the satisfaction of these universal needs, mankind presents the appearance and follows the methods of a mob when it ought to follow the method of an army. In place of disorderly individual effort, each man doing what he pleases, the Socialist wants organised effort and a plan. And while the scientific man seeks to make an orderly map of the half-explored wilderness of fact, the Socialist seeks to make an orderly plan for the half-conceived wilderness of human effort. That and no other is the essential Socialist idea.

2.6 SIDNEY AND BEATRICE WEBB

As classical Fabianism came under attack in the second decade of the century, not least from the Guild Socialists, the Webbs were prompted to reformulate their position. This they did in their *A constitution for the socialist commonwealth of Great Britain* (1920), described by Beatrice as 'the summing up of our observation and reasoning about political and industrial organisation'.

Today it seems, in the Labour and Socialist world, that the vital question is who should give orders and who should obey them – whether the government of industry shall be 'from above' or 'from below'. In the ensuing years of ever-increasing socialisation this controversy will become largely meaningless. Paradoxical as this may seem today, we venture on the prediction that, from the stand-point of personal authority, it will matter far less than at present exactly how the executive command is apportioned. In industry no less than in political administration, the combination of Measurement with Publicity is today already undermining personal autocracy. The deliberate intensification of this *searchlight of published knowledge* we regard as the corner-stone of successful Democracy. The need for final decision will remain not merely in emergencies but also as to policy; and it is of high importance to vest the responsibility for a decision, according to the nature of the case, in the right hands. But a great deal of the old autocracy, once deemed to be indispensable in government departments and capitalist industry alike, is ceasing to be necessary to efficiency, and will, accordingly, as Democracy becomes more genuinely accepted, gradually be dispensed with. A steadily increasing sphere will, except in matters of emergency, be found for consultation among all grades and sections concerned, out of which will emerge judgments and decisions arrived at, very largely, by common consent. This common consent will be reached by the cogency of accurately ascertained and authoritatively reported facts, driven home by the silent persuasiveness of the public opinion of those concerned. The Works Committee, the District Council, the National Board, the Social Parliament itself, will have before them, not merely the spontaneous promptings of their members' minds, and not even only the information provided by their own officials, but much more. To such committees and councils there will come, as a matter of course, a stream of reports from independent and disinterested experts . . .

Democracy cannot afford to dispense with complication in its administrative machinery, because only by an extensive variety of parts, and a deliberately adjusted relation among those parts, can there be any security for the personal freedom and independence in initiative of the great mass of individuals, whether as producers, as consumers or as citizens. It is only by systematically thinking out the function that each person has to perform, the sphere that must be secured to each group or section, the opportunities in which each must be protected, and the relation in which each must stand to the others and to the whole, that in any highly developed society the ordinary man can escape a virtual, if not a nominal, slavery. Those impatient democrats who will not take the trouble to understand the problem, and who petulantly demand, at the same time, the elaborations and refinements of civilisation and the anarchy and simplicity of the primitive age, cannot in the nature of things ever be gratified. The condition of any genuine Democracy, of the wide diffusion of any effective freedom, is such a systematic complication of social machinery as will negative alike the monarchical and the capitalist dictatorships, and prevent the rise of any other. The price of liberty – of individual variety and specialisation 'in widest commonalty spread' – is the complication of a highly differentiated and systematically co-ordinated social order.

2.7 HAROLD LASKI

Harold Laski, like Cole and Tawney, gave intellectual leadership to British socialism for some thirty years. As an academic political theorist, he explored the nature of the State, initially as a pluralist and then in the 1920s as a Fabian (and later still as a Marxist). His massive *A grammar of politics* (1925), from which this extract comes, came to be regarded as a textbook of Fabian political science.

Social organisation, therefore, does not present a single problem in relation to its government. On the one hand, it is fairly simple to construct a government for each function in society in terms of the particular purpose each embodies. But no man's activities are confined to a single function. It is necessary to safeguard his interests as a user of services he has no part in producing. It is essential, in other words, to protect him as a consumer. The co-ordination of functions is the sphere in which, to that end, the State must operate. It has so to organise the conditions of their lives that the individual members of the State are assured of reasonable access to those goods without which they cannot fulfil their vocations as men. Where their needs are identical as undifferentiated persons, at least at some minimum level, it is essential to have a single centre of control to achieve them. That does not mean that the State itself will, as the controlling body, provide directly the response to such needs. It means only, that it will so direct the functions which produce the required services as to secure effective conditions of response. In an aspect of this kind, the State is obviously a public service corporation . . .

That the State is, in some form or another, an inevitable organisation will be apparent to anyone who examines the human nature that we encounter in daily life. But to admit that it is inevitable is not to admit that it is entitled to moral pre-eminence of any kind. For, after all, the State is not itself an end, but merely the means to an end, which is realised only in the enrichment of human lives. Its power and the allegiance it can win depend always upon what it achieves for that enrichment. We are, that is to say, subjects of the State, not for its purpose, but for our own. Realisable good means always some happiness won for the lives of persons, or it means nothing. Power, therefore, must seek the widest possible distribution of such happiness. We are entitled to suspect the State save as we see under its aegis the unfettered growth of human personality. We are entitled to condemn it save as its powers are used deliberately to defeat the forces which stand in the way of that growth. Ultimately, at least, the minds of men can give service to no end less than the realisation of what is best in themselves. They can give allegiance to no lesser ideal. They exercise most truly their citizenship when they seek with wisdom a release from the servitude, alike material and spiritual, that is born of the perversion of power . . .

The manner in which property is distributed will always, in a system so largely individualist as our own, determine also the distribution of economic power. And it is inevitable that economic power should, in its turn, chiefly determine the distribution of political power also. For those who can decide not only what is to be produced but, also, the manner of its production clearly command the working lives of other men. Their decisions, doubtless, will be quite largely influenced by considerations in which economic motives have only a partial place. They will make concessions to the demands of humanitarianism, as in the Factory Acts. They will yield, as in the establishment of the check-weighman in a colliery, to the power of combination among the workers. But, at the base, the political system will practically reflect their interests to the degree that they are united in their consciousness of them. And in an age, like our own, of vast concentration of industrial capital it is unlikely that such consciousness will be lacking. Unless, therefore, the power of property is to dominate the rights of personality in a community, it is necessary to limit the opportunities of which it may seek to take advantage.

3.1 R. H. TAWNEY: EQUALITY

Tawney's *Equality* (first published in 1931) is a classic of British
socialism and remains the reference point for much contemporary
democratic socialist argument on the subject. Attacking the English
'religion of inequality', Tawney distinguished between relevant and
irrelevant inequalities and outlined a strategy for eliminating the
former. This elimination had to take account of different types of
inequality, including inequalities of power, and had as its object nothing
less than the creation of a society in which there was common access to
what Tawney liked to call the 'means of civilisation'.

Everyone who is not blind realizes, indeed, that, if the issue between individualism and socialism is merely a matter of the structure and mechanism of industry, then it has, in large measure,
already been decided. Everyone sees that the characteristic of the
phase on which the economic system is now entering will, as far as
the larger and more essential undertakings are concerned, be some
form of unified direction under public control. But then, if that is
all that the issue means, though technically interesting, it is not of
any great moment, except to specialists. Organisation is important,
but it is important as a means, not as an end in itself; and, while
the means are debated with much zeal and ingenuity, the end, unfortunately, sometimes seems to be forgotten. So the question
which is fundamental, the question whether the new organisation,
whatever its form and title, will be more favourable than the old to
a spirit of humanity and freedom in social relations, and deserves,
therefore, that efforts should be made to establish it, is the object
of less general concern and less serious consideration than the
secondary, though important problem, which relates to the pro-
cedure of its establishment and the technique of its administration.

It is rarely considered, and more rarely finds overt expression in the world of public affairs. The reason is simple. An indifference to inequality, as the foreign observers remark, is less the mark of particular classes than a national characteristic. It is not a political question dividing parties, but a common temper and habit of mind which throws a bridge between them. Hence even those groups which are committed by their creed to measures for mitigating its more repulsive consequences rarely push their dislike of it to the point of affirming that the abolition of needless inequalities is their primary objective, by the approach to which their success is to be judged, and to the attainment of which other interests are to be subordinated. When the press assails them with the sparkling epigram that they desire, not merely to make the poor richer, but to make the rich poorer, instead of replying, as they should, that, being sensible men, they desire both, since the extremes both of riches and poverty are degrading and anti-social, they are apt to take refuge in gestures of deprecation. They make war on destitution, but they sometimes turn, it seems, a blind eye on privilege . . .

What the working-class movement stands for is obviously the ideal of social justice and solidarity, as a corrective to the exaggerated emphasis on individual advancement through the acquisition of wealth. It is a faith in the possibility of a society in which a higher value will be set on human beings, and a lower value on money and economic power, when money and power do not serve human ends. But that movement is liable, like all of us, to fall at times below itself, and to forget its mission. When it does so, what it is apt to desire is not a social order of a different kind, in which money and economic power will no longer be the criterion of achievement, but a social order of the same kind, in which money and economic power will be somewhat differently distributed.

Its characteristic fault is not, as is sometimes alleged, that the spirit behind it is one of querulous discontent. It is, on the contrary, that a considerable number among those to whom it appeals are too easily contented – too ready to forget fundamental issues and to allow themselves to be bought off with an advance in wages, too willing to accept the moral premises of their masters, even when they dispute the economic conclusions which their masters draw from them . . .

Heaven takes, to paraphrase Homer, half the virtue from a man, when, if he behaves like a man, he may lose his job; and it is not for one who has not experienced the wage-earners' insecurity to be critical of the wage-earners' patience. But it would be better, never-theless, both for them and for the nation as a whole, if they were more continuously alive, not only to their economic interests, but to their dignity as human beings. As it is, though they resent poverty and unemployment, and the physical miseries of a prolet-ariat, they do not always resent, as they should, the moral humili-ation which gross contrasts of wealth and economic power necess-arily produce. While they will starve for a year to resist a reduction in wages, they still often accept quite tamely an organisation of in-dustry under which a dozen gentlemen, who are not conspicuously wiser than their neighbours, determine the conditions of life and work for several thousand families; and an organisation of finance which enables a handful of bankers to raise and lower the economic temperature of a whole community; and an organisation of justice which makes it difficult . . . for a poor man to face the cost of obtaining it; and an organisation of education which still makes higher education inaccessible to the great majority of working-class children, as though such children had, like anthropoid apes, fewer convolutions in their brains than the children of the well-to-do.

They denounce, and rightly, the injustices of capitalism; but they do not always realise that capitalism is maintained, not only by capitalists, but by those who, like some of themselves, would be capitalists if they could, and that the injustices survive, not merely because the rich exploit the poor, but because, in their hearts, too many of the poor admire the rich. They know and complain that they are tyrannized over by the power of money. But they do not yet see that what makes money the tyrant of society is largely their own reverence for it. They do not sufficiently realise that, if they were as determined to maintain their dignity as they are, quite rightly, to maintain their wages, they would produce a world in which their material miseries would become less unmanageable, since they would no longer be under a kind of nervous tutelage on the part of the minority, and the determination of their economic destinies would rest in their own hands . . .

Psychologists tell us that the way to overcome a complex is not to suppress it, but to treat it frankly, and uncover its foundations. What a community requires, as the word itself suggests, is a com-mon culture, because, without it, it is not a community at all. And evidently it requires it in a special degree at a moment like the pre-sent, when circumstances confront it with the necessity of giving a new orientation to its economic life, because it is in such circumstances that the need for co-operation, and for the mutual confidence and tolerance upon which co-operation depends, is particularly pressing. But a common culture cannot be created merely by desiring it. It must rest upon practical foundations of social organisation. It is incompatible with the existence of sharp contrasts between the economic standards and educational opportunities of different classes, for such contrasts have as their result, not a common culture, but servility or resentment, on the one hand, and patronage or arrogance, on the other. It involves, in short, a large measure of economic equality – not necessarily in the sense of an identical level of pecuniary incomes, but of equality of environment, of access to education and the means of civilisation, of security and independence, and of the social consideration which equality in these matters usually carries with it . . .

It is obvious, indeed, that, as things are today, no redistribution of wealth would bring general affluence, and that statisticians are within their rights in making merry with the idea that the equalisation of incomes would make everyone rich. But, though riches are a good, they are not, nevertheless, the only good; and because greater production, which is concerned with the commodities to be consumed, is clearly important, it does not follow that greater equality, which is concerned with the relations between the human beings who consume them, is not important also. It is obvious, again, that the word 'Equality' possesses more than one meaning, and that the controversies surrounding it arise partly, at least, because the same term is employed with different connotations. Thus it may either purport to state a fact, or convey the expression of an ethical judgment. On the one hand, it may affirm that men are, on the whole, very similar in their natural endowments of character and intelligence. On the other hand, it may assert that, while they differ profoundly as individuals in capacity and character, they are equally entitled as human beings to consideration and respect, and that the well-being of a society is likely to be increased if it so plans its organisation that, whether their powers are great or small, all its members may be equally enabled to make the best of such powers as they possess . . .

The equality which . . . these thinkers emphasize as desirable is not equality of capacity or attainment, but of circumstances, institutions, and manner of life. The inequality which they deplore is not inequality of personal gifts, but of the social and economic environment. They are concerned, not with a biological phenomenon,

R. H. Tawney: Equality

but with a spiritual relation and the conduct to be based on it. Their view, in short, is that, because men are men, social institutions – property rights, and the organisation of industry, and the system of public health and education – should be planned, as far as is possible, to emphasize and strengthen, not the class differences which divide, but the common humanity which unites, them.

Such a view of the life which is proper to human beings may, of course, be criticised, as it often has been. But to suppose that it can be criticised effectively by pointing to the width of the intellectual and moral differences which distinguish individuals from each other is a solecism, an *ignoratio elenchi*. It is true, of course, that such differences are important, and that the advance of psychology has enabled them to be measured with a new precision, with results which are valuable in making possible both a closer adaptation of educational methods to individual needs and a more intelligent selection of varying aptitudes for different tasks. But to recognise a specific difference is one thing; to pass a general judgment of superiority or inferiority, still more to favour the first and neglect the second, is quite another. The nightingale, it has been remarked, was placed in the fourth class at the fowl show . . .

It is true, again, that human beings have, except as regards certain elementary, though still sadly neglected, matters of health and development, different requirements, and that these different requirements can be met satisfactorily only by varying forms of provision. But equality of provision is not identity of provision. It is to be achieved, not by treating different needs in the same way, but by devoting equal care to ensuring that they are met in the different ways most appropriate to them, as is done by a doctor who prescribes different regimens for different constitutions, or a teacher who develops different types of intelligence by different curricula. The more anxiously, indeed, a society endeavours to secure equality of consideration for all its members, the greater will be the differentiation of treatment which, when once their common human needs have been met, it accords to the special needs of different groups and individuals among them.

It is true, finally, that some men are inferior to others in respect of their intellectual endowments, and it is possible – though the truth of the possibility has not yet been satisfactorily established – that the same is true of certain classes. It does not, however, follow from this fact that such individuals or classes should receive less consideration than others, or should be treated as inferior in respect of such matters as legal status, or health, or economic arrangements, which are within the control of the community . . .

Everyone recognizes the absurdity of such an argument when it is applied to matters within his personal knowledge and professional competence. Everyone realises that, in order to justify inequalities of circumstance or opportunity by reference to differences of personal quality, it is necessary . . . to show that the differences in question are relevant to the inequalities. Everyone now sees, for example, that it is not a valid argument against women's suffrage to urge, as used to be urged not so long ago, that women are physically weaker than men, since physical strength is not relevant to the question of the ability to exercise the franchise, or a valid argument in favour of slavery that some men are less intelligent than others, since it is not certain that slavery is the most suitable penalty for lack of intelligence.

Not everyone, however, is so quick to detect the fallacy when it is expressed in general terms. It is still possible, for example, for one eminent statesman to ridicule the demand for a diminution of economic inequalities on the ground that every mother knows that her children are not equal, without reflecting whether it is the habit of mothers to lavish care on the strong and neglect the delicate; and for another to dismiss the suggestion that greater economic equality is desirable, for the reason apparently, that men are naturally unequal. It is probable, however, that the first does not think that the fact that some children are born with good digestions, and others with bad, is a reason for supplying good food to the former and bad food to the latter, rather than for giving to both food which is equal in quality but different in kind, and that the second does not suppose that the natural inequality of men makes legal equality a contemptible principle . . .

Many services are supplied by collective effort today which in the recent past were supplied by individual effort or not supplied at all, and many more, it may be suspected, will be so supplied in the future. At any moment there are some needs which almost everyone is agreed should be satisfied on equalitarian principles, and others which they are agreed should be met by individuals who purchase what their incomes enable them to pay for, and others, again, about the most suitable provision for which opinions differ. Society has not been prevented from seeking to establish equality in respect of the first by the fear that in so doing it may be perpetrating a scientific impossibility. Nor ought it to be prevented from moving towards equality in respect of the second and third, if experience suggests that greater equality in these matters also would contribute to greater efficiency and to more general happiness . . .

How men in given circumstances tend to behave, and how, as a consequence, wealth tends in such circumstances to be distributed, are subjects about which valuable and illuminating, if necessarily tentative, generalisations have been produced by economists. But their behaviour, as economists have often told us, is relative to their circumstances; and the distribution of wealth depends, not wholly, indeed, but largely, on their institutions; and the character of their institutions is determined, not by immutable economic laws, but by the values, preferences, interests and ideals which rule at any moment in a given society. These values and preferences are not something fixed and unalterable. On the contrary, they have changed repeatedly in the past, and are changing today; and the distribution of wealth has changed, and is changing, with them . . .

Mumbo-Jumbo is a great god, who, if he is given his head, is disposed to claim, not only economics, but the whole world, as his kingdom, and who is subtle enough to deceive even the elect . . . And, when his prophets are so much alarmed by the symptoms of increasing equality, and by the demand for its still further increase, that they declare that equality is a scientific impossibility, they ought not, indeed, to be treated unkindly, or hewn in pieces before the Lord, like the prophets of an earlier Mumbo-Jumbo; but they should be asked to undergo, for the sake both of themselves and of their neighbours, what to nimble minds, with a gift for quick and sweeping generalisation, is sometimes a hardly less painful discipline. They should be asked to study the facts. The facts, they will find, show that the distribution of wealth in a community depends partly, at least, upon its organisation and institutions – its system of property rights, its economic structure, its social and financial policy – and that it is possible for it to give these matters a bias either towards greater equality or towards greater inequality, because different communities, at different times, have done, in fact, both the one and the other.

Perhaps, therefore, the remote Victorian thinkers, like Arnold and Mill, who dealt lightly with Mumbo-Jumbo, and who commended equality to their fellow-countrymen as one source of peace and happiness, were not speaking so unadvisedly as at first sight might appear. It is the fact that, in spite of their varying characters and capacities, men possess in their common humanity a quality which is worth cultivating, and that a community is most likely to make the most of that quality if it takes it into account in planning its economic organisation and social institutions – if it stresses lightly differences of wealth and birth and social position, and establishes on firm foundations institutions which meet common needs, and are a source of common enlightment and common enjoyment. The individual differences of which so much is made, they would have said, will always survive, and they are to be welcomed, not regretted. But their existence is no reason for not seeking to establish the largest possible measure of equality of environment, and circumstance, and opportunity. On the contrary, it is a reason for redoubling our efforts to establish it, in order to ensure that these diversities of gifts may come to fruition.

It is true, indeed, that even such equality, though the conditions on which it depends are largely within human control, will continue to elude us. The important thing, however, is not that it should be completely attained, but that it should be sincerely sought. What matters to the health of society is the objective towards which its face is set, and to suggest that it is immaterial in which direction it moves, because, whatever the direction, the goal must always elude it, is not scientific, but irrational. It is like using the impossibility of absolute cleanliness as a pretext for rolling in a manure heap, or denying the importance of honesty because no one can be wholly honest.

It may well be the case that capricious inequalities are in some measure inevitable, in the sense that, like crime and disease, they are a malady which the most rigorous precautions cannot wholly overcome. But, when crime is known as crime, and disease as disease, the ravages of both are circumscribed by the mere fact that they are recognised for what they are, and described by their proper names, not by flattering euphemisms. And a society which is convinced that inequality is an evil need not be alarmed because the evil is one which cannot wholly be subdued. In recognising the poison it will have armed itself with an antidote. It will have deprived inequality of its sting by stripping it of its esteem.

So to criticise inequality and to desire equality is not, as is sometimes suggested, to cherish the romantic illusion that men are equal in character and intelligence. It is to hold that, while their natural endowments differ profoundly, it is the mark of a civilised society to aim at eliminating such inequalities as have their source, not in individual differences, but in its own organisation, and that individual differences, which are a source of social energy, are more likely to ripen and find expression if social inequalities are, as far as practicable, diminished. And the obstacle to the progress of equality is something simpler and more potent than finds expression in the familiar truism that men vary in their mental and moral, as well as in their physical characteristics, important and valuable though that truism is as a reminder that different individuals require different types of provision. It is the habit of mind which thinks it, not regrettable, but natural and desirable, that different sections of a community should be distinguished from each other by sharp differences of economic status, of environment, of education and culture and habit of life. It is the temper which regards with approval the social institutions and economic arrangements by which such differences are emphasised and enhanced, and feels distrust and apprehension at all attempts to diminish them.

The institutions and policies in which that temper has found expression are infinite in number. At one time it has coloured the relations between the sexes; at another, those between religions; at a third, those between members of different races. But in communities no longer divided by religion or race, and in which men and women are treated as political and economic equals, the divisions which remain are, nevertheless, not insignificant. The practical form which they most commonly assume – the most conspicuous external symptom of difference of economic status and social position – is, of course, a graduated system of social classes, and it is by softening or obliterating, not individual differences, but class gradations, that the historical movements directed towards diminishing inequality have attempted to attain their objective. It is, therefore, by considering the class system that light upon the problem of inequality is, in the first place at least, to be sought, and it is by their attitude to the relations between classes that the equalitarian temper and philosophy are distinguished from their opposite.

A society which values equality will attach a high degree of significance to differences of character and intelligence between different individuals, and a low degree of significance to economic and social differences between different groups. It will endeavour, in shaping its policy and organisation, to encourage the former and to neutralise and suppress the latter, and will regard it as vulgar and childish to emphasise them when, unfortunately, they still exist. A society which is in love with inequality will take such differences seriously, and will allow them to overflow from the regions, such as economic life, where they have their origin, and from which it is difficult wholly to expel them, till they become a kind of morbid obsession, colouring the whole world of social relations . . .

Since life is a swallow, and theory a snail, it is not surprising that varieties of class organisation should be but inadequately represented in the terminology of political science. But the absence of a word to describe the type of society which combines the forms of political democracy with sharp economic and social divisions is, none the less, unfortunate, since it obscures the practical realities which it is essential to grasp. The conventional classification of communities by the character of their constitutional arrangements had its utility in an age when the principal objective of effort and speculation was the extension of political rights. It is economic and social forces, however, which are most influential in determining the practical operation of political institutions, and it is economic and social relations that create the most urgent of the internal problems confronting industrial communities. The most significant differences distinguishing different societies from each other are, in short, not different forms of constitution and government, but different types of economic and social structure.

Of such distinctions the most fundamental is that which divides communities where economic initiative is widely diffused, and class differences small in dimensions and trivial in their effects, from those where the conditions obtaining are the opposite – where the mass of mankind exercise little influence on the direction of economic enterprise, and where economic and cultural gradations descend precipitately from one stratum of the population to another. Both types may possess representative institutions, a wide franchise and responsible government; and both, therefore, may properly be described as democracies. But to regard them as, on that account, resembling each other – to ignore the profound differences of spirit and quality between a democracy in which class divisions play a comparatively unimportant part in the life of society, and a democracy where the influence of such differences is all-pervasive – is to do violence to realities. It is like supposing that all mammals have the same anatomical structure, or that the scenery of England resembles that of Switzerland because both countries lie in the temperate zone. Such varieties should be treated by political scientists as separate species, and should be given distinctive names. The former contain large elements, not merely of political, but of social, democracy. The latter are political democracies, but social oligarchies . . .

Thus a class system which is marked by sharp horizontal divisions between different social strata is neither, as is sometimes suggested, an indispensable condition of civilisation nor an edifying feature of it. It may, as some hold, be inevitable, like other misfortunes to which mankind is heir, but it is not lovable or admirable. It is the raw material out of which civilisation has to be made, by bringing the blind economic forces under rational control and sifting the gold of past history from its sand and sediment. The task of the spirit, whatever the name most appropriate to describe it, which seeks to permeate, not merely this fragment of society or that, but the whole community, with reason and mutual understanding, is not to flatter the natural impulses which have their origin in the fact of class, but to purify and educate them. It is to foster the growth of a classless society by speaking frankly of the perversions to which the class system gives rise and of the dangers which accompany them.

The forms which such perversions assume are, of course, innumerable, but the most fundamental of them are two. They are privilege and tyranny. The first is the insistence by certain groups on the enjoyment of special advantages which are convenient to themselves, but injurious to their neighbours. The second is the exercise of power, not for the common benefit, but in order that these special advantages may be strengthened and consolidated.

It is the nature of privilege and tyranny to be unconscious of themselves, and to protest, when challenged, that their horns and hooves are not dangerous, as in the past, but useful and handsome decorations, which no self-respecting society would dream of dispensing with. But they are the enemies, nevertheless, both of individual culture and of social amenity. They create a spirit of domination and servility, which produces callousness in those who profit by them, and resentment in those who do not, and suspicion and contention in both. A civilized community will endeavour to exorcise that spirit by removing its causes. It will insist that one condition, at least, of its deserving the name is that its members shall treat each other, not as means, but as ends, and that institutions which stunt the faculties of some among them for the advantage of others shall be generally recognised to be barbarous and odious. It will aim at making power, not arbitrary, but responsible, and, when it finds an element of privilege in social institutions, it will seek to purge it . . .

Most social systems need a lightning-conductor. The formula which supplies it to our own is equality of opportunity. The conception is one to which homage is paid today by all, including those who resist most strenuously attempts to apply it. But the rhetorical tribute which it receives appears sometimes to be paid on the understanding that it shall be content with ceremonial honours. It retains its throne, on condition that it refrains from meddling with the profitable business of the factory and market-place. Its credit is good, as long as it does not venture to cash its cheques. Like other respectable principles, it is encouraged to reign, provided that it does not attempt to rule.

The content of the idea has been determined by its history. It was formulated as a lever to overthrow legal inequality and juristic privilege, and from its infancy it has been present in negative, rather than positive terms. It has been interpreted rather as freedom from restraints than as the possession of powers. Thus conceived, it has at once the grandeur and the unreality of a majestic phantom. The language in which it is applauded by the powers of this world sometimes leaves it uncertain which would horrify them most, the denial of the principle or the attempt to apply it . . .

It is possible that intelligent tadpoles reconcile themselves to the inconveniences of their position, by reflecting that, though most of them will live and die as tadpoles and nothing more, the more fortunate of the species will one day shed their tails, distend their mouths and stomachs, hop nimbly on to dry land, and croak addresses to their former friends on the virtues by means of which tadpoles of character and capacity can rise to be frogs. This conception of society may be described, perhaps, as the Tadpole Philosophy, since the consolation which it offers for social evils consists in the statement that exceptional individuals can succeed in evading them. Who has not heard it suggested that the presence of opportunities, by means of which individuals can ascend and get on, relieves economic contrasts of their social poison and their personal sting? Who has not encountered the argument that there is an educational 'ladder' up which talent can climb, and that its existence makes the scamped quality of our primary education – the overcrowded classes, and mean surroundings, and absence of amenities – a matter of secondary importance? And what a view of human life such an attitude implies! As though opportunities for talent to rise could be equalised in a society where the circumstances surrounding it from birth are themselves unequal! As though, if they could, it were natural and proper that the position of the mass of mankind should permanently be such that they can attain civilisation only by escaping from it! As though the noblest use of exceptional powers were to scramble to shore, undeterred by the thought of drowning companions!

It is true, of course, that a community must draw on a stream of fresh talent, in order to avoid stagnation, and that, unless individuals of ability can turn their powers to account, they are embittered by a sense of defeat and frustration. The existence of opportunities to move from point to point on an economic scale, and to mount from humble origins to success and affluence, is a condition, therefore, both of social well-being and of individual happiness, and impediments which deny them to some, while lavishing them on others, are injurious to both. But opportunities to 'rise' are not a substitute for a large measure of practical equality, nor do they make immaterial the existence of sharp disparities of income and social condition. On the contrary, it is only the presence of a high degree of practical equality which can diffuse and generalise opportunities to rise. The existence of such opportunities in fact, and not merely in form, depends, not only upon an open road, but upon an equal start. It is precisely, of course, when capacity is aided by a high level of general well-being in the *milieu* surrounding it, that its ascent is most likely to be regular and rapid, rather than fitful and intermittent . . .

If a high degree of practical equality is necessary to social well-being, because without it ability cannot find its way to its true vocation, it is necessary also for another and more fundamental reason. It is necessary because a community requires unity as well as diversity, and because, important as it is to discriminate between different powers, it is even more important to provide for common needs. Clever people, who possess exceptional gifts themselves, are naturally impressed by exceptional gifts in others, and desire, when they consider the matter at all, that society should be organised to offer a career to exceptional talent, though they rarely understand the full scope and implications of the revolution they are preaching. But, in the conditions characteristic of large-scale economic organisation, in which ninety per cent of the population are wage-earners, and not more than ten per cent employers, farmers, independent workers or engaged in professions, it is obviously, whatever the level of individual intelligence and the degree of social fluidity, a statistical impossibility for more than a small fraction of the former to enter the ranks of the latter; and a community cannot be built upon exceptional talent alone, though it would be a poor thing without it. Social well-being does not only depend upon intelligent leadership; it also depends upon cohesion and solidarity. It implies the existence, not merely of opportunities to ascend, but of a high level of general culture, and a strong sense of common interests, and the diffusion throughout society of a conviction that civilisation is not the business of an elite alone, but a common enterprise which is the concern of all. And individual happiness does not only require that men should be free to rise to new positions of comfort and distinction; it also requires that they should be able to lead a life of dignity and culture, whether they rise or not, and that, whatever their position on the economic scale may be, it shall be such as if fit to be occupied by men.

3.2 HAROLD LASKI: CAPITALIST DEMOCRACY

In the 1930s, influenced by the economic and political crisis of 1931 in Britain and by the rise of fascism in Europe, Harold Laski abandoned his liberal collectivism in favour of a neo-Marxism. In a series of influential books (and through his role in the Left Book Club) Laski did much to shape thinking on the Left in the 1930s. He argued, as in this extract from his *Democracy in crisis* (1933), that capitalist democracy was fatally flawed because of its contradiction between a formal political equality and an economic inequality and that this contradiction would have dramatic consequences, from which Britain was unlikely to be immune.

What is the essence of the position thus revealed? Political democracy developed in response to the demand for the abrogation of privilege. In modern European history its cause was the liberation of a commercial middle class from domination by a landholding aristocracy. To free itself, that middle class formulated a body of liberal generalisations which culminated in the widespread grant of universal suffrage. Their underlying philosophy was the well-known Benthamite argument, that since each man in a political democracy was to count for one, and not more than one, and since each was, on the whole, the best judge of his own interest, universal suffrage would permit the translation of the majority will into the substance of legislation. Sinister interest, it was urged, belonged only to a few; privilege could not resist the onset of numbers. Representative democracy, on the basis of equal and universal suffrage, would mean the creation of a society in which the equal interest of men in the results of the social process would be swiftly recognised. The rule of democracy was to be the rule of reason. The party which best grasped the purpose of the electorate would win a majority in the legislature, and it would use the normal, constitutional forms to give effect to that purpose.

The flaw in the argument was an obvious one. It assumed the absolute validity of the form of the political state regardless of the economic character of the society it was supposed to represent. It did not see that each economic regime gives birth to a political order which represents the interests of those who dominate the regime, who possess in it the essential instruments of economic power. In a feudal society, broadly speaking, sovereignty belonged to the owners of land; custom was registered, legislation was made, in their interest. In a capitalist society, quite similarly, sovereignty belonged to the owners of capital; and custom was registered, legislation made, in their interest also. The simplest test of this truth in any society is the analysis of the working of the Courts. And if their decisions be scrutinised, it will always be found that, in the last analysis, they are inexplicable except upon the basis of their effort to defend the sovereignty of the owners of economic power. The framework of a legal system is always geared to that end. Liberty means liberty within the law, and the purpose of the law is the protection of some given *status quo*. Its substance is always the result of a struggle to widen an existing basis of privilege. Those who share in this may on occasion be tempted to the surrender of an occasional outwork; they have always defended to the last the possession of the inner citadel.

It is in the perspective of these general truths that the history of parliamentary democracy must be set. It has been successful in the difficult task of enabling the outworks of the capitalist system to be surrendered to its opponents; it has at no point solved the central problem of the inner citadel's surrender. It has discovered ways and means of graceful compromise, wherever compromise has been possible; it has not proved that it forms the natural road to a new equilibrium when the differences between men are ultimate. For we have to acknowledge the grim fact that, at the parting of the ways, men in the possession of actual sovereignty choose to fight rather than to abdicate. In Great Britain, no doubt, the genius for compromise has been peculiarly outstanding, though that is most largely due to the fact that the ultimate issues have never been raised. In other European countries this has not been the case, and a break with the old legal order has invariably become imperative in order to find the necessary conditions of a new equilibrium. The power to compromise while compromise is still possible is perhaps the rarest quality in history.

And if the character of the struggle involved in the historic process be analysed, its root will be found always to lie in the unending problem of equality. Those who are denied access to privilege seek to destroy privilege. It may present itself under the most various forms – religious, social, economic, political. It may be accepted for a period as part of an order of nature; the abolition of the prerogatives of the House of Lords was hardly thinkable to the eighteenth century. But, sooner or later, those excluded from privilege resent their exclusion, and it is then only a matter of time before they attack it. And unless they can be convinced that the maintenance of the privilege is directly associated with their own good, the choice offered to the society is always one between concession and violence.

Anyone who considers the natural history of parliamentary democracy in these terms will have no difficulty in realising the crisis that is before it. The people was taught by the ideology of its early triumphs that the conquest of political power meant that they would be masters of the state. They found, indeed, that having conquered it, the way lay open to acquisitions unattainable under any other system. But they found, also, that to have won formal political power was not to have gained the mastery they sought. They realised that the clue to authority lay in the possession of economic control. When they sought to move by the ordinary constitutional means to its conquest as well, they found that the fight had to be begun all over again. Not only was this the case, but the essential weapons lay in their opponents' hands. The Courts, the Press, the educational system, the armed forces of the state, even, in large degree, the bureaucracy, were instruments operating towards their defeat. If they maintained law and order, they maintained that subtle atmosphere upon which the security of economic privilege depended. If they sought its overthrow by violence, in ordinary circumstances the organised power of the state was on their opponents' side. If they became the government by the methods sanctioned in constitutional law, they found, first, that they could not count upon its instruments of action, and, second, that their opponents were not always prepared to observe the traditions they themselves respected. They discovered, in a word, that agreements peacefully to disagree could only be maintained when the subjects of contention were not deemed valuable enough, by either side, to justify resort to violence.

This may be put in another way. The Industrial Revolution brought the middle classes to power, and they evolved a form of state – capitalist democracy – which seemed most suited to their security. Capitalist democracy worked admirably so long as the environment was stable enough to maintain the self-confidence of its governing class. But inherent in it was a new struggle for power. It offered a share in political authority to all citizens upon the unstated assumption that the equality involved in the democratic ideal did not seek extension to the economic sphere. The assumption could not be maintained. For the object of political power is always the abrogation of privilege; and that abrogation can only be postponed when the conquests of the new regime are so great that it can offer a constantly increasing standard of life to the masses. That happened in the nineteenth century, and parliamentary democracy then seemed to all but a few prophets of woe to fulfil all the conditions of security the new governing class demanded. That class, however, failed to foresee two things. It did not realise how rapid would be the changes in environment due to scientific discovery; how accelerated, therefore, would have to be the adaptability of the political system to a new economic atmosphere. Nor did it understand that the association of nationalism with statehood, the domination of both by the vested interests of the propertied class, would place technical barriers in the way of capitalist expansion at the very moment when this was most necessary. The system, accordingly, faced the dilemma that at the very moment, again, when its productive processes were at their maximum power it could not solve the problem of distributive justice; to maintain itself, it had to lower the standard of life just when democratic expectation looked to its dramatic expansion proportionately to the increase in productive power. And since that democratic expectation was accompanied by the knowledge that political authority belonged to the people, it was wholly natural that they should seek to solve the dilemma for themselves. They hoped, in a word, to solve the problem of political justice by obtaining possession of the sources of productive power.

The disintegration of parliamentary democracy, if this analysis is correct, is then due to the fact that the leaders of the class who dominate it cannot meet the demands made upon them. The new class which has arisen to political authority, dissatisfied with the results of the present state, seeks to reorganise it in its own interest. The rise of a new class to political power is always, sooner or later, synonymous with a social revolution; and the essential characteristic of a social revolution is always the redistribution of economic power. Here, it may be urged, is the centre of the *malaise* in representative democracy, the root of the crisis it confronts. A new society is struggling to be born within the womb of the old; it finds the forms of that old society resist its effort at emergence. It is, I think, wholly natural that if those forms should be found too inflexible to permit the easy birth of the new order, an attempt should be made to break them . . .

The crisis of capitalist democracy is essentially a crisis of authority and discipline. The power to secure obedience to its principles has decreased because men increasingly refuse to accept its ends as obviously just. In whatever realm we examine the claim of law to respect, it is clear that its power over its subjects has declined. And that decline is not merely due . . . to the enactment of unwise statutes in some particular field of behaviour. It is not the outcome of a growth of conscious and deliberate lawlessness valued for its own sake. The great mass of people today, as in Burke's time, have no interest in the manufacture of disorder. Disrespect for authority is not due to some sudden burst of enthusiasm for anarchy; it is rooted in a disbelief in the principles for which authority has been organised in a capitalist society . . .

If we apply to capitalist democracy the argument I have been making, its implications are sufficiently explicit. The tendencies we call socialism challenge capitalist assumptions in much the same way as Christianity challenged paganism some two thousand years ago. Socialism, like Christianity, has reached that stage where it cannot be suppressed by persecution, and has become militant in temper because the conditions of victory are within its grasp. It has, it should be insisted, all the characteristics of a great religion – its dogmas, its missionaries, its sects acutely divided from one another, its priests, its fanatics, its martyrs. There was a stage when it seemed possible for capitalist society to make terms with its demands. Had the social service state emerged, most notably in England, a generation earlier – at the time, above all, when Carlyle was preaching the folly of *laissez-faire* industrialism – it might well have been that the adjustments could have been effected which would have permitted the old gospel to absorb the new. The liberalism, indeed, of T. H. Green and his school was nothing so much as an attempt to discover the foundations of such a compromise. But it was made too late. The wealth of capitalist society before the 'seventies had not been expended upon those social objects which were a necessity for it to assure itself against attack; and when it turned, after that period, to the effort of reconstruction, it had not the capacity for expansion which enabled it at once to maintain the standards of private expenditure to which it had

accustomed its votaries and to satisfy the expectations of those influenced by its critics. As always happens in the history of such an
effort, the concessions it made to these only led to further demands; and the votaries of the old way of life found that what was
challenged was not merely the adequacy of concessions they could
no longer afford, but the very principle which permitted them to
be in a position to make concessions. What was attacked, in a
word, was not the excrescences of capitalism, but the foundations
upon which it rested.

And it is these foundations upon which capitalist democracy re-
lies for the maintenance of its discipline. It praises their value with
none of the old power to carry conviction; indeed, as I have earlier
insisted, it is not even confident of its power to carry conviction to
itself. Every experiment it makes by way of accommodation breaks
down. The more widely it extends the boundaries of citizenship –
the experience of Rome is notable in this regard – the wider is the
gap revealed in its defences. It admits its opponents to power; it
finds that a brief experience of their policy threatens its fundamental equilibrium. Nor is experience in the industrial field at all
different. Co-partnership, profit-sharing, the system of joint industrial councils, the Mond – Turner conferences – to speak of British
effort alone – were all attempts, more or less sincerely made, to
find immediate terms between a capitalist and a socialist society;
they all illustrate the same truth that the doctrines in battle
together are mutual and exclusive opposites between which there is
no prospect of final adjustment. A society can no more make peace
between the motives of private profit and public service than it can
continue half-slave and half-free. There is absent from its foundations that area of common agreement about fundamentals which
makes possible the unity needful for peace. Men think too differently who live so differently in such a commonwealth to know
how the basis of accord can be found.

And this is seen the more intensely because the votaries of either
way of life attach such intense significance to their rival creeds. To
ask from the capitalist a peaceful abdication is like asking a pagan
Emperor to admit the intellectual compulsion of Christianity. He
denies its principles; he feels none of its emotional sanctions. One
has only to scrutinise the case made by the defenders of capitalist
society against their critics to see how profoundly this is the case.
For them, socialism is against human nature; it is the creed of the
unsuccessful; it is the destruction of that freedom which is the arm
of man's striving; it takes all the joy and colour from life in the in-

terest of a dead and drab level of unromantic equality. All to which socialism appeals as the basis of its system of values is at variance with all that gives meaning to the quality of capitalist dogmas.

There cannot be discipline in such a society because the conditions upon which discipline depends are absent. We cannot overestimate the importance of this situation. For outside a society that has no need of compulsions – and such a society we have not yet experienced – the need for discipline is vital if order and security are to be preserved. By discipline I mean a cheerful acceptance of law by reason of approval for the conditions the law is seeking to make. If law cannot, in any given equilibrium, achieve that discipline, the movement to a new plane of action where it again becomes possible of achievement is inevitable. That is why revolution supervenes in historic experience whenever the capacity to rule of some particular system of government has been exhausted. For that exhaustion simply implies that the conditions upon which the rulers can maintain the necessary discipline of the society are not acceptable to the ruled, or, at least, unacceptable to such portion of the ruled as are prepared to make a bid for power . . .

On this hypothesis, the *malaise* of capitalist democracy is incurable while it remains capitalist, for the simple reason that it is against the conditions inherent in capitalism that men revolt. The system, that is, has lost the power to win assent to its hypotheses. Its leaders are trying to make laws which shall fulfil its postulates when it is exactly these that are denied. It can, indeed, not improbably make such laws if it is prepared to enforce them without regard to the consequences of enforcement; but it must then be prepared, first, to take the risk which always attends a government careless of its means, and, second, to abandon the conventions of its constitution. It may, indeed, be driven to both these adventures in order to preserve the essential features of capitalism; but, obviously, it could not then indulge the pretence that it was in any sense a democracy . . .

What, in short, begins as an attack upon democracy, ends, when it is analysed, as an attack upon the values to which the principle of democracy is subordinated. That principle, in essence, is a simple one. It is the assertion that men and women have an equal claim upon the common good; that, therefore, no social order can for long endure in which that principle is inherently denied. For the denial, sooner or later, involves the society in contradictions of which the result is necessarily an attack upon its foundations. It loses stability because it cannot justify the consequences of its operation upon the terms which have produced those contradictions. Its privileges cease to seem natural. Its values no longer commend themselves. Its logic fails to seem the dictates of irresistible nature. It comes to be examined as an historic process, and it is observed that it was the outcome of a special set of conditions which no longer obtain. The demand is made for a revision of its essence, and its capacity to survive becomes a function of its ability to respond to the new demands made upon it.

The question, that is, we have to answer is not whether democracy will survive, but whether capitalist democracy will survive, for that is the system which is attacked. For the masses, I believe, it is not attacked because it is regarded as inherently wrong, though that is the main motive of its outstanding critics; it is attacked because it is unsuccessful. The results it can now secure do not justify the claims made upon its behalf. And a social order that is in decay is like a beleaguered city, every place in its defences appears a contingent point of attack. It is challenged because every differentiation of treatment that is revealed is no longer capable of defence on the ground that it adds to its success. Men did not resent the immense fortunes of the early industrial magnates because they felt the exhilaration of conditions where so many seemed to have hope of wealth also. But when these, too, had become a settled and privileged aristocracy, which had to guard its treasure with the same passion as the old, it was no longer the object of confidence. Because, too, it has shaped all the principles and institutions of the society to its needs, it was entirely natural that the same suspicion should attach to them as was cast upon their makers. Discipline goes into the melting-pot because the authority from which it is derived has lost its energising principle . . .

When, therefore, indiscipline emerges in a people, I believe it to be due, not to inherent defects of its character, but to conditions external to it. The revolt of the masses is a perfectly intelligible phenomenon. The results it was led to expect from the discipline it accepted have not followed from its imposition in a continuous and orderly way. It is no effective answer to its demands to insist – as there is ground for insisting – that its position represents a solid improvement upon anything that it has known in the past. The issue does not present itself in that way. Its roots are far more spiritual than material in character. The French people had probably improved their material position in the years just before the Revolution, but that improvement only made them resent the more profoundly their exclusion from the privileges the aristrocracy enjoyed.

The present ownership of economic power, and its kindred divorce from public responsibility, acts upon the masses in a similar way. The more real their access to the good life, the more they resent the barriers which remain in their path; and if these are stoutly defended, the pressure against them only becomes proportionately the more keen. The business of any social order which encounters this temper is to reform itself, for the alternative is inevitably the kind of festering resentment at its inadequacies which, if unappeased, issues into revolution . . .

I have been concerned here to argue that a political democracy is bound by its very nature to resent, and ultimately, therefore, to seek to overthrow, distinctions among its citizens which are built upon wealth or birth. It will therefore move, slowly it may be, but nevertheless inevitably, to the organisation of an institutional framework in which the advantages of either are suppressed. It will move slowly so long as the society shows itself capable of making the adjustments by consent within a reasonable time. But those adjustments, of themselves, produce an egalitarian temper which feels the burden of remaining inequalities much more fiercely than was the case when they seemed, by their extent, a part of the fixed order of nature. As soon as the adjustments die down, the demand for their continuance becomes more vehement. The long refusal, in England, to establish a national system of education produced far less resentment than the attempt to economise upon it in the post-war years. Men bore the price of unemployment much more cheerfully half a century ago than they have done since the establishment of insurance against its more terrible consequences.

If, then, political democracy means a continuous movement towards equality, there cannot be a halt to its progress over any considerable period without challenge. A temporary panic, like the financial crisis of 1931, may persuade men to a temporary postponement of its benefits, but it is upon the very definite condition that they are demonstrably temporary in character. But the resumption of this progress is, for those who have enforced its suspension, a function of economic recovery. To attempt it on other terms is, for them, an impossible adventure. We then reach a position in which, in the absence of economic recovery, the purpose of political democracy is stultified by the confinement of economic advantage to a narrow circle. It is explained, of course, that the economies effected are consolidation rather than regression; but if this is widely challenged, as, notably, it is widely challenged with ourselves, it will not be for long believed. Sooner or later a change in popular opinion will put the party of challenge into power; and if their opponents cannot reconcile themselves to the resumption of the egalitarian movement, there is no alternative but the suspension of constitutional government. It is the half-instinctive realisation of how closely we approximate to this position which explains the decline in the zeal for liberty. Men now interpret so differently the ends that politics must serve that the victory of one set of principles is to its opponents in the nature of a catastrophe. And if the victory can be prevented by fighting, it is in human nature, even in English human nature, to fight . . .

The governing class, in such a capitalist democracy as ours, has the simple alternative of fighting for its position of privilege or of showing itself able consistently to improve the standard of life. If it cannot achieve the latter objective, it cannot satisfy the conditions implicit in universal suffrage. Either it must force the abandonment of that experiment – and this, in itself, may well involve revolution – or it must be prepared deliberately to abdicate its privileged position because the force of numbers is against it. That abdication will not, I think, display itself as natural to men whose historic expectations suffer sudden and violent disappointment; it is hardly in human nature that it should so so. One can see how large-scale economic recovery might permit the resumption of the policy of concessions. But there is a wide margin between concessions and abdication. Depression in a few brief years has already produced an atmosphere in which the whole philosophy of concession has been seriously called into question. When it is the remaking of the social order that is demanded, is it likely that men will refuse the challenge?

3.3 G. D. H. COLE: LIBERAL SOCIALISM

Like Laski, G. D. H. Cole also had a considerable influence on British socialist thought in the 1930s and 1940s. He revived the Fabian Society and set in motion much of the policy discussion that prepared Labour for its post-war assumption of power, and also provided British socialists with an important source of economic analysis throughout this period. At the end of the 1930s Cole sought to restate the philosophy of 'liberal socialism' (as he now called it) in the light of the political and economic lessons of that troubled decade. This was his theme in this essay on 'A socialist civilisation', from the Fabian volume *Programme for victory* (1941).

The problem that I am called upon to face . . . is that of discussing the tasks that are before us in our attempt to build a Socialist civilisation.

What are the principles which Bevin and Morrison and the other Labour Ministers should have in mind when they are confronting their major tasks inside the Government? What kind of Socialist civilisation should they try to bring about, and at any rate to lay the foundations of during the war? They *could* take as their model either of two systems which are actually in existence in the world today. They *could* take the economic system of the Soviet Union, or they *could* take the economic system of Nazi Germany. These are two working models of twentieth-century ways of social organisation which are actually working; and they both differ from the ways of living to which we are accustomed in this country in that they are based on twentieth-century, and not on nineteenth-century, technique. We, on the other hand, are still living under institutions which were set up and continue to be administered in the light of nineteenth-century technique, nineteenth-century notions, and nineteenth-century ways of life. Both Nazi Germany and the Soviet Union, whether we like them or not, have been conceived basically in terms of the economic conditions, the underlying powers of production, existing in the twentieth century. It would be possible for our statesmen here to make up their minds that the best thing they could do would be to try to bring about in Great Britain a full Communist form of organisation such as the Russians have been attempting to build up, based on an omnipotent State which would take over and direct all the instruments of production, based on a complete destruction of the bourgeoisie, and a new class structure which would know no classes of the old sort but, if it had classes or class division at all (and that, of course, its creators would deny), would rest them not on property or inheritance but on the exercise of function, on the importance of the contribution that this man or that man was making to the common cause. Our statesmen *could* set to work to build a civilisation of the sort, conscious that it could be built only after a terrific struggle against our own vested interests and a terrific holocaust of habits of living that are deeply engrained in my being and yours, in the whole British middle class and in a large part of the British working classes as well.

Or, on the other hand, our statesmen *could* take the Nazi State as their model, and seek to build up a State-controlled economic system which would leave capitalist property still in being but subordinate the exercise of capitalist rights to the over-riding rights of the State, allowing the capitalists to retain their property and their incomes from property subject to their doing the things which the State wants them to do, producing the goods which the State wants them to produce, employing the persons whom the State wants them to employ, investing their capital where the State wishes it to be invested, and so on. Our leaders *could* say that we had better try to establish a State-controlled capitalism, based on a system of economic planning, on making all the classes in society fit together in terms of a general social plan which the State would dictate. That is the ideal of State-controlled capitalism...

There you have two working models. The one is a model of a completely State-run economic system, in which the State takes over the ownership of all the basic industries, and all the control of the way in which those industries are to be run; in which the State becomes the director of further technical advance, the means of applying mass production to the full and of using all the latest scientific discoveries for the purpose of increasing the total volume of output; in which the State aims primarily at raising the standard of living of the people by these means...

That is one ideal – the ideal that there should be built up a completely State-run society in which the State would be the controller and the embodiment of the new technical forces of mass production and enforce the development of these powers upon the whole people. Over against that, there is the alternative model, based on the conception of a capitalism controlled and dominated by a powerful State machine which, without abolishing property rights or economic distinctions, would compel every subject to subserve a general economic and political plan.

I dislike both those models of twentieth-century organisation. I dislike anything that subordinates the individual as completely to the machine as do both Communism and State Capitalism in the forms in which we see them at work in the world today... But deeply as I dislike these Leviathans, deeply as I want to live in a social environment which leaves large scope for diversity and individual and group initiative and is not all shut up within a basic uniformity prescribed by the State, I have always to remind myself that I am, after all, living not in Utopia, but in twentieth-century Europe, and that the technical developments of the twentieth century render certain models of social organisation which one can conceive in one's mind visionary utopias for us and for our time. The very situation prescribes certain basic principles on which any society that has a chance of survival under twentieth-century conditions has to be founded. The characteristics of centralised planning and control which are common to Nazi Germany and to the Soviet Union are not accidents: they are the direct outcome of certain technical conditions, and are indispensable, in some measure, to any twentieth-century society that is to rest on solid foundations. They have to be accepted as part of the order of our universe: upon them we have to build as best we can, being the possessors of great scientific powers which we have not yet learned the art of controlling and subordinating to the nobler human desires.

Given man as he is, given these forces as they are, it is inevitable that any society capable of standing the test of the struggle for existence under twentieth-century conditions shall have built into its very foundations this common element of centralised planning and control that exists both in Nazi Germany and in the Soviet Union. We have to assume a large-scale, planned social order; we have to assume that the control of the uses made of the major powers of production will be in the hands of a central authority; we have to assume that the great majority of men will have to work within the limits set by this great machine; and we have to admit that any attempt to build a society that does not accept these basic conditions is doomed to failure. If we try, in the name of liberty, in the name of individuality, in the name of anything else that we hold dear, to stand in the way of the development of these great technical forces, we shall be doing nothing to build a new democratic order that will have in it the elements of victory and of stability.

This means that we cannot restore, even if we would, either the old capitalism or the old objectives of Labour Parties or Social Democratic Parties which expected capitalism to stay steady while they modified its evil social consequences, to continue in effective operation while they gradually got ready to supersede it, and to consent to be superseded as fast as they could persuade people to pass laws restraining it from doing this or that, and establishing little bits of semi-Socialism here and there. We have to take it for granted that the new order must be a highly centralised and basically planned order in its method of handling all the essential services, and that the foundations of this new order must be laid at once. I say this, not because I like it, but because it is true, and it does not matter whether I like it or not. But, having said it, I go on to ask what chance there is within this new order of saving whatever has been valuable and remains valuable in the civilisation which was gradually built up under capitalism in the course of the nineteenth century, and is now visibly tottering to its fall.

Nineteenth-century capitalism, after all, had very considerable values... Through the past century the sphere of freedom was being continually enlarged, in the sense that individuals or groups were able more and more to break loose from an imposed uniformity of conduct... That kind of diversity, and the tolerance which alone makes it possible in a community which means to go on living together as a community, is one of the values of nineteenth-century capitalism which I, at any rate, want to preserve. But how far can we preserve that tolerance, that right to live our own lives, that right to behave in different ways, under the conditions which now face us – the conditions which impose upon us centralised planning and control as sheer necessities if we are to survive at all?

This is the great question that confronts us in building our Socialist civilisation for tomorrow. The Communists obviously threw away a great deal that was good when they made their revolution. Making it against an old order far more reactionary than ours, and under much more difficult conditions, because they were badly lacking in skilled man-power, in technicians and organisers of every sort, and faced by a terrible ignorance and lack of civilisation, bred of long oppression, among their people, they were compelled to insist on a degree of uniformity in conduct and behaviour and, above all, on a degree of uniformity in thought, without which their attempt to build a new social system could hardly have succeeded at all. They had to be all Marxists together; they had to inculcate a common philosophy and, to a large extent, a common way of behaviour, because that was the means of giving solidarity and unity of direction to the new society which they were trying to consolidate. As against that, we in Western Europe start with enormous advantages – with an abundance of technicians of every kind and with an abundance of persons used to some measure of freedom and responsibility who possess the qualities of competence and education needed for carrying out the essential tasks of Socialist construction. We possess also a tradition of getting along together somehow even when we differ, of not enlarging differences on one point into differences on all points, of not dividing ourselves into sects that cannot play football together because they cannot agree about politics. That is a valuable tradition which lives among us and will make all the difference if we can reconcile it with wholehearted endeavour in the building of a new society. The doubt is whether this very tolerance, this very habit of not quarrelling about everything because we quarrel about politics, is part of the 'fatty degeneration of democracy', as the Nazis would teach us to believe, or is a quality of civilised living, which men can preserve, and at the same time act in forthright fashion in adapting it to the needs of a radically different social order.

What fundamentally differentiates us, who belong to the Fabian Society and to the Labour Party, from Communists and from all who believe that the new civilisation can be built only by a sharp break with the old traditions, not only in politics but in everything else as well, is the belief that it is possible to build the new society without throwing overboard those values which are our heritage from the past, developed under a capitalism which once allowed room for them to grow, but now, in its new monopolistic phase, has shown its incapacity to sustain them, or to yield to us anything further of the same order of value. We Fabians believe that it is possible to carry over into the new society values developed under the old order, but not inseparably bound up with nineteenth-century ways of conducting our economic affairs. We believe that it is possible to build a Socialist civilisation without throwing over-board all the institutions that grew up under capitalism, good and bad alike. We believe that we need cast away only those things which necessarily belong to a capitalist society and are not capable of being adapted to the needs of a Socialist society. We believe, however, that, while this can be done, there is no certainty that it will be done. If we have to choose between a vast sacrifice of these older values, a vast sacrifice of the things that we believe to be good in the society in which we are now living, and our desire to con-struct a new, Socialist civilisation, there is no doubt which way our choice should go. We should be prepared to sacrifice all these ex-isting values if need be; but if we can create the new society with-out that sacrifice it will be an infinitely better society and will be built with far less human suffering, and with far fewer growing pains of transition, than if we have to tear everything down first, and then begin building up again amid the ruins of all our habits and traditional standards . . .

What, in outline, are the essential qualities that we must build into the walls and strong places of our new City? That we must make it strong, goes without saying: there must be no room in it for idleness or for parasites; for the City cannot be strong unless it can find scope for all its citizens to labour in the common service. We cannot therefore any longer allow the business or idleness of any man to depend on the fiat of some other man, or some great imper-sonal company, that sees, or does not see, a prospect of profit from employing him. The Right to Work, and therewith the Right to Leisure after work, must be built into our new foundations. But

the Right to Work implies the power to provide work. It implies
that the society as a whole, and not some private employer, is to be
the arbiter in deciding what work is to be done. It implies the collective planning and control of the industrial effort of the people,
with need, not profit, as the criterion of worthwhileness in setting
men to work. The Right to Work is the corner-stone of Socialism,
because it implies Socialism.

But—can we have the Right to Work without imposing the
tyranny of the State upon the people? There is no unemployment,
none that matters, in the Soviet Union – or in Nazi Germany. But is
there any freedom, either? Can we abolish unemployment without
introducing what Mr. Hilaire Belloc has called 'The Servile State'?

Why not? The conditions imposed on us by modern industrial
technique require that the factory and the mine shall be organised
for production in accordance with a general plan, and that it shall
not be left to private proprietors to decide whether it is or is not
worth while to employ these instruments of production. But there
is no need, even in time of war – much less in time of peace – to
apply to the main body of the workers any compulsion to work in a
particular establishment. In wartime, it may be necessary to order a
few key men, highly skilled workers, to go where their services are
most urgently needed, and it is very necessary to make sure that all
are engaged on some form of nationally useful work. Under a
socialised economic system the worker can be left full freedom to
change his place of employment or his job – indeed, he can be given
much more freedom than he has now, by making it easier for men
who have made a wrong choice at the outset to learn a new trade.
This will not happen automatically under Socialism; but it can
happen, if we want it to happen, and that it should happen is fully
consistent with the technical conditions of twentieth century production.

It is one clear lesson of the war that it is the employer, the business firm, and not the workers, that have to be disciplined in the
interest of maximum output. It is the individualism of business in
some trades, and equally the restrictiveness which develops wherever capitalist businesses shed their individualism and join together
in combines and trade associations, that hamper the productive
effort. Organise the factories and bring them under a common
direction seeking not maximum profit but maximum production of
useful goods, and there will be no need to coerce labour. Labour,
with its strong tradition of trade union solidarity behind it, will
organise itself for the task of co-operating in the common plan. It is

doing this today, with signal success; what stands in the way is the rooted fear of business men that if they throw down the barriers in the way of higher production, the post-war world will become glutted with goods for which there will be no market when the abnormal demands of warring States have ceased.

The workman can have freedom under the new large-scale industrialism provided that the employer is not left free to damp down production in order to preserve his profits. But this implies that the State will be able to find markets for everything that can be produced. This in turn implies something else. The Nazis have been able to banish unemployment because from their very advent they have been producing intensively with a view to war. Under such conditions, full employment is quite consistent with a low standard of living for the mass of the people. War preparation involves a low standard, because it, like war itself, diverts a large part of the national manpower and machine-power to meeting the special demands of the Government. But under the conditions of peace full employment requires a high standard of living among the main body of the people, as a means of distributing the expanding output of industry.

In this country standards of living are already relatively high, and the demand for new capital equipment can be met, even if we decide on very large measures of economic reorganisation, by a tiny fraction of our total productive resources. If we can but get rid of the need to prepare for war, and use all our resources for improving standards of living, we have all the ingredients to our hands for making a rapid advance in the arts of life. Managerial capacity and manual skill are ours in abundance: it is the want of central drive and direction towards a diffused welfare that holds us back.

In order to achieve this drive, we shall have to base incomes on what we can produce, instead of limiting production to what incomes can buy. The employer who refrains from production for fear of glutting the market thereby destroys the market and helps to make his fears come true. It is an essential part of any planning for welfare, such as Socialism connotes, that incomes shall be planned to correspond to productive capacity, and shall be well diffused. 'Money is like muck, not good unless it be well spread.' Adequate consumers' demand requires that incomes shall not be left, any more than production, to be settled by the higgling of the market, but shall be planned so as to yield the largest possible sum-total of welfare.

Socialism, however, though it involves a generous approach to economic equality, is not wholly a bread-and-butter question. As I have said, it is also, and ultimately, a question of the spirit of man. As giant power spreads over the world, as the units of production grow larger and the units of business control much larger still, the mass of men pass more and more under the domination of the machine. Immensely greater power to control the lives of the many passes into the hands of the few – as long as the few are allowed to own and manipulate the machines. This is true not only of industry, or of warfare: it is true of propaganda also, with its new techniques of psychological approach. Individualism and *laisser-faire* quite change their practical meaning when the individual comes to mean in practice a great capitalist trust or a newspaper syndicate with unlimited capital at its back. It is useless to wish these giants away, or to sigh for the joys of an age of little things. There can be no peace for the soul of man, and no space for the individual to live his own life, till we have learnt by collective action to subordinate these monsters to our needs.

This is our task today and tomorrow – to subdue these giants to our will without making them at the same time the masters of our spirit. I am not a Communist, but a good Fabian Socialist, precisely because I fear that a Communist Revolution, by sweeping too much away, would enthrone in the minds of the new generation the iron spirit of the mass-producing machine, whereas a milder Socialist Revolution could bring to the control of the machine the liberal spirit that values difference, and reckons suffering at a high rate in the scale of things to be put down.

But the danger is that this liberal spirit may be perverted into mere negation, or into sloth. It is disastrously easy to make tolerance an excuse for inaction and to mistake laziness and cowardice for judicious caution and a humane temper. It is easy to do nothing, on plea of the danger of doing the wrong thing. These perversions are disastrous in the world of today, when science is forcing upon all men vast readjustments in their ways of life, and every new discovery can be seized upon as a weapon of rapine unless it is promptly harnessed to creative use. Every invention, every advance in man's knowledge, is *michin mallecho* unless it is collectively controlled in the service of the common people. Socialism is, in the last resort, simply the means to this control. A Socialist civilisation is one in which the past victories of humanity are not thrown away, or bombed into unrecognizable fragments because they have been misapplied, but are used as a basis for further conquests in the interests of ordinary, decent people. The trouble is that these ordinary, decent people, who claim for the most part nothing better than to be let alone, cannot be let alone until the world has settled its fate anew. The bombs will fall upon them, the giant machine will bind them to the will of its masters, the megaphones will blare propaganda at them, and they will live unquiet lives, until they themselves realise that, for very peace and quietness, they must do for themselves what no political sect can do without them – claim their right to be free, not by turning their backs on the juggernauts that ride over them, but by facing manfully the task of bringing these monsters under collective, democratic Socialist control.

3.4 JOHN STRACHEY

John Strachey's political career was a remarkable odyssey, ranging from a brief flirtation with Oswald Mosley to ministerial office in the 1945 Labour Government. However, in the 1930s Strachey emerged as the most effective and influential exponent in Britain of a Marxist analysis of contemporary events, a role facilitated by his collaboration with Laski and Gollancz in the Left Book Club. This extract is from his celebrated account of *The coming struggle for power* (1932).

The capitalist system is dying and cannot be revived. That is the conclusion to which any honest investigator of the actual facts and possibilities of the present situation must be driven.

The end of that phase of the history of the peoples of the West which began five hundred years ago, carries such enormous implications with it that nearly everyone stands too dumbfounded to admit what is happening. And even those who do admit the fact of finality, are reluctant to realise a tenth of its consequences. The gradual and fatal decay of all those societies which are based upon the capitalist system of production, and the rise of another and alternative way of carrying on life, are the two sides of a process, too gigantic to be easily apprehended. But we may be assured of one thing: the death of capitalism and the substitution of another economic system in its place, will leave no single side of life unaltered. Religion, literature, art, science, the whole of the human heritage of knowledge will be transformed. For no aspect of human life can remain unaffected by a change in the way in which human life itself is maintained. And the new forms, whether higher or lower, which these principal concepts of man's imagination will assume, will depend on what new economic system will succeed the capitalist system. On the character of this new basis will depend whether human knowledge and skill flourish and expand so that a new and less miserable, or (if you prefer it) more glorious, epoch in human history is made possible, or whether they relapse and decay, as they have done so many times before, until nearly all the little gains which men have so painfully won are lost again, and the slow long task of revival from a very simple level of life has to be begun again . . .

Those possibilities of subtle and imperceptible social readjustments which seem so real in Britain are utterly out of the question in most of the rest of the world, and consequently communist theory and communist methods are the only ones which apply to the social conditions of nine-tenths of the inhabited globe. And if this is the case, then we may be assured that in a very short while they will apply also to such countries as Great Britain. Britain has her own history and consequently her own peculiar characteristics: but if we suppose that she will be allowed to work out her destiny in isolation, unaffected by the events which are unfolding themselves in the rest of the world, then we delude ourselves. The truth is rather that Britain is quite peculiarly vulnerable to the reactions of events which may take place at the other side of the globe. Her whole economy is based to an unparalleled degree upon profits drawn from the exploitation of her Empire. Colonial revolts already menace essential parts of her system. The social reactions which are bound to follow the crash of the high-piled pyramid of her superprofits, may well be especially violent and sudden. If communist theory and practice is the only possible policy for the working class of the world as a whole, then it is the only possible policy for the workers of Great Britain also.

3.5 DOUGLAS JAY

Douglas Jay, economist and Labour politician, was one of a group of socialist economists (including Gaitskell and Durbin) who in the 1930s drew upon the work of Keynes and the 'new economics' to counter Marxism and to present a revised economic case for socialism. This extract is from Jay's *The socialist case* (1937).

The principles of redistribution – the modifications, that is to say, which it is proposed to introduce into the system of private capitalism and free prices – must be dependent on the flaws inherent in the system. Some of these flaws are inherent in the legal framework and some in the price system itself; and there must consequently be two main types of reform: alteration of the framework and interference with the system. It was argued . . . that almost all the major distortions and injustices of the price system spring from the inequality of incomes, and that the worst *and* most unjustifiable inequalities spring from the institution of inheritance. It follows, therefore, that inheritance, and its consequence, inherited income, ought as far as possible to be abolished. And on the possibility of thus altering the legal framework of the price system without destroying the system itself, even Professor Hayek is with us... Socialists should therefore change the laws so as substantially to abolish inheritance. On the substance of this there should be no compromise whatever. For inheritance is at once the chief cause of inequality and of the resulting poverty, and the most indefensible of all the trappings of modern capitalism. The payment of inherited incomes is not morally justifiable, because the recipients make no real effort or sacrifice in return; and it is not economically justifiable, because the passive service of merely refraining from consuming one's capital is one that can be performed with equal efficiency by the State. Moreover just because inheritance is associated with the family, it inevitably produces a propertied class, with all its attendant evils. The abolition of unearned incomes and the consequent social ownership of property must be the centre and the heart of socialism. The traditional socialist belief that unearned incomes are the main removable cause of poverty and inequality is true and of dominating importance. The tendency of socialists lately to think less of the dispossession of property and more of organisation, 'planning', efficiency, and so on, is in many ways unfortunate. What society fundamentally needs is not so much planning as socialism...

Socialists have been mistaken in making ownership of the means of production instead of ownership of inherited property the test of socialisation... It is not the ownership of the means of production as such, but ownership of large inherited incomes, which ought to be eliminated. Indeed, the official Marxist definition of socialism, as propagated by Mr John Strachey for instance, denotes a state of affairs which would be perfectly compatible with all the most unbridled abuses of private capitalism. Socialism by this definition means the abolition of private ownership of the means of production. But supposing, as might happen in Russia, that the State owned all the means of production, but that at the same time there was a class of rich rentiers living entirely on the interest on Government securities, and handing them on freely up to 100 per cent to their children. It would be possible, on Mr Strachey's definition, to build up an entirely idle class of millionaire rentiers, and to say that 'socialism' had nevertheless been achieved. If we are to have the substance and not the shadow, therefore, we must define socialism as the abolition of private unearned or inherited incomes rather than of the private ownership of the means of production.

3.6 EVAN DURBIN

Evan Durbin's early accidental death deprived British socialism of a considerable talent. His book *The politics of democratic socialism* (1940), from which this extract comes, prefigured much post-war revisionist writing. His aim was to come to terms with the political and economic experience of the 1930s in presenting the case 'for the maintenance and extension in our society of the twin principles of democracy and socialism'.

The problem of policy can . . . be defined as the search for a method whereby the virtues of capitalism – rationalism and mobility – can be combined with democratic needs – security and equality – by the extension of the activity of the State upon an ever-widening and consistent basis. This, at least, is the problem for those of us who reject the doctrine that the only economic hope of mankind must for ever lie in a competitive and free enterprise economy. It is then, to the problem of extended State control that we must now turn, equipped in part for the task with the psychological and economic evidence now at our disposal . . .

I wish to argue that the only conceivable route to a better social order lies in the pathway of democracy, and that the political method of democratic government is an essential principle, not an accidental accompaniment, of any just society.

If by the 'socialist commonwealth' we mean a society in which a larger measure of social justice has been established through the instrumentality of a planned economy, then I believe that the democratic method is an inherent part of socialism, and cannot be separated from it – any more than batting can be separated from cricket or love from life. They are all necessary parts of a complex whole . . .

We reach then this final position – that the democratic method is not only essential for the achievement of socialism, but that it is part of that achievement. In so far as we are democratic we are already, in some degree, socialist; and to betray democracy is to betray socialism.

There is a complex and important sense in which socialism is necessary to democracy – the sense in which capitalism is incompatible with democracy. But there is a very simple and much more obvious sense in which democracy is necessary to socialism. It is not that democracy is the pleasantest, or most efficacious, or most certain method of achieving socialism, but that it is the only method; that all other hopes and all other programmes are mistaken and illusory. Democracy is not related to socialism as gilt to the gingerbread, or cream to coffee – a decorative addition or a great improvement; but as air to breathing, as coal to fire, as love to life – the indispensable means, the *fons et origo* of all our social hopes . . .

I am left with a practical problem to face. If the economic system is in urgent need of reform, and if the maintenance of democracy is an essential condition of social justice, how can the one be used to secure the other? How can expansionist and egalitarian policies be secured through the practice of the democratic method? The democratic socialist must discover such a strategy.

3.7 GEORGE ORWELL

The writer George Orwell was a libertarian socialist who fought against fascism in Spain and satirised totalitarianism in such celebrated works as *Animal farm* and *Nineteen-eighty four*. Orwell was also an acute observer of English society and of its socialist possibilities. These concerns are reflected in this extract from his important but neglected wartime book *The lion and the unicorn: socialism and the English genius* (1941).

It has become clear in the last few years that 'common ownership of the means of production' is not in itself a sufficient definition of Socialism. One must also add the following: approximate equality of incomes (it need be no more than approximate), political democracy, and abolition of all hereditary privilege, especially in education. These are simply the necessary safeguards against the reappearance of a class-system. Centralised ownership has very little meaning unless the mass of the people are living roughly upon an equal level, and have some kind of control over the government. 'The State' may come to mean no more than a self-elected political party, and oligarchy and privilege can return, based on power rather than on money . . .

It is only by revolution that the native genius of the English people can be set free. Revolution does not mean red flags and street fighting, it means a fundamental shift of power. Whether it happens with or without bloodshed is largely an accident of time and place. Nor does it mean the dictatorship of a single class . . . What is wanted is a conscious open revolt by ordinary people against inefficiency, class privilege and the rule of the old. It is not primarily a question of change of government. British governments do,

broadly speaking, represent the will of the people, and if we alter
our structure from below we shall get the government we need...
Right through our national life we have got to fight against privilege, against the notion that a half-witted public schoolboy is better for command than an intelligent mechanic. Although there are
gifted and honest *individuals* among them, we have got to break
the grip of the moneyed class as a whole. England has got to
assume its real shape. The England that is only just beneath the
surface, in the factories and the newspaper offices, in the aeroplanes
and the submarines, has got to take charge of its own destiny...

Nations do not escape from their past merely by making a revolution. An English Socialist government will transform the nation
from top to bottom, but it will still bear all over it the unmistakable
marks of our own civilisation, the peculiar civilisation which I discussed earlier...

It will not be doctrinaire, nor even logical. It will abolish the
House of Lords, but quite probably will not abolish the Monarchy.
It will leave anachronisms and loose ends everywhere, the judge in
his ridiculous horsehair wig and the lion and the unicorn on the sol-
dier's cap-buttons. It will not set up any explicit class dictatorship.
It will group itself round the old Labour Party and its mass following will be in the trade unions, but it will draw into it most of the
middle class and many of the younger sons of the bourgeoisie. Most
of its directing brains will come from the new indeterminate class of
skilled workers, technical experts, airmen, scientists, architects and
journalists, the people who feel at home in the radio and ferro-
concrete age. But it will never lose touch with the tradition of compromise and the belief in a law that is above the State. It will shoot
traitors, but it will give them a solemn trial beforehand and occasionally it will acquit them. It will crush any open revolt promptly
and cruelly, but it will interfere very little with the spoken and
written word. Political parties with different names will still exist,
revolutionary sects will still be publishing their newspapers and
making as little impression as ever. It will disestablish the Church,
but will not persecute religion. It will retain a vague reverence for
the Christian moral code, and from time to time will refer to England as 'a Christian country'. The Catholic Church will war against
it, but the Noncomformist sects and the bulk of the Anglican
Church will be able to come to terms with it. It will show a power
of assimilating the past which will shock foreign observers and
sometimes make them doubt whether any revolution has happened.
But all the same it will have done the essential thing.

Part four
1945–1964

4.1 C. A. R. CROSLAND: REVISIONISM

In the post-war period, Anthony Crosland emerged as a key contributor
to the theoretical debate on the future direction of British socialism that
followed the demise of the 1945–51 Labour governments. His
contribution to *New Fabian essays* (1952) had suggested the need for a
radical revision of the socialist position because of the changed character
of capitalism, and this argument formed the basis for his subsequent
account of *The future of socialism* (1956), from which this extract is
taken. This wide-ranging and influential work set the terms of much of
the debate between the 'revisionists' and 'fundamentalists' of British
socialism in this period.

It is surely time . . . to stop searching for fresh inspiration in the
old orthodoxies, and thumbing over the classic texts as though they
could give oracular guidance for the future. The first need now, in
R. H. Tawney's words, 'is to treat sanctified formulae with judicious irreverence and to start by deciding what precisely is the end
in view'.

The need for a restatement of doctrine is hardly surprising. The
old doctrines did not spring from a vacuum, or from acts of pure
cerebration performed in a monastery cell. Each was the product of
a particular kind of society, and of minds reacting to that society.
Since this external factor was not constant and unchanging, the
doctrines changed through time. And as society has changed again
since before the war, so again a restatement of objectives is called
for. The matter can be put quite simply. Traditional socialism was
largely concerned with the evils of traditional capitalism, and with
the need for its overthrow. But today traditional capitalism has
been reformed and modified almost out of existence, and it is with a
quite different form of society that socialists must now concern
themselves. Pre-war anti-capitalism will give us very little help.

The traditionalists may comfort themselves by reflecting that this will not be the first time that socialism has been restated; nothing is more traditional in the history of socialist thought than the violent rejection of past doctrines. Marx expended prodigious energy in flaying the Utopian and Owenite brands of socialism that held the field before him. The Fabians used less vitriolic pens, but were as vehement in rejecting Marx as Marx had been in rejecting Owen. Neither owed anything significant to previous doctrine. Thus even revisionism is hallowed by an appeal to the past; and the common-sense view that the more is achieved, the less relevant traditional dogmas become, need not be thought heretical.

But it will, nevertheless, be unpopular. I am not thinking simply of the fact that people dislike new ideas, and hate to be jolted out of the old, familiar habits of mind: but of a more subtle reason why revisionism has, historically, always been resented. This is because many working-class militants, and still more some middle-class people who have espoused the workers' cause, feel their whole status and psychological security to depend on preserving a traditional, proletarian philosophy of class-struggle.

For the middle-class socialist, this is because he may think that he must prove himself more royalist than the king – that he must be combatively traditional and doctrinal in order to be accepted as a good comrade, to win the approval of the workers, and feel that he really 'belongs' to their party; in politics, as in religion, the most rigid attachment to dogma is often to be found amongst the converts. And for the working-class activist, devoting his entire energies to the socialist movement, both his social status and emotional certainty depend on the conviction that militant struggle is necessary; it is only on this assumption that his life makes sense. Revisionism, by casting doubts on the need for militancy, or suggesting that the class-struggle is now rather out-of-date, challenges both his social and emotional security; if class-conscious anti-capitalism is obsolete, what is his status as a militant, and what his purpose in life? Hence the anger with which criticisms of militancy or class-struggle are often greeted . . .

And there is now an additional psychological reason for resenting revisionism, stemming from the very success of the socialist movement. Mr Raymond Aron has correctly observed that 'Socialism has ceased in the West to be a myth because it has become a part of reality' – not, of course, a complete reality, but sufficiently so to be no longer a myth. Labour Governments have been in power, and have found responsibility harsher and quite different from anything they expected; while full employment and social security have destroyed the rationale of much of the old emotional enthusiasm.

Revisionism draws attention to this new reality. It is an explicit admission that many of the old dreams are either dead or realised; and this brutal admission is resented. It is resented, first, because it destroys the old simplicity, certainty, and unquestioning conviction. 'The will to Socialism', wrote G. D. H. Cole before the war, 'is based on a lively sense of wrongs crying for redress.' And when the wrongs were so manifest, we all knew what to do, and where the enemy was, and what was the order of battle; it was exhilarating to fight for such clear-cut and obviously righteous aims. But now the certainty and simplicity are gone; and everything has become complicated and ambiguous. Instead of glaring and conspicuous evils, squalor and injustice and distressed areas, we have to fuss about the balance of payments, and incentives, and higher productivity; and the socialist finds himself pinioned by a new and unforeseen reality.

And the objective has become not only less clear-cut, but also . . . less urgent; hence it no longer excites the same crusading spirit. But people want something to crusade about; and even the partial fulfilment of a dream leaves a feeling of lassitude and anti-climax. 'Oh, how I should like to begin all over again!' cries Olof in Strindberg's play at the moment when the Reformation triumphs; 'it was not victory I wanted – it was the battle!'; and many socialists, deep down, feel much the same. A people enjoying full employment and social security has lost its dreams, and lost the need to struggle; and the activists in consequence feel restless and frustrated. That is why they resent revisionist thinkers who compel them to face the new reality, and try to delude themselves instead that all the old enemies – capitalist barons, Wall Street, exploiting profiteers – are still there, waiting to be attacked. 90% of resolutions at Annual Conference today are Quixotic tilts at objects still hopefully seen as 'outrageous giants of that detested race'; unfortunately, there are too few Sancho Panças to point out that they are really only windmills.

If we are to reformulate socialist doctrine, the first task is clearly to decide what precise meaning is to be attached to the word 'socialism'.

This is not an easy question to answer. The word does not describe any present or past society, which can be empirically observed, and so furnish unimpeachable evidence for what is or is not 'socialism'. Thus statements about socialism can never be definitely verified; and we cannot treat it as being an *exact* descriptive word at all. There is therefore no point in searching the encyclopaedias for a definitive meaning; it has none, and never could.

This can easily be seen by considering the numerous and... often inconsistent meanings attached to the word by people who have called themselves 'socialists'. Marx, defining it as the 'nationalisation of the means of production, distribution, and exchange', meant something quite different from Proudhon, who defined it as consisting of 'every aspiration towards the amelioration of our society'. Sir William Harcourt, declaring in 1892 that 'we are all socialists now', evidently had a different version from his contemporary Bradlaugh, to whom socialism meant that 'the State should own all wealth, direct all labour, and compel the equal distribution of all produce'. And any history of socialist thought will provide dozens of different definitions, some in terms of ownership, some of cooperation, some of planning, some of income-distribution; and it soon becomes simply a matter of subjective personal preference which is chosen as the 'correct' one. Many definitions, moreover, are so vague as to be virtually meaningless; one can read almost anything, for example, into Sidney Webb's definition: 'the economic side of the democratic ideal'.

The confusion has become worse inasmuch as the word is also charged with a high degree of emotional content, and so has acquired a range of purely persuasive meanings. It is either used to denote or win approval, as in Hitler's National 'Socialism' and 'Socialism' in Eastern Europe, or when Left-wing weeklies attack a policy which they dislike as not being 'Socialist'; or pejoratively, as when Right-wing Americans speak of 'creeping Socialism'.

But the worst source of confusion is the tendency to use the word to describe, not a certain kind of society, but particular policies which are, or are thought to be, means to attaining this kind of society, or realising these attributes. To rescue the word from these confusions, and the debasement referred to above, one must begin by asking what, if anything, is common to the beliefs of all, or almost all, of those who have called themselves socialists. The only constant element, common to all the bewildering variety of different doctrines, consists of certain moral values and aspirations; and people have called themselves socialists because they shared these aspirations, which form the one connecting link between otherwise hopelessly divergent schools of thought.

Thus the word first came on the modern scene with the early nineteenth-century Owenites, whom Marx contemptuously termed 'Utopian' socialists. They based their 'socialism' explicitly on an ethical view of society, a belief in a certain way of life and certain moral values. The means by which they thought this 'good society' could be attained are irrelevant today; and in fact they were quickly challenged by other socialist schools of thought, since when a continuous debate has proceeded, with no agreement, about what constituted the most suitable means. This debate would have no particular interest today, but for the fact that all the protagonists tried to appropriate the word 'socialism' to describe the particular means which they themselves favoured.

Thus Marx appropriated it for the collective ownership of the means of production on the false assumption ... that the pattern of ownership determined the character of the whole society, and that collective ownership was a sufficient condition of fulfilling the basic aspirations. And generally the word came to be applied to policies for the economic or institutional transformation of society, instead of to the ultimate social purposes which that transformation was intended to achieve; so one often hears socialism equated not only with the nationalisation of industry, but with government planning, or redistribution, or state collectivism. This of course is quite unhelpful, for although people may agree on ends, they may legitimately disagree about means. Moreover, the means most suitable in one generation may be wholly irrelevant in the next, and in any case (still more significant) a given means may lead to more than one possible end, as indeed has happened with each of the policies just mentioned.

Thus if, for example, socialism is defined as the nationalisation of the means of production, distribution and exchange, we produce conclusions which are impossible to reconcile with what the early socialists had in mind when they used the word: such as, that Soviet Russia is a completely socialist country (much more so, for instance, than Sweden) – even though it denies almost all the values which Western socialists have normally read into the word. Similarly, if socialism is defined as economic collectivism or State control of economic life, then Nazi Germany would correctly have been called a socialist country. But in neither case would the end-result be described as socialism by most socialists; the means of nationalisation and planning have proved adaptable to more than one purpose, which shows how unwise it is to identify the means with the end.

Not only is it unwise, but it is also semantically and historically incorrect. The various schools of thought which have called themselves, and been called by others, 'socialist' – Owenites and Marxists, Fabians and Christian Socialists, Syndicalists and Guild Socialists – have differed profoundly over the right means; and no one means has a better title to the label 'socialist' than any other. The one single element common to all schools of thought has been the basic aspirations, the underlying moral values. It follows that these embody the only logically and historically permissible meaning of the word socialism; and to this meaning we must now revert.

These ethical and emotional ideals have been partly negative – a protest against the visible results of capitalism – and partly positive, and related to definite views about the nature of the good society; though of course negative and positive strands are often intertwined.

Perhaps one can list them roughly as follows. First, a protest against the material poverty and physical squalor which capitalism produced. Secondly, a wider concern for 'social welfare' – for the interests of those in need, or oppressed, or unfortunate, from whatever cause. Thirdly, a belief in equality and the 'classless society', and especially a desire to give the worker his 'just' rights and a responsible status at work. Fourthly, a rejection of competitive antagonism, and an ideal of fraternity and co-operation. Fifthly, a protest against the inefficiencies of capitalism as an economic system, and notably its tendency to mass unemployment. The first three formed the basis of socialism as 'a broad, human movement on behalf of the bottom dog' (G. D. H. Cole). The first and last were censures on the material results of capitalism; while the other three stemmed from an idealistic desire for a just, co-operative and classless society.

(I have listed only the social and economic aspirations. But of course underlying them, and taken for granted, was a passionate belief in liberty and democracy. It would never have occurred to most early socialists that socialism had any meaning except within a political framework of freedom for the individual. But since this political assumption is shared by British Conservatives as well as socialists, no further reference is made to it.)

As thus formulated, even these basic aspirations are not all equally relevant to present-day society. Some are expressed in language adapted to conditions that no longer exist, and in particular are too negative in character. This is natural, for they were, in large part, a reaction against the actual results of pre-war capitalism; and with two million unemployed, widespread poverty and malnutrition, and appalling slums set against a background of flamboyant wealth amongst the richer classes, it was natural that the negative desire to abolish evils should outweigh more positive and detailed aspirations.

But to the extent that evils are remedied and injustices removed, negative statements become less and less appropriate. And they are seen to be inappropriate by the electorate, a growing section of which has no recollection of unemployment, or poverty, or dole queues, and finds Labour propaganda which plays on the themes and memories of the 1930s quite incomprehensible. To a population which has lost its fears, and now has every hope of a rapidly rising standard of living, a negative protest against past wrongs is merely a bore.

Thus even when we go back to the basic aspirations, we still find the same, welcome, difficulty that the pace of change has overtaken the doctrine, and a re-formulation is needed. Of course if a Tory Government were to re-create all the old evils, matters would be simple. New thinking could be set aside 'for the duration', and negative statements would again suffice. But it is not likely that the Tories will act so recklessly, or that mere periodic counter-attacks to regain lost positions will remove the need for a map of the new terrain.

How should we re-formulate these aspirations today in such a way as to preserve their basic emotional and ethical content, yet discarding what is clearly not germane to present-day conditions? Of the original five, the first and last are rapidly losing their relevance in a British context. Such primary poverty as remains will disappear within a decade, given our present rate of economic growth; and the contemporary mixed economy is characterised by high levels both of employment and productivity and by a reasonable degree of stability. In other words, the aspirations relating to the economic consequences of capitalism are fast losing their relevance as capitalism itself becomes transformed.

But the remaining three more positive ideals, described above as stemming either from a concern with the 'bottom dog', or from a vision of a just, co-operative and classless society, have clearly not been fully realised. No doubt we should phrase them differently today, but their basic content is still perfectly relevant. We have plenty of less fortunate citizens still requiring aid; and we certainly have not got an equal or classless society, nor one characterised by 'co-operative' social relations . . .

The co-operative aspiration has at least been partially fulfilled, in that society is much less aggressively individualistic and competitive than a century ago; and indeed the trend toward 'sociability' is now so strong that we are more likely to be deprived of solitude than company. On the other hand we do not yet live in a co-operative Utopia. Most people still work mainly for personal gain, and not for the social good; and the ideal of communal, co-operative participation has scarcely begun to be realised in industry.

Now there are one or two specific directions in which a clear choice exists between more or less competition – most notably in education . . . There are one or two further directions in which a less clear choice exists between more or less communal activity, e.g. housing development and town planning. Furthermore, the *sense* of co-operation in industry may spread as management grows more progressive and enlightened; and a gradual increase in equality will itself . . . still further diminish the intensity of competition. But beyond this, at our present state of knowledge, we cannot go. We cannot assert definitely what would be the effect either on personal contentment, or attitudes to work, or the quality of our society, of a wholesale effort to suppress the motive of personal gain, or to elevate collective at the expense of individual relationships: nor can we even begin to see a feasible institutional framework within which these changes could be brought about: nor can we be sure that even if they were practicable, they might not lead to serious losses in other directions, such as privacy, individuality, personal independence, equality of opportunity, or the standard of living.

While, therefore, I realise that as a matter of verbal precision the co-operative ideal is certainly embraced by the word 'socialism', and while I accept that it would clearly be in some sense 'better' if there were a more general awareness of a common social purpose, I do not feel able, in what is intended to be a reasonably definite and practical statement of socialist aims, to include this as part of the goal. I shall no doubt be corrected by those with clearer views.

The two remaining aspirations – the concern with social welfare, and the desire for an equal and classless society – still have a perfectly clear relevance. The first implies an acceptance of collective responsibility and an extremely high priority for the relief of social distress or misfortune, in contrast to the much lower priority which

it would receive in a 'free' economy guided mainly by an individualistic philosophy. This is the contemporary version of the traditional welfare and social-service philosophy of the Labour movement, and of the instinct to side automatically with the less fortunate and those in need.

There is plenty of residual social distress in Britain. It is now
caused less by primary poverty, though this can still be found, than
by secondary poverty, natural misfortune, physical or mental ill-
ness, the decline in the size of the family, sudden fluctuations in income, and deficiencies in social capital. These last, for all the high
level of average personal spending, are still appalling – ugly towns,
mean streets, slum houses, overcrowded schools, inadequate hos-
pitals, under-staffed mental institutions, too few homes for the
aged, indeed a general, and often squalid, lack of social amenities.

The relief of this distress and the elimination of this squalor is
the main object of social expenditure; and a socialist is identified as
one who wishes to give this an exceptional priority over other
claims on resources. This is not a matter of the overall vertical
equality of incomes; the arguments are humanitarian and com-
passionate, not egalitarian. It is a matter of priorities in the distribution of the national output, and a belief that the first priority
should always be given to the poor, the unfortunate, the 'have-
nots', and generally to those in need; from which follows a certain
view about collective social responsibility, and thence about the
role of the state and the level of taxation. This represents the first
major difference between a socialist and a conservative.

The second distinctive socialist ideal is social equality and the
'classless society'. The socialist seeks a distribution of rewards, status, and privileges egalitarian enough to minimise social resentment, to secure justice between individuals, and to equalise opportunities; and he seeks to weaken the existing deep-seated class stra-
tification, with its concomitant feelings of envy and inferiority, and
its barriers to uninhibited mingling between the classes. This belief
in social equality, which has been the strongest ethical inspiration
of virtually every socialist doctrine, still remains the most characteristic feature of socialist thought today.

It is significant that these aspirations are not now primarily economic in character. The worst economic abuses and inefficiencies
of modern society have been corrected; and this is no longer the
sphere, as it has been for the greater part of the life of modern
socialism, in which reforms are most urgently required. It is true,

of course, that Britain still faces a serious economic problem – the problem of external solvency. But this is a problem common to both parties; and so far as specifically socialist policy is concerned, the battle is not mainly on this front.

It is also obvious that these ideals are much less pertinent to Britain, than to Britain's relations with the outside world. It is in the backward nations that the real poverty exists; and the inequality between those nations and Great Britain is far more glaring than the inequality between rich and poor in Britain. That is why the most obvious fulfilment of socialist ideals lies in altering not the structure of society in our own country, but the balance of wealth and privilege between advanced and backward countries. This I do not discuss, for this book, as I made clear in the Preface, is about the British domestic scene and even within Britain these ideals are not yet fully realised. But socialists must always remember that inter-national now surpass inter-class injustices and inequalities.

The ideals have so far merely been stated. They have not been justified in detail, nor any evidence adduced to show that their further fulfilment would definitely improve our society. All that has been argued is that they constitute 'socialism' in the only legitimate sense of the word, and that they are not embodied in our present society to such an extent that most people would describe it as socialist.

A few people would, it is true, so describe it – not explicitly, but by implication. That is, they take the view that we are at, or anyway in sight of, the final objective. This of course is a plausible view only if we select those more modest aspirations which have largely been fulfilled and define these, and these alone, as socialism. Thus if we were to say, as G. D. H. Cole once did before the war, that 'the Socialist has two main enemies to fight – poverty and enslavement', it would follow that we now nearly have socialism in Britain, since we have very little poverty or enslavement.

Examples of such definitions can be found. Perhaps the most striking is the Frankfurt Manifesto of the reborn Socialist International in 1951, in which (after a preamble so vague as to be almost meaningless) the whole emphasis is placed on democratic planning, which is regarded as the basic condition of socialism. The purposes of planning are defined as 'full employment, higher production, a rising standard of life, social security and a fair distribution of income and property' – purposes which (at least if one omits the one word 'property') are either not peculiar to socialists, or else are largely achieved already in Britain and Scandinavia.

Now it is true that the planned full-employment welfare state, which has been the outcome of the first successful spell of Labour government, is a society of exceptional merit and quality by historical standards, and by comparison with pre-war capitalism. It would have seemed a paradise to many early socialist pioneers. Poverty and insecurity are in process of disappearing. Living standards are rising rapidly; the fear of unemployment is steadily weakening; and the ordinary young worker has hopes for the future which would never have entered his father's head. There is much less social injustice; the economy works efficiently; and the electorate, as the Labour Party discovered at the last election, is in no mood for large-scale change, and certainly not for the complete overthrow of the present system. Many liberal-minded people, who were instinctively 'socialist' in the 1930s as a humanitarian protest against poverty and unemployment, have now concluded that 'Keynes-plus-modified-capitalism-plus-Welfare-State' works perfectly well; and they would be content to see the Labour Party become (if the Tories do not filch the role) essentially a Party for the defence of the present position, with occasional minor reforms thrown in to sweeten the temper of the local activists.

Yet this is not socialism. True, it is not pure capitalism either; and it does fulfil some part of the traditional socialist aspirations, and to this extent has socialist features. Yet it could clearly be a great deal more socialist than it is – not, as people sometimes think, because it now has only 25% public ownership and is not fully planned down to the minutest detail, any more than Soviet society *is* more socialist because it has 100% public ownership and complete state planning: but simply because the traditional socialist ideals could be more fully realised than they are. To put the matter simply, we have won many important advances; but since we could still have more social equality, a more classless society, and less avoidable social distress, we cannot be described as a socialist country . . .

One may at this stage briefly summarise, without attempting to justify, the reasons for wanting to move forward, and to alter what is admitted to be a prosperous and generally tolerable society; and the value judgments which underlie this wish. Lord Attlee recently remarked, looking back on his early days, that 'I joined the socialist movement because I did not like the kind of society we had and I wanted something better'. Why should anyone say the same today?

There are, I believe, three answers. First, for all the rising material standards and apparent contentment, the areas of avoidable distress and physical squalor, which were referred to above, are still on a scale which narrowly restricts the freedom of choice and movement of a large number of individuals. Secondly (and perhaps more intractable), we retain a disturbing amount, compared with some other countries, of social antagonism and class resentment, visible both in politics and industry, and making society less peaceful and contented than it might be. Thirdly, the distribution of rewards and privileges still appears highly inequitable, being poorly correlated with the distribution of merit, virtue, ability, or brains: and, in particular, opportunities for gaining the top rewards are still excessively unequal.

This significant residue of distress, resentment, and injustice affords a *prima facie* justification for further social change – as I think, and shall argue, in a socialist direction. It may not justify the same *saeva indignatio* as mass unemployment and distressed areas before the war – rather a purposeful, constructive, and discriminating determination to improve an already improved society. But the belief that further change will appreciably increase personal freedom, social contentment, and justice, constitutes the ethical basis for being a socialist.

4.2 JOHN STRACHEY: LAST STAGE CAPITALISM

Influenced by the work of Keynes and its assimilation by socialists like Douglas Jay, John Strachey had revised his views on the economic prospects of capitalism and moved away from his earlier Marxism. In the 1950s he embarked on an ambitious exploration of the relations between capitalism, socialism and democracy that sought to draw upon both Keynesian and Marxist insights. This project produced his impressive account of *Contemporary capitalism* (1956), from which this extract comes. The theme of the book turned on the relations between a maturing democracy and a 'last stage capitalism', and on the ability of the former to transform the latter.

Socialist thinking must begin with the study of capitalism. This is as true for the evolutionary as for the revolutionary tradition, for the Webbs as for Marx. It is this which marks the distinction between the attempt genuinely to comprehend and control the development of human society, and mere dreaming. This is the distinction between what has been called 'scientific' and 'Utopian' socialism. What is to be can only emerge from what is.

Renewed attempts to assess the nature of contemporary capitalism are overdue. Capitalist society in 1955 is a very different thing from what it was 100 years ago when the socialist *critique* of it was first undertaken, or even from what it was 50 years ago when most of the current socialist conceptions of it were first formulated. Socialists will not succeed very well in their task of social transformation until and unless they form a clear idea of what capitalism has become and is becoming . . .

In this connection it may be useful to define the place of Marxism in this study . . . For Marxism contains astringent truths about human society in general, and about the society in which we live in particular; it contains truths which are hard to take because they ask us to strip off the illusions which are for many their comfort in a terrifying world. It would be tragic indeed if those truths, once seen, were to be lost sight of. An attempt is made, then, to take a modest step in the indispensable process of re-integrating Marxism with the Western cultural tradition from which it derives, but from which it has widely diverged. The aim is to see Marxism neither as an anathematised heresy, nor yet a gospel, but as one, partial, brilliant, rich, prejudiced, but precious, contribution to our cultural heritage.

Nevertheless it must be acknowledged that immense dangers are inherent in the use of any method as sweeping and comprehensive as Marx's . . . The profoundly anti-theoretical tradition of British sociological thought in general, and of the British Labour movement in particular, has always been acutely aware of such dangers . . . All grand theories and systems are seen as mere stumbling-blocks to true insight.

Such has always been the mental climate of this country, made explicit in the British empirical tradition. Nor has recent experience done anything but confirm that tradition. For the evidence of our times proclaims that no one theory, neither Marxism nor any other, has proved to be in itself an adequate 'guide to action'. In the hurricanes of the twentieth century those who have relied on one such unique guide have, as often as not, fared even worse than those who have trusted to empiricism, instinct, insight and sheer luck to see them through. Yet just because of all this, what is now, perhaps, chiefly needed is to strive to remember that empiricism also can become a dogma. In Britain and America we are only too ready to make a virtue out of our own intellectual laziness, and to plume ourselves, not only on freedom from enslavement to 'a theory', which is prudent, but on sheer ignorance of political and economic *theory* in any shape or form. The sceptical and empirical tradition, pushed to this point, degenerates into mere illiteracy. The truth is that the more we reject any one all-sufficient theory, the greater is the obligation upon us to achieve a command over the whole range of political and economic thinking. Otherwise we shall inevitably repeat all the tedious re-discoveries of the auto-didact. In a word, the complexities of social phenomena are a reason for viewing with scepticism any vast unifying hypothesis which is interpreted as giving all the answers, and giving them once and for all. But these complexities are no excuse for abandoning the task of interpretation as hopeless: that way lies despair, mysticism and the mutilation of the intellect . . .

No-one who has lived and worked in the British Labour movement for over a quarter of a century can doubt the grave disadvantages of the anti-theoretical tradition when carried to excess. If the stock-in-trade of ideas, theories, plans and aspirations of a reforming movement does not grow at least in step with its practical activities, a painful hiatus may occur. The very success of such a movement in carrying out the main parts of its traditional programme may, as in the case of the British Labour movement after the 1945–51 government, produce a sense almost of bankruptcy. 'Stout Cortez' in Keats' sonnet did not confront the Pacific ocean with a greater air of 'wild surmise' than that with which some members of the British Labour movement confronted the new state of things which they had themselves brought into being in Britain by the middle of the twentieth century . . .

Paradoxical in the extreme as it may seem, what has impelled me to write this sort of book is, precisely, the conviction that issues of social morality are supreme. They are supreme, but for that very reason impossible, for me at least, to deal with abstractly and except by the implications of the discussion of concrete economic and political facts. For what has made men's efforts at social improvement so partially successful at best, and at worst so tragically abortive, has been insufficient comprehension of the ways and means by which their objectives may be reached. I find it difficult to contemplate with equanimity the amount of honest, selfless, and sometimes heroic, social and political effort which, even in my own experience, I have seen run to waste and turn, first to futility, then to disillusionment and bitterness, so that in the end it becomes actively pernicious, for lack of such *comprehension*. That is why it seems to me that at this particular moment of history it is more useful to discover social inter-connections than to exhort . . .

You can change the very nature of a bowl of cream merely by stirring it. As you stir, it will begin to coagulate; lumps will appear in the once smooth and perfect liquid. At length you will transform the whole bowl into a solid; the cream will be butter.

For half a century now some such process has been at work within the economic system. The powerful hand which has solidified by stirring the once fluid medium of our economic relations is competition . . . From being a grinding power of social disintegration, it began to build up new relationships and new institutions: it became integrating, solidifying and constructive. In the smooth liquid of the perfectly competitive market the solid bodies of substantial new social and economic institutions began to form, modifying and in the end destroying the homogeneity of the medium.

To drop the simile, the competitive process, by its own ruthless strength, and in accordance with its own inner logic, continually creates bigger and fewer units with which to fight out the competitive battle. It does so because, on the whole and in the end, the larger units prove to have superior competitive power. It does so by carrying far further an integrating process which had in fact been at work, underneath the destructive atomising process, from almost the beginning of capitalism . . . Such giant units are now the dominant, although by no means universal, economic institutions of our period. They have become the decisive *dramatis personae* of contemporary economic life . . .

We shall further assert that this tendency has now reached a point at which it has all-important consequences. But why should this be so? It is by no means self-evident that we should attach any special significance to this growth in the size, and shrinkage in the number, of the units which do the competing in our essentially (it is still assumed) competitive economic system. Is there any reason to suppose, it may be asked, that the mere growth in the size of the competitors will have changed the nature of the contest?

There are such reasons. A whole literature analysing and discussing them already exists. Indeed two whole literatures exist, each of which seeks to construct a different diagram or model for the study of the new stage of capitalism which has come into being. On the other hand, and in spite of the existence of these literatures, much of our political life is still lived on the basis of assumptions and preconceptions appropriate to the previous phases of capitalism alone. Many of both the supporters and of the opponents of capitalism today conduct a battle over the ghost of an economy which no longer inhabits the earth. Both, consequently, misunderstand or misinterpret the reality about them, by applying to it categories and concepts which have little relevance left in them. And finally, this new and culminating stage of capitalism has appeared in the world in very different forms, according to the political environment in which it has arisen.

In this chapter we shall seek to do no more than list the reasons which have caused an increase in the size, and a decrease in the number, of the competitors within the economic system, to change the nature of capitalism. They have changed its nature in the sense that the laws of development of the older stage of the system no longer fully apply to the new stage. Extreme theoretical confusion and ghastly practical mistakes, therefore, result from supposing that the new model will behave in the old way. The following list of reasons is conclusive, it will be submitted, in showing that a new and distinct stage of our extant economic system, namely capitalism, now exists in the advanced industrial communities. But they do not show that the system as such, that capitalism itself, has been abolished, as it undoubtedly has been in Russia, for example. To use the biological analogy – imperfect but graphic – the extinction of the species and its supersession by another would be a change of a different order of magnitude. The species is still recognisably itself; but it has undergone a mutation . . .

It is the ability of the producers in some, but not in all, of the spheres of production to affect prices, instead of merely being affected by them, that is the root of the matter . . . The social consequences of this have helped to draw the State – usually against its will – into the productive process. The State in this more active role may itself be used by the oligopolies to enhance their price fixing policies. On the other hand, if the oligopolists do not control the State, the rest of the community – the wage earners and the farmers in particular – will certainly try to use its power to protect themselves against the otherwise overweening power of the oligopolists.

Thus the ability to influence prices will inevitably sap the automatic, self-regulating character of the economy: it will consequently provoke and require more and more State intervention, and will lead to an intensified struggle for the now all-important levers of economic power which will be in the hands of the State. At the same time the conduct and the ownership of the main enterprises of the economy are becoming separated, and, largely consequentially, the key function of accumulation is taking on a new and semi-collective character. Finally the growing integration of society has enabled its theoreticians to measure it, and so, potentially at least, to comprehend and to control it.

Thus the characteristics of the last stage of capitalism both make possible a much higher degree of social control and at the same time make such control imperative. We here catch a glimpse of the concept that the new stage may be either far worse than the old if it is uncontrolled, or if it is controlled solely in the interests of the oligopolists; but that, on the other hand, it may be superior, both in stability and equity, to the old stage, if it is controlled adequately and in the interests of the population as a whole.

Many names, favourable and unfavourable, have been suggested for the new stage which capitalism has entered. These names have often better expressed the desires, the prejudices and the passions of those who have coined them than the character of the thing described. Thus Marxists, when the symptoms of oligopoly first appeared, called the new stage 'Monopoly Capitalism' or 'Imperialism'. On the other hand, liberal, conservative and social democratic writers have now begun to use such terms as the Mixed Economy, the Managerial State, Statism, the Welfare State, Progressive Capitalism, Fair Dealism, State Capitalism, the First Stage of Socialism, and so on and so forth. The one thing common to these terms is that they pick out the particular characteristic of our present economy which the writer desires to emphasise. For example, one social analyst sees that the State now plays a far more active role than formerly, and calls the new stage statism; another emphasises the decay of competition and refers to monopoly; a third sees chiefly the vast outward, expansive drive of the system and calls it Imperialism; a fourth considers the much greater attention given to the human needs of the population at home to be its main feature, and calls it the Welfare State; while a fifth, concentrating attention upon the growing divorce between the ownership and the control of productive resources, calls it the Managerial State.

It may be that it is not possible adequately to subsume under one name the various important respects in which mid-twentieth century capitalism differs from the previous version of the system. It may, therefore, be better to call it simply 'the last stage of capitalism'. No doubt even that title is equivocal, since the word 'last' may be used in the sense of latest, or in the sense of ultimate. I mean it in both senses. Thus the narrative undoubtedly carries the implication that this latest stage of capitalism is the ultimate one, and will be succeeded not by still a third version of the system, but by something which it would be manifestly an abuse of language to call capitalism at all.

No doubt such a prediction will be considered rash. The system has shown itself to be much more protean than was once supposed. May it not suffer, or achieve, another mutation, as marked as that of the last fifty years, and survive in some still newer form? This seems improbable. After all, some third of the world's population already live in communist societies, which, whatever mutations they also may experience (and it is greatly to be hoped that they experience many), are not likely to return to anything which could be correctly called capitalism. True the larger part of the rest of the world's population live in underdeveloped societies which are only approaching the capitalist stage. They are approaching it, however, in a way which suggests that they do not mean to stay long in it, even if they traverse it.

All this is by no means to prejudice the question of how long the present stage will endure or the respects in which it will continue to evolve, until the point is reached at which it can no longer usefully be called capitalism.

There is no mystery about what has caused the standard of life of the wage earners to rise, roughly in step with the rise in the national income. Many other factors, such as the rise of productivity, have been a necessary condition: nevertheless the operative factor, without which the rise would not in fact have taken place, has been the growing power of the people. And by 'the people' I mean that 90% of the British population who have usually received . . . about half the national income. It is this which has prevented the innate tendencies of the capitalist system from working themselves out in the ever increasing misery of the wage earners . . .

We reach the paradoxical conclusion that it has been, precisely, the struggle of the democratic forces *against* capitalism which has saved the system. It has done so not only by making tolerable the conditions of life of the wage earners, but also by keeping open the indispensable market for the final product which the self-destructive drive of capitalism to a more and more inequitable distribution of the national income would otherwise have closed. Thus democracy has had far reaching economic consequences. It has determined, within limits sufficiently wide to be profoundly significant, the actual distribution of goods and services between persons and classes of persons. It has gone far to determine, in plain English, who shall be rich and who shall be poor, and how rich and how poor they shall be . . .

If . . . contemporary democracy is the diffusion of power in the political field, it has obvious analogies with a diffusion of ownership and wealth in the economic field. We have noted, however, that the natural drive of the capitalist system, in all its stages, a drive to be overcome only with the utmost difficulty, if at all, is to a greater and greater concentration of ownership and wealth. As we saw, it has proved possible, by means of the separation of ownership and management, by high redistributary taxation, and by other such devices, to separate to some extent the concentration of economic power and control (necessitated by the new techniques) from an ever more outrageously inequalitarian distribution of income. But the underlying economic tendency is strongly inequalitarian and centralising: and therefore it is potentially anti-democratic.

Thus the main trends in the political and economic fields are running in opposite directions. The extension of the franchise and its increasingly effective use, the consolidation of trade unionism, and the other factors which we have noted, have diffused political power through the major last stage capitalisms to a varying but significant degree. But in the same decades, economic power has been steadily concentrated into the hands of the major oligopolies. Such contradictory trends can hardly co-exist indefinitely. One must overcome and absorb the other; for political power and economic power are, in the last resort, merely aspects of one indivisible whole, namely power itself. It is this contradiction which has led those who have thought most realistically about contemporary democracy to depict it always in highly dynamic terms. It is a trend or process rather than a state . . .

This hitherto unresolved contradiction between the trend of our political life towards the diffusion of power, and of our economic life towards the concentration of power, is a major factor in the contemporary situation. So far the diffusion of political power has just about succeeded in offsetting the effects of the concentration of economic power. It is this which has falsified the prediction of ever increasing misery and by so doing enabled the economic system to function. But now economic power is reaching a critical degree of concentration which threatens to become incompatible with the still growing diffusion of political power. Economic power threatens to submerge political power unless political power can at the critical moment obtain control of economic power . . .

In the end the power of contemporary democracy must encroach upon capitalism until its last stage also has been completed: or, alternatively, capitalism must encroach upon democracy until this young, vulnerable and experimental method of government has been destroyed. That is why the struggle to preserve and to extend democracy both in time and in space is likely to be a crucial feature of the politics of the second half of the twentieth century, at any rate in those highly developed societies which are the primary objects of our study.

The methods by which last stage capitalism encroaches upon democracy are subtle rather than direct . . . What is to be apprehended is not, then, a direct attack. What is not only likely but inevitable – indeed it is taking place without ceasing – is an attempt, largely unconscious, on the part of capital, highly organised and integrated in the oligopolies, to manipulate and distort, and if necessary frustrate, the workings of contemporary democracy to its own advantage. Again, there is no need to postulate a high degree of conscious intention. It is often an error to attribute to social forces much self-consciousness. It is rather that the oligopolies, working quite naturally to further their own interests, come into conflict with this or that aspect of democracy and seek to modify it to suit themselves. But the sum of those modifications and manipulations, if they did not encounter successful opposition, would spell out the end of effective democracy.

This is another important 'special case' of the process which we have been studying throughout this volume; a special case of the consequences of the reduction of the units in any sphere of the productive system to a small number of large firms. It will be recalled that this process had exceptionally far reaching consequences in the case of banking . . . A reduction in the number of banks to the typical handful of oligopolies transformed the very nature of banking from being a humble handmaid of industrial production and commerce, useful for storing and pooling spare surpluses, into a mighty engine of control, capable, if acting in step with the State, of modifying the whole economic climate of the society in question. Now we must note other cases in which the process of 'oligopolisation', spreading from the strictly economic field into every part of contemporary society, has critically important consequences. The first of these examples is afforded by the Press and the other media of mechanised expression, such as broadcasting and television . . .

Here we have a cardinal instance of how the development of

capitalism in its last stage automatically enroaches on democracy. The dissemination of news and opinion has become a branch of big business and, like other big business, has passed into the oligopolistic stage. As such it becomes the quasi-monopoly of a handful of great firms, just as does the manufacture of motor cars, or chemicals, or steel, or half a dozen other products. But the dissemination of news and opinion is no ordinary productive process. It is closely bound up with the existence of effective democracy. Experience has indeed shown that in favourable circumstances it is possible for democracy to function even when almost all the media of mass expression are in the hands of only one of the main political tendencies. But there is a limit to the monopolisation of opinion which democracy can stand and yet continue to be effective. If *all* the effective media of expression come into the hands of one political tendency – and it will be, of course, the pro big capital political tendency – then it is almost impossible for the electorate to make a rational choice. That is why such issues as the control of television are, and are felt to be, of immense importance. These issues – and not, in the main, constitutional forms, will be what really matter in the political struggles of the second half of the century . . .

The oligopolisation of the media of expression is an example of a general tendency. Just as the units of production have become few and large, so have almost all the other institutions of the national life. And for the same reason. Modern techniques depend upon large units and central control for their application, not only in the productive process itself, but in administration, and even in such apparently less relevant spheres as political and cultural life . . .

It is a commonplace that the increase in size and decrease in number, which characterises the institutions of contemporary society, poses acute questions for democracy. But the general tendency is not usually linked with the specific mutation of the economy into its oligopolistic phase. And for this reason there is a failure to distinguish between two separate aspects of democracy which are affected in different ways. It is true that democracy, if it is to fulfil its function of diffusing power, must seek in one way or another to draw an ever growing proportion of the population into active participation in the running of the country. And the growth in size, and the centralisation, of our institutions undoubtedly creates serious problems in this respect. Nevertheless even for the purposes of participation a growth in size may not be all loss. A small master may be a great tyrant. And a large organisation may by careful arrangements secure very real possibilities of participation on the part of its members.

But, after all, participation is only one aspect – although no doubt it is the highest aspect – of democracy. The more immediate task for democracy is to secure ultimate *control* over the main national institutions. Such control has been fairly effectively secured in the case of our political institutions. It is a most rough and ready sort of control. Nevertheless, because of the competitive political process . . . it is a very real thing. One way of describing the first purpose of socialism is to write that it is an attempt to secure the same kind and the same degree of overall democratic control in the case of our major economic institutions, the oligopolistic firms. And for this simpler purpose of democracy the growth in size and scale is by no means wholly adverse. True, it may threaten the very existence of democracy, in the ways we have described, *if* that overall democratic control is not progressively achieved. But at the same time it makes such overall democratic control possible, as well as necessary. In spite of sustained attempts to deny it, the fact that the administrators of a publicly owned corporation are ultimately responsible to elected representatives of the whole population, instead of to a motley, ever changing, but relatively very narrow, group of shareholders, is of crucial importance. It may, or may not, make much visible difference to the day to day conduct of the concern: but it will, in the end, if it becomes the predominant form of ownership in the economy, condition the whole character of society.

Thus the essence of the matter which we are discussing is that it is not so much the growth of size and scale in itself, as that growth combined with the ownership of the great corporations by wholly irresponsible shareholders, which menaces democracy. Capitalism in its last stage, when it is progressively outgrowing the forms of ownership which were once appropriate to it, threatens to turn upon what was once its own political counterpart, namely democracy.

Thus the interaction between capitalism and democracy is seen to be exceedingly complex and dynamic. The character of both has been, and continues to be, transformed. On the one hand democracy has ceased to be the method by which different sections of the ruling class, such as the landlords and the industrialists in nineteenth century Britain, fought out, and compromised over, the question of which should rule, with the, at most, partial and intermittent intervention of the wage earners. It has become, in the advanced, last stage capitalisms, a method by which, on the one hand, the wage earners as a whole and, on the other, the property owners as a whole, seek to fight out, and to compromise over, the question of which of them shall control the economy.

Simultaneously, the structure of the economy has become modified in such a way that it imperatively requires a central regulating authority in order to function at all. It has lost its automatic, self-regulatory characteristics and has become far more centralised and concentrated. It has become last stage capitalism. This simultaneous transformation of the natures of democracy and capitalism is causing the tension within our societies to mount. For the transformation of capitalism makes it indispensable that *someone* should regulate it. And the transformation of democracy sharply poses the question of which class, or as we traditionally say in British public life, which *interest*, is to do the regulating. It is a most ambitious attempt to decide such a question as that by democratic means. And yet at the mid-point of the century it is possible to say that, on the whole, at least in Britain and America, the democratic method is showing possibilities of being able successfully to undertake this critical task . . .

The main tendency of an unmodified last stage capitalism is deeply antagonistic to democracy. But if democratic institutions are strong enough, as they have been in Britain and America, to modify the 'set' of the economy, then these modified economic tendencies begin, in turn, to help democratic institutions to maintain and extend themselves. If, to put the matter more specifically, the democratic countervailing pressures can once become strong enough to make the distribution of the national income significantly more favourable to the mass of the population than it would 'naturally' have been, then the wage earners and farmers begin to acquire a vested interest in democracy. They find that democratic institutions really can be valuable to them. Moreover their improved economic position, rising as we have seen much above a subsistence level, instead of falling below it, gives them access to those educational and cultural facilities which are almost indispensable to the effective exercise of democratic rights. Not only materially, but in every way, they begin to have, and to feel that they have, what is often called 'a stake in the country'. They become, in Marxist terminology, increasingly de-proletarianised.

Both Marxist and conservative observers have insufficiently noticed that this process of acquiring 'a stake in the country' need not necessarily, and indeed will not typically, consist in acquiring a nest egg of property. A right to an Old Age Pension, to adequate Unemployment Benefit, to a Free Health Service, and to the other main features of the Welfare State, plus a right to normally uninterrupted employment at trade union rates of wages, plus satisfactory educational facilities provided by the community, plus publicly developed housing, all amount to a substantial stake in the country, even if the wage earners in general have no significant quantity of investments. Once such 'rights' as these have been acquired, democracy becomes much more strongly entrenched than before. For then the struggle to maintain and extend democracy can be undertaken as a struggle to preserve known, tangible and valued rights, and not merely as a struggle to achieve theoretically desirable ideals. Thus it is vital that democratic institutions should have been established, and effectively used, at a relatively early point in the development of a last stage capitalism. For then only will they have the opportunity to become strong enough to withstand the anti-democratic pressures to which they will sooner or later be subjected . . .

When we remind ourselves of the way in which our democratic institutions really work: when we recollect how much by way of maturity, steadiness and insight the effective use of those institutions demands of the wage earners and farmers: when we recollect, also, that they must exercise those qualities amidst the screech and din of the counter-propaganda of capital, we also may sometimes be tempted to doubt the democratic cause. But such doubts are not only unworthy, they are also futile. No one can assess the true chances of democracy in the long struggle which lies ahead of it. Nor should we attempt to do so. The thing to do is not to speculate on the chances of the struggle: the thing is to engage in it. For if none can know the outcome, all can know that the preservation, development and final triumph of democracy offer the only tolerable future for societies such as ours. Even if democracy's chances were very small (which I do not believe), the experience of the first half of the twentieth century proves that it would still be our duty to devote ourselves to its preservation. For the struggle of democracy is in our type of society the decisive aspect of every other form of social struggle. It is true that we shall often find ourselves fighting for other causes: for peace, for liberty, for socialism, for equality. But the outcome of these particular struggles will depend on whether contemporary democracy can be preserved and made into an effective instrument of social transformation. Everything else will be won or lost on this battlefield.

4.3 RAYMOND WILLIAMS: CULTURAL REVOLUTION

The writer and critic Raymond Williams expressed many of the cultural concerns of the New Left in the late 1950s and early 1960s and exercised a wide influence. His *Culture and society* (1958) was a pioneering and contextual history of the idea of culture in Britain, and its sequel *The long revolution* (1961) extended this account into an analysis of cultural institutions and contemporary problems. The extract here is based upon the final section of this latter book, in which Williams reflects upon the current condition of the 'long revolution' embracing political, economic and cultural patterns and directed towards a common culture rooted in socialist 'meanings and values'.

As we enter the 1960s, the effective historical patterns of British society seem reasonably clear. The industrial revolution, in an important technical phase, is continuing. The cultural expansion, again with new technical developments, also continues. In the democratic revolution, Britain has recently been mainly in a defensive position, as the colonial peoples move to emancipation. At home it is generally assumed that the democratic process has been essentially completed, with parliamentary and local government solidly established on universal suffrage, and with the class system apparently breaking up. Britain seems, from these patterns, a country with a fairly obvious future: industrially advanced, securely democratic, and with a steadily rising general level of education and culture.

There is substantial truth in this reading. It is not only the general consensus, but most attempts to challenge it seem unreasonable; even powerful local criticisms do not fundamentally disturb the sense of steady and general advance. Yet in deeper ways, that have perhaps not yet been articulated, this idea of a good society naturally unfolding itself may be exceptionally misleading. It is perhaps an intuitive sense of this that has given such emotional force to the total denunciations, the sweeping rejections, so characteristic of recent years, for even when these can be shown to be based on selective evidence and particular minority tensions, the experience they attest is still not easily set aside.

It seems to me that the first difficulty lies in the common habit of supposing our society to be governed by single patterns, arrived at by averaging the overall trends in familiar categories of economic activity, political behaviour and cultural development. As I see the situation, we need quite different forms of analysis, which would enable us to recognise the important contradictions within each of the patterns described, and, even more crucially, the contradictions between different parts of the general process of change. It is not only that the analysis should be more flexible, but that new categories and descriptions are needed, if all the facts are to be recognised. In particular fields we have made some progress with these, but in our most general descriptions we are all still visibly fumbling, leaving an uncertainty easily exploited by the blandest versions of a natural and healthy evolution, and certainly not redeemed by such general nostrums as the fight for socialism, which remains, after all, in terms of this country, almost wholly undefined.

We have to observe, for example, that the ordinary optimism about Britain's economic future can be reasonably seen as simple complacency. It is very far from certain that on present evidence and given likely developments the directions and rate of growth of the economy guarantee us, over say fifty years, a steadily rising standard of living in this economically exposed and crowded island. Both the rapid rate of economic growth elsewhere, and the certainty of steady industrialisation of many areas now undeveloped, seem ominous signs for a country so dependent on trade and in fact given its prosperity by its early industrial start (now rapidly being overtaken) and by its Empire (now either disappearing or changing its character). Long-term thinking of this kind is in fact beginning, but the gap between thinking and vigorous action to implement it seems no ordinary inertia, but the consequence of habits which, in other parts of our life, seem satisfactory and even admirable. The deep revulsion against general planning, which makes sense again and again in many details of our economic activity, may be really disabling in this long run. And this revulsion is itself in part a consequence of one aspect of the democratic revolution – the determination not to be regimented. Here is a substantial contradiction that I think now runs very deep. The very strong case for general planning, not simply to avoid waste but to promote essential development, research and reorganisation, is practically nullified by a wholly creditable emotion: that we reject the idea of this kind of economic system controlling our lives. True, we are controlled now and will continue to be controlled by a quite different system, with its own denials and rigidities, but in the first place this is very much harder to identify, and secondly, by its very structure and ideology, it appears to offer, and in just enough places does offer, the feeling of freedom. It seems unlikely that the case for general planning will ever be widely accepted until not only do its forms seem sensible, but also its methods seem compatible with just this feeling of freedom. Democratic planning is an easy phrase, but nobody really

knows how it would work, and the spectacular successes of economic planning elsewhere have after all not co-existed with any general
democracy. This is the severe damage of the contradiction, because
it is then easy to suppose that we have found good reasons for not
planning, when in fact the need remains urgent and the problems
will not disappear because on balance we find them too difficult to
solve . . .

Unless we achieve some realistic sense of community, our true
standard of living will continue to be distorted. As it is, to think
about economic activity in the limited terms of the consumer and
the market actually disguises what many of us are doing, and how
the pattern of economic life is in any case changing. Even now,
one person in four of the working population is engaged neither in
production nor in distribution, but in public administration and
various forms of general service. For a long time this proportion
has been steadily rising, and it seems certain that it will continue
to rise. Yet it is a kind of economic activity which cannot be explained, though it may be distorted, by such descriptions as the
consumer and the market . . . The product of this kind of work,
which one in four of us give our time to, is almost wholly in terms
of life and experience, as opposed to things. What kind of accounting is adequate here, for who can measure the value of a life and an
experience? Some parts of the process can be reduced to more
familiar terms: medicine saves working days, education produces
working skills, sport creates fitness, entertainment keeps up morale.
But we all know that every one of these services is directed, in the
end, to larger purposes: doctors work just as hard to save the life of
a man past working age; every school teaches more than direct
working skills, and so on. To impose an accounting in market
terms is not only silly but in the end impossible: many of the results of such effort are not only long-term and indirect, but in any
case have no discoverable exchange value. The most enlightened
ordinary reaction is to put these activities into a margin called 'life'
or 'leisure', which will be determined as to size by the shape of
'ordinary' economic activity. On the other hand, if we started not
from the market but from the needs of persons, not only could we
understand this part of our working activity more clearly, but also
we should have a means of judging the 'ordinary' economic activity
itself. Questions not only of balance in the distribution of effort and
resources, but also of the effects of certain kinds of work both on
users and producers, might then be adequately negotiated. The
danger now, as has been widely if obscurely recognised, is of fitting

human beings to a system, rather than a system to human beings. The obscurity shows itself in wrong identification of the causes of this error: criticism of industrial production, for example, when in fact we should starve without it; criticism of large-scale organisation, when in fact this extension of communication is the substance of much of our growth; criticism, finally, of the pressures of society, when in fact it is precisely the lack of an adequate sense of society that is crippling us.

For my own part I am certain, as I review the evidence, that it is capitalism – a particular and temporary system of organising the industrial process – which is in fact confusing us. Capitalism's version of society can only be the market, for its purpose is profit in particular activities rather than any general conception of social use, and its concentration of ownership in sections of the community makes most common decisions, beyond those of the market, limited or impossible. Many industrial jobs, as now organised, are boring or frustrating, but the system of wage-labour, inherent in capitalism, necessarily tends to the reduction of the meaning of work to its wages alone. It is interesting that the main unrest of our society – the running battle which compromises any picture of a mainly contented and united country – is in this field of wages. Whenever there is an important strike, or threat of a strike, we tend to react by defining a different conception of work – service to the community, responsibility to others, pulling together. The reaction is quite right: work ought to mean these things. But it is hypocritical to pretend that it now does, all the way through. While the light comes on when we press the switch, we take for granted just these qualities, but ordinarily fail to acknowledge, with any depth, the needs of the man who made the light possible. If we want to stop strikes, we have to carry the reaction right through, for this system of bargaining for labour necessarily includes, as a last resort, as in all other bargaining, the seller's refusal of his labour at the price offered. Strikes are an integral part of the market society, and if you want the advantages you must take the disadvantages, even to the point of dislocation and chaos. While we still talk of a labour market, as despite long protest many of us continue to do, we must expect the behaviour appropriate to it, and not try to smuggle in, when it becomes inconvenient, the quite different conception of common interest and responsibility. The moral disapproval of strikers is shallow and stupid while the system of work is based on the very grounds of particular profit which we there condemn.

What is happening to capitalism in contemporary Britain? We are told that it is changing, but while this is obviously true it can be argued that the patterns of thinking and behaviour it promotes have never been more strong. To the reduction of use to consumption, already discussed, we must add the widespread extension of the 'selling' ethic – what sells goes, and to sell a thing is to validate it – and also, I think, the visible moral decline of the labour movement. Both politically and industrially, some sections of the labour movement have gone over, almost completely, to ways of thinking which they still formally oppose. The main challenge to capitalism was socialism, but this has almost wholly lost any contemporary meaning, and it is not surprising that many people now see in the Labour Party merely an alternative power-group, and in the trade-union movement merely a set of men playing the market in very much the terms of the employers they oppose. Any such development is generally damaging, for the society is unlikely to be able to grow significantly if it has no real alternative patterns as the ground of choice. I remember that I surprised many people, in *Culture and Society*, by claiming that the institutions of the labour movement – the trade unions, the co-operatives, the Labour Party – were a great creative achievement of the working people and also the right basis for the whole organisation of any good society of the future. Am I now withdrawing this claim, in speaking of moral decline? The point is, as I see it, that my claim rested on the new social patterns these institutions offered. I recognise that the motives for their foundation, and consequently their practice, must be seen as mixed. Sectional defence and sectional self-interest undoubtedly played their part. But also there was this steady offering and discovery of ways of living that could be extended to the whole society, which could quite reasonably be organised on a basis of collective democratic institutions and the substitution of co-operative equality for competition as the principle of social and economic policy. In the actual history, there has been a steady pressure, from the existing organisation of society, to convert these institutions to aims and patterns which would not offer this kind of challenge ... If I seem eccentric in continuing to look to these institutions for effective alternative patterns, while seeing all too clearly their present limitations, I can only repeat that they can go either way, and that their crisis is not yet permanently resolved ...

The central point, in this contentious field, is that the concepts of the organised market and the consumer now determine our economic life, and with it much of the rest of our society, and that challenges to them have been so effectively confused that hardly any principled opposition remains, only the perpetual haggling and bitterness of the wage claim and the strike. It is difficult to believe that we shall remain satisfied by this situation, which is continually setting us against each other and very rapidly promoting patterns of crude economic cynicism, yet to which no clear and practical alternative exists. The challenge to create new meanings, and to substantiate them, will have to be met if that apparently obvious future is in fact to be realised.

The progress of democracy in Britain is deeply affected by what is happening in the economy, but also by other factors. The aspiration to control the general directions of our economic life is an essential element of democratic growth, but is still very far from being realised. Beyond this general control lies a further aspiration, now equally distant and confused. It is difficult to feel that we are really governing ourselves if in so central a part of our living as our work most of us have no share in decisions that immediately affect us. The difficulties of a procedural kind in ensuring this share are indeed severe, and because of the variety of institutions in which we work there is no single answer. Yet if the impulse is there, some ways can be found, and steadily improved from experience . . .

Our main trouble now is that we have many of the forms of democracy, but find these continually confused by the tactics of those who do not really believe in it, who are genuinely afraid of common decisions openly arrived at, and who have unfortunately partly succeeded in weakening the patterns of feeling of democracy which alone could substantiate the institutions . . .

It is clear, on balance, that we do not get enough practice in the working of democracy, even where its forms exist. Most of us are not expected to be leaders, and are principally instructed, at school and elsewhere, in the values of discipline and loyalty, which are real values only if we share in the decisions to which they refer. Those who are expected to be leaders are mainly trained to the patterns of leadership, . . . centred on the general development of confidence – but in fact that a leader should be self-confident enough to be capable of radical doubt is rarely mentioned and rarely taught. The necessary practice of the difficult processes of common decision and execution is left, on the whole, to hit or miss, and the result, not unexpectedly, is often both. A weakening of belief in the possibility of democracy is then inevitable, and we prefer to lament the 'general indiscipline' (trade-union leaders cannot control their members, party leaders are not firm enough; it is all sloppy discussion, endless talk, and then people behaving unreasonably) rather than nourishing and deepening the process to which in any case, in any probable future, we are committed.

The counterpart of this feeling, reinforced by the actual history of democratic institutions in this country, is an approach to government which in itself severely limits active democracy. A tightly organised party system and parliament seem to have converted the national franchise into the election of a court. As individuals we cast one national vote at intervals of several years, on a range of policies and particular decisions towards which it is virtually impossible to have one single attitude. From this necessarily crude process, a court of ministers emerges (in part drawn from people who have not been elected at all), and it is then very difficult for any of us to feel even the smallest direct share in the government of our affairs . . .

At this critical point, the relative absence of democracy in other large areas of our lives is especially relevant. The situation can be held as it is, not only because democracy has been limited at the national level to the process of electing a court, but also because our social organisation elsewhere is continually offering non-democratic patterns of decision. This is the real power of institutions, that they actively teach particular ways of feeling, and it is at once evident that we have not nearly enough institutions which practically teach democracy. The crucial area is in work, where in spite of limited experiments in 'joint consultation', the ordinary decision process is rooted in an exceptionally rigid and finely-scaled hierarchy, to which the only possible ordinary responses, of the great majority of us who are in no position to share in decisions, are apathy, the making of respectful petitions, or revolt. If we see a considerable number of strikes, as the evidence suggests, as revolts in this sense, we can see more clearly the stage of development we have reached . . .

One other field in which the growth of democracy seems urgently necessary is the ordinary process of decision about the development of our communities. This has been approached, but is still very muddled, and it is unfortunately true that there is even more dissatisfaction, and consequent apathy, about local government than about the national court. Authoritarian patterns at the centre seem to be widely reproduced in our local councils, where much more of the process is in the open and within our ordinary experience, unfortunately in its ordinary course giving far too much evidence of how easily democracy is distorted. Still, the problems here are quite widely understood, and the active struggle against distortion is encouraging. More seriously, behind this struggle is a familiar inertia of old social forms. Housing is an excellent example, because the common provision of homes and estates is so obviously sensible, in principle, and is already extending beyond the mere relief of exceptional need. Why then does such an extension, or further extension, leave many of us quite cold? One answer, certainly, is the way such houses and estates are commonly managed, by supposedly democratic authorities . . . Why should the management of a housing estate not be vested in a joint committee of representatives of the elected authority and elected representatives of the people who live on it? While general financial policy obviously rests with the whole community, there is a wide area of decision, on the way the houses are used and maintained, on estate facilities, and on any necessary regulations, which could be negotiated through such channels more amicably and I think more efficiently. If this experiment has been tried, we should know more about it and consider extending it. If it has not been tried, here is an immediate field in which the working of democratic participation could be tested. Labour councils, in particular, ought continually to be thinking in these ways, for there is great danger to the popular movement if its organisations are persistently defensive and negative (as in the ordinary Tenants' Association), and it is Labour which has most to lose if it allows democracy to dwindle to a series of defensive associations and the minimal machinery of a single elected administration. The pressure has been to define democracy as 'the right to vote', 'the right to free speech', and so on, in a pattern of feeling which is really that of the 'liberty of the subject' within an established authority. The pressure now, in a wide area of our social life, should be towards a participating democracy, in which the ways and means of involving people much more closely in the process of self-government can be learned and extended . . .

The extension of culture has to be considered within the real social context of our economic and political life. My studies of the growth of particular cultural institutions showed a real expansion, which of course is continuing, but showed also the extent to which this was affected or determined by other facts in the society. In the 1960s, the rate of growth seems promising, and we are busy with plans to maintain and increase it. Yet here, very clearly, is a major contradiction easily overlooked by following a simple rising graph, for while real art and argument are being more widely enjoyed, the distribution of a bewildering variety of bad art and bad argument is increasing even more rapidly. We are reaching the point where the contradiction between these different lines and rates of growth is serious and inescapable, yet even those who see this situation feel particularly uncertain about what can be done...

Instead of the ritual indignation and despair at the cultural condition of 'the masses' (now increasingly uttered even by their supposed friends) it is necessary to break through to the central fact that most of our cultural institutions are in the hands of speculators, interested not in the health and growth of the society, but in the quick profits that can be made by exploiting inexperience. True, under attack, these speculators, or some of them, will concede limited policies of a different kind, which they significantly call 'prestige'; that is to say, enough to preserve a limited public respectability so that they will be allowed to continue to operate. But the real question is whether a society can afford to leave its cultural apparatus in such irresponsible hands.

Now I think many people feel the strength of this question, but feel even more strongly the difficulties of any possible alternative. Steady and particular encouragement, in the obvious limited fields, is quite widely approved, but any attempt to tackle the whole situation runs into major difficulties. For it is obvious that the amount of capital and effort required, to make any substantial change, can come only from public sources, and to this there are two objections. The first is the question whether such resources are really available, on the scale required. This goes back to the difficulty discussed earlier: that we find it almost impossible to conceive the financing of social policy out of the social product, and have never learned a system of accounting which would make this possible or even visible. For it is true, of course, that the present investment comes from the society and economy as a whole. The supply of advertising money (the contemporary equivalent of manna) can only come in the end from us, as workers and buyers, though it is now routed through channels that give control of this social capital to very limited groups. If we can realise that we are paying for the existing cultural system, by one kind of organisation of the economy, we need not be frightened by the scale of resources required, since that organisation is in fact subject to change. We should be much clearer about these cultural questions if we saw them as a consequence of a basically capitalist organisation, and I at least know no better reason for capitalism to be ended. It is significant that the liveliest revolt against the existing system, particularly among the new young generation, is in precisely these cultural terms.

But then the second objection is deeply involved with this point. What is the alternative to capitalism? Socialism. What is a socialist culture? State control. There are many good liberals, and many anxious socialists, who draw back if this is the prospect. Better even the speculators, they say, than the inevitable horde of bureaucrats, official bodies, and quite probably censorship.

This difficulty has a representative significance. It is not only in cultural questions, but in the whole area of thinking about change in our society, that this knot is tied. Here is the deepest difficulty in the whole development of our democracy: that we seem reduced to a choice between speculator and bureaucrat, and while we do not like the speculator, the bureaucrat is not exactly inviting either. In such a situation, energy is sapped, hope weakens, and of course the present compromise between the speculators and the bureaucrats remains unchallenged . . .

It is urgent to define the alternative principle, which I think can only be that when the producers cannot themselves own the means of their work, these must be owned by the community in trust for the producers, and an administration set up which is capable of maintaining this trust. The difficulties here are obvious, but all administration and constitution-making in fact proceed from an emphasis of what is desirable, and I believe that if we can agree that this end is desirable, no society is better qualified from experience to devise adequate practical methods . . .

Would the quality of our cultural life be improved by such measures? I feel certain that it would, in the real energies that would be released, but I am not thinking in terms of any overnight transformation. I say only that the channels would be more open, that the pressure for quick profit would be lifted, and that a more genuine range of choices would be made available. My whole case about social change is, moreover, that the interdependence of elements which I described as a matter of theory is an argument for conceiving change on the widest possible front: the changes in emphasis in our economy, in our ordinary working relationships, in our democratic institutions, and in education are all relevant to cultural change in this more explicit field . . .

The human energy of the long revolution springs from the conviction that men can direct their own lives, by breaking through the pressures and restrictions of older forms of society, and by discovering new common institutions. This process necessarily includes both success and failure. If we look back over recent centuries, the successes are truly spectacular, and we ought to keep reminding ourselves of them, and of the incomprehension, the confusion, and the distaste with which the proposals for things now the most ordinary parts of reality were received. At the same time the failures are evident: not only the challenging failures, as new and unrealised complexities are revealed, but also the straight failures, as particular changes are dragged back into old systems, and as ways of thinking deeply learned in previous experience persist and limit the possibility of change. We tend to absorb the successes and then to be preoccupied by the hard knots of failure. Or as we approach the failures, to see if anything can be done, we are distracted by the chorus of success . . .

If the existing meanings and values could serve the new energies, there would be no problem. The widespread dissent, and growing revolt, of the new young generation are in fact the growth of the society, and no policy is relevant unless conceived in these terms. The most useful service already performed by the new generation is its challenge to the society to compare its ideals and its practice. This comparison . . . is the first stage of new learning. People get a sense of reality, and of their own attitudes to it, from what they learn of a whole environment. It is one thing to offer certain meanings and values and ask people to consider and if possible accept them. Yet we all naturally look, not only at the meanings and values, but at their real context. If, for example, we are to be co-operative, responsible, non-violent, where exactly, in our actual world, are we expected to live? Is the economy co-operative, is the culture responsible, are the politics non-violent? If these questions are not honestly answered, propagation of the values as such will have little effect. The degree of evasion will be matched by a degree of contempt, and this can as easily degenerate into cynical apathy as grow into protest and new construction. The only useful social argument is that which follows the meanings and values through to the point where real contradictions are disturbing or denying them. Then, with the real situation admitted, the stage of contemptuous comparison and dissent may pass into constructive energy. For my own part, I see the present situation as a very critical phase in the long revolution, because it is by no means certain, in the short run, whether the new and constructive stage will be reached in time. There are many warning signs of dissent and boredom being capitalised, as a new kind of distraction. The cult of the criminal, the racketeer, the outsider, as relevant heroes of our society, is exceptionally dangerous, because it catches up just enough real feeling to make the heroism seem substantial, yet channels them towards those parodies of revolution often achieved in modern history in the delinquent gang or even in fascism. These destructive expressions can only occur when, in the widest sense, the society is in a revolutionary phase. It is not time then for the reasoned catalogues of sober achievement, but for new creative definitions. The contradictions between an apparently contented society and a deep current of discontent emerging mainly in irrational and ugly ways is our immediate and inescapable challenge.

A growing number of people, in recent years, have been trying to describe new approaches and to make them practical. They have, of course, been widely dismissed as utopians or extremists. But how did they seem at the time, those men we look back to who 'in opposition to the public opinion of the day', 'outraging their contemporaries', 'challenging the general complacency', somehow live with us and even seem tame and 'limited by their period'? Working for something new, a writer or thinker easily identifies with these men, and of course may be wholly wrong: not everything new is in fact communicated and lived. But the reasonable man, tolerantly docketing the extremists of his day: who is he exactly? For he too identifies with these figures from the past; it is usually where he learned to be reasonable. And then who is left for that broad empty margin, the 'public opinion of the day'?

I think we are all in this margin: it is what we have learned and where we live. But unevenly, tentatively, we get a sense of movement, and the meanings and values extend. I have tried to describe some possible ways forward, and ask only for these to be considered and improved. But what I mainly offer is this sense of the process: what I have called the long revolution. Here, if the meaning communicates, is the ratifying sense of movement, and the necessary sense of direction. The nature of the process indicates a perhaps unusual revolutionary activity: open discussion, extending relationships, the practical shaping of institutions. But it indicates also a necessary strength: against arbitrary power whether of arms or of money, against all conscious confusion and weakening of this long and difficult human effort, and for and with the people who in many different ways are keeping the revolution going.

4.4 R. H. S. CROSSMAN

Richard Crossman, Labour intellectual and politician, edited the collection of *New Fabian essays* (1952) which was designed to provide 'a new analysis of the political, economic and social scene as a basis for reformulating socialist principles'. This extract is from Crossman's own essay 'Towards a philosophy of socialism'.

This is the point of departure for a modern theory of socialism. Instead of regarding social change as tending towards the enlargement of freedom, we must assume that increased concentration of power, whether in the form of technological development or social organisation, will always produce exploitation, injustice and inequality in a society, unless the community possesses a social conscience strong enough to civilize them. Human institutions will always be not merely amoral but immoral, as Reinhold Niebuhr showed in his famous book, unless they are moralised by individual men and women aware of this proclivity and waging unceasing war against it. Every economic system, whether capitalist or socialist, degenerates into a system of privilege and exploitation unless it is policed by a social morality, which can only reside in a minority of citizens. Every political party degenerates into office-seeking, unless its leaders are faced by an opposition within the ranks. Every Church becomes a vested interest without its heretics, and every political system, including democracy, ossifies into an oligarchy. Freedom is always in danger, and the majority of mankind will always acquiesce in its loss, unless a minority is willing to challenge the privileges of the few and the apathy of the masses.

In the nineteenth century this challenge was the task of liberalism. Today it has fallen to socialism. But we cannot fulfil it so long as we base our policy on the materialist fallacy that material progress *makes* men either free or equal. One particularly vicious form of this fallacy is the belief that economics are the determinant factors in social change and that, if we achieve economic justice, we automatically secure human freedom...

Marx saw that, though capitalism was the enemy, the Industrial Revolution was 'objectively progressive', a stage in social development. Yet, as soon as capitalism reached maturity, it became a system of privilege and exploitation. Today the enemy of human freedom is the managerial society and the central coercive power which goes with it. And yet the Political Revolution has been 'objectively progressive', in the sense that the instruments of mass communication and coercion, if restrained by social morality, *can* be used to enlarge freedom. Just as capitalism *could* be civilised into the Welfare State, so the managerial society *can* be civilised into democratic socialism...

The planned economy and the centralisation of power are no longer socialist objectives. They are developing all over the world as the result of the Political Revolution, and the process is accelerated by the prevalence of war economy. The main task of socialism to-day is to prevent the concentration of power in the hands of *either* industrial management *or* the state bureaucracy – in brief, to distri-bute responsibility and so to enlarge freedom of choice. This task was not even begun by the Labour Government.

4.5 ANEURIN BEVAN

Nye Bevan was the outstanding politician of the Left in the 1950s, leader of the parliamentary 'Bevanites' who defended a traditional socialist fundamentalism ('Bevanism') against the new revisionists. Bevan's *In place of fear* (1952), from which this extract comes, was a revealing sketch of his conception of democratic socialism.

Thus, judged from any angle, the relations between public and private enterprise have not yet reached a condition where they can be stabilised. That is why it is so foolish for certain Labour men to preach 'consolidation' at this stage. Before we can dream of con-solidation, the power relations of public and private property must be drastically altered. The solution of the problems I have been dis-cussing cannot be approached until it becomes possible to create a purposive and intelligible design for society. That cannot be done until effective social and economic power passes from one order of society to another.

At the moment we are between two worlds. We have lost the propulsions of one and we have not yet gained the forward thrust of the other. This is no place in which to halt.

That is not to say a halting place cannot be reached. I think it can. It is clear to the serious student of modern politics that a mixed economy is what most people of the West would prefer. The victory of Socialism need not be universal to be decisive. I have no patience with those Socialists, so-called, who in practice would socialise nothing, while in theory they threaten the whole of private property. They are purists and therefore barren. It is neither pru-dent, nor does it accord with our conception of the future, that all forms of private property should live under perpetual threat. In almost all types of human society different forms of property have lived side by side without fatal consequences either for society or for one of them. But it is a requisite of social stability that one type of property ownership should dominate. In the society of the future it should be public property. Private property should yield to the point where social purposes and a decent order of priorities form an easily discernible pattern of life. Only when this is accomplished will a tranquil and serene attitude take the place of the all-pervading restlessness that is the normal climate of competitive society.

4.6 IRIS MURDOCH

The contributors to *Conviction* (1958), a collection of essays by representatives of the post-war generation of socialist intellectuals, discussed the future direction of British socialism in face of the existing 'stalemate state' described by the volume's editor, Norman Mackenzie. An interesting contribution came from the writer and philosopher Iris Murdoch ('A house of theory'), the concluding section of which appears here.

The problem of the transformation of labour is not only the original centre of Socialist thought, it is the problem of the managerial society. Even to pose it with enough clarity would help to counteract the movement of talent and interest toward the levels of bureaucratic control and to send it back toward the levels of the unskilled. But for such an idea to be fruitful, a source of inspiration and controversy, it needs to be presented as an autonomous moral conception, independent of, and ultimately sovereign over, the mere notions of efficiency and rational 'tidying up' of capitalist society into which Socialism is in danger of degenerating.

If we seek here for inspiration in our own tradition we have not far to look. The Guild Socialists dissented on precisely this point from their less ambitious and more purely Benthamite colleagues, in that the latter were concerned with the damage done to the consumer and the former with the damage done to the producer. The Guild Socialists were deeply concerned with the destruction of community life, the degradation of work, the division of man from man which the economic relationships of capitalism had produced: and they looked to the transformation of existing communities, the trade unions, the factories themselves, for the restoration of what was lost. Such ideas were and are easy targets for mockery, and in the old Guild Socialist form were doubtless quite impracticable; and they faded from the scene partly because they were tied to inadequate techniques, and partly because the conception of the Welfare State presented an easier and more obviously urgent and attractive target. With its achievement it is necessary to renew our study of the more difficult and fundamental problems of capitalism. We cannot live without the 'experts'. But the true 'open society' in the modern world is one in which expertise is not mysterious; and the only way to prevent it from becoming mysterious is continually to subordinate its activities to a lively and *interested* public opinion: and this in turn will languish without 'theories'. The Welfare State marks the successful end of the first road along which the Socialist movement in this country elected to travel. It is time now to go back and explore the other road, to go back to the point of divergence, the point not so very far back at which we retained as a living morality ideas which were common to Marx and to William Morris.

4.7 RICHARD TITMUSS

Richard Titmuss, pioneer practitioner of the academic discipline of social administration, followed Tawney in subjecting social and economic policy to the test of moral values and social purpose. This extract is from his influential Fabian pamphlet on *The irresponsible society* (1960).

Underlying the notions of continued economic growth is the assumption of a dwindling role for Government. The public services are increasingly seen, as Galbraith says, as an incubus; an unnecessary, doctrinaire burden on private enterprise. The act of affirmation, the positive political decision about equality and its correlate freedom, becomes harder to make as the majority of voters (and not just the top 10 per cent) grow richer. Negatively, they assume – insofar as they are helped to think about these matters at all – that the unseen mechanisms of a more prosperous market will automatically solve the problems of the poverty of dependency, the slums of obsolescence, the growth of irresponsible power and all the contradictions that flow from undirected or misdirected social policies.

As society grows in scale and complexity, new social needs are created; they overlap with and often accentuate the more classical forms of dependent needs. Many of these new needs are born of the disservices of technological and scientific change which, in turn, give rise to new concentrations of self-interested professional and economic power. These needs call for services and social amenities; things which, in Galbraith's analysis, do not easily lend themselves to private production, purchase and sale. If inequalities are not to grow, individual and territorial, and if public meanness is not to become public squalor, these things should be provided for everyone if they are provided for anyone.

The growth of a 'Pressure Group State', generated by more massive concentrations of interlocking economic, managerial and self-regarding professional power, points in the other direction; towards more inequality; towards the restriction of social rights and liberties and the muffling of social protest among a large section of the population. The growing conservatism of professionalism, of the imposed inequalities resulting from the decisions of congeries of social power, were remarked, with extraordinary foresight, by Graham Wallas in his chapter on 'Professionalism' in *Our social heritage* in 1921. He was concerned as I have been (though in a much more limited context) with the fundamental problem of reinterpreting social equality and personal liberty in the conditions of a new age and a changed society.

Those aspects of economically determined power with which I have been chiefly concerned function, if not socially controlled, as accelerators of inequality; inequalities in the distribution of income and wealth, educational opportunity, vocational choice, pension expectations, and in the right to change one's job, to work in old age, and in other spheres of individual and family need. Some part of this process is expressed through the multiplication and division of occupational and fiscal benefits. Some part is traceable to the separation of 'ownership' from the rights of stockholding, and the organised concentration of control over the 'economic surplus' which represents a primary source of power in our society. The answers lie in many fields and forms of public ownership, public responsibility, and public accountability. The expansion and reshaping of social policy is but one.

To grow in affluence then does not mean that we should abandon the quest for equality. In some senses at least the quest becomes harder to undertake as the cruder injustices of yesterday are reduced and blurred. But new forms and manifestations of social injustice take their place. To substitute the professional protest for the social protest and the arbitrary power of the city for the accountable power of the Commons is no answer. No answer for ourselves; no prescription for a participating democracy; no example for Africa and the poverty-stricken peoples of the world. It is simply the mark of an irresponsible society.

4.8 E. P. THOMPSON

E. P. Thompson, social historian and biographer of William Morris, was a leading participant in the New Left and remains an outstanding figure within contemporary British socialism. In this extract from the New Left volume *Out of apathy* (1960) Thompson offered a characteristic sketch of the British socialist tradition, and it is appropriate to include it as a post-script here.

Will Britain founder under old habits, rotting institutions, its hull encrusted with nostalgia, drifting half-waterlogged into the twenty-second century, a bourgeois Spain among the socialist nations? It would be foolish to be sanguine. But foolish also to underestimate the long and tenacious revolutionary tradition of the British commoner.

It is a dogged, good-humoured, responsible, tradition: yet a revolutionary tradition all the same. From the Leveller corporals ridden down by Cromwell's men at Burford to the weavers massed behind their banners at Peterloo, the struggle for democratic and for social rights has always been intertwined. From the Chartist camp meeting to the dockers' picket line it has expressed itself most naturally in the language of moral revolt. Its weaknesses, its carelessness of theory, we know too well; its strengths, its resilience and steady humanity, we too easily forget. It is a tradition which could leaven the socialist world.